The IDEA MAGAZINE FOR TEACHERS®
MAILBOX®

2007–2008 YEARBOOK

The Education Center, Inc.
Greensboro, North Carolina

The Mailbox® 2007–2008 Intermediate Yearbook

Managing Editor, *The Mailbox* Magazine: Peggy W. Hambright

Editorial Team: Becky S. Andrews, Diane Badden, Kimberley Bruck, Karen A. Brudnak, Kitty Campbell, Tazmen Carlisle, Chris Curry, Lynette Dickerson, Sarah Foreman, Margaret Freed (COVER ARTIST), Theresa Lewis Goode, Marsha Heim, Lori Z. Henry, Dorothy C. McKinney, Sharon Murphy, Jennifer Nunn, Mark Rainey, Kelly Robertson, Hope Rodgers, Eliseo De Jesus Santos II, Rebecca Saunders, Barry Slate, Zane Williard

ISBN10 1-56234-854-X
ISBN13 978-156234-854-0
ISSN 1088-5552

Printed in the United States of America.

The Education Center, Inc.
P.O. Box 9753
Greensboro, NC 27429-0753

Look for *The Mailbox® 2008–2009 Intermediate Yearbook* in the summer of 2009. The Education Center, Inc., is the publisher of *The Mailbox*®, *Teacher's Helper*®, *The Mailbox*® BOOKBAG®, and *Learning*® magazines, as well as other fine products. Look for these wherever quality teacher materials are sold, call 1-800-714-7991, or visit www.themailbox.com.

Contents

Seasonal ideas
&
Reproducibles

My superhero name: _Supergirl_

Also known as: _Madison_

My strengths and abilities:
organizing, doing math, showing
respect, being kind and caring,
being generous, giving good
compliments

How I will use my strengths and
abilities to help my classmates:
I will help them organize their
desks. I can help them with math
too. I will be kind and caring, and
I will respect all of my classmates.
I will compliment my classmates
for the great things they do.

Our Class Superheroes
Getting acquainted, building a class community

To get ready for this super first-day activity, have each child
complete a form like the one shown to describe her superhero
qualities. Next, have her draw herself wearing superhero attire.
Then have her cut out her drawing and glue it and her completed
form onto construction paper. After a sharing session, post the projects on
a display titled "Our Class Superheroes."

Jean Perkins, Coleman Elementary, Coleman, MI

Build a Yearbook
Yearlong collaborative project

Label a large sheet of paper for each school month. Post the papers in order on a wall. As the year progresses, have student volunteers list events, activities, books read, and other notes about the month on the appropriate sheet. Also clip to each sheet photos taken during the month. At the end of the year, form a small group for each month. Have each group use its chart to write a one-page summary of the assigned month. Also have the group arrange the month's photos on a second page. After compiling the groups' pages, make copies of the resulting yearbook so each child can take one home as a special memento.

Brooke Blake, Wentworth Elementary, Wentworth, NH

Summer Points
Back-to-school icebreaker

Get to know your new students quickly and easily by creating a "Summer Points" form like the one shown. One at a time, read each summertime activity listed on the form. Ask students who participated in the activity over the summer to raise their hands. Then announce the activity's point value and have those students note the number on scrap paper. After you've read the entire list, have students total their points. Award a small prize to the students with the highest and lowest point totals.

Carolyn Hart, Taylorsville Elementary, Taylorsville, NC

Summer Points	
Activity	**Points**
1. took swimming lessons	10
2. read a book	5
3. caught lightning bugs on a summer night	5
4. went to camp	20
5. looked for seashells on a beach	5
6. went horseback riding	10
7. made a gift for a friend or family member	20
8. went to an amusement park	5
9. visited relatives out of state	15
10. participated in a summer library program	25
11. flew on an airplane	20
12. helped make homemade ice cream	10
13. worked in the family garden	20
14. went on a picnic	10
15. got paid for a summer job	25
16. ate watermelon	5
17. got a new pet	10
18. visited a historic site	20
19. went bike riding with a friend	5
20. had a summer birthday	10
21. took music lessons	20
22. played a summer sport	5
23. cooked a meal for your family	15
24. reorganized your bedroom	10
25. saw a snake	10
26. washed a family car	10
27. slept past noon	5
28. went fishing	15
29. went to a family reunion	10
30. were excited about coming back to school	30

I Predict!
Back-to-school activity, writing

To generate excitement about the year ahead, write on a transparency a summary of the curriculum and activities your new class will experience this year. Underline 15–18 words or phrases; then list them in order on the board. Challenge each student to use all of the words in the order listed to write a prediction about the upcoming year. Have students share their finished summaries with the class or in small groups. Then display your original selection so students can compare their predictions with your summary.

Kelly Clark, Kerr Elementary, Pittsburgh, PA

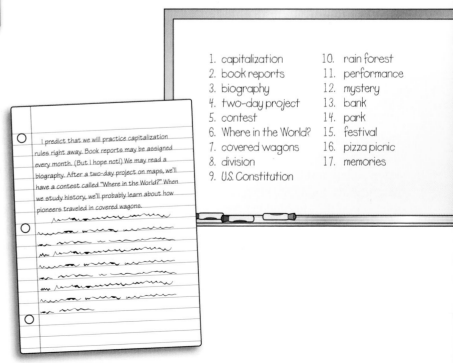

Time for Open House!

Ideas for Making Parent Night a Huge Success

GET-TO-KNOW-THE-TEACHER BROCHURE

Open house is a perfect time for satisfying parents' curiosity about who is teaching their child. So create a colorful, easy-to-read pamphlet that contains a letter of introduction, information about your educational background and teaching philosophy, and, if desired, a supply list and tips for success. Place the folded brochures in a basket by the door for parents to take home.

Dawn M. Rispinto, Ellsworth Elementary, Ellsworth, OH

CONTACT CARD

Show your openness to communicating with parents by making a simple business card. Label the card with your name and the school's name, address, and phone number. Laminate the cards and attach a magnetic strip to the back of each one. Then put a card on each child's desk for the parent to take home and mount near a phone. This small gesture goes a long way toward forming positive relationships!

Kristine Toland, Bayview Elementary, Belford, NJ

BREAKING THE ICE

Before open house, have students create self-images to put on their chairs using tagboard, markers, yarn, and old wallpaper books. Also have each child leave on her desktop an index card labeled with a clue to her identity. Once parents have found the correct seats, have them write their child a note on the back of the clue and leave it on the desk for the next day. At the end of the meeting as a reward for coming, present each parent with a "Parent's Free Homework Pass" to use on a night when uncontrollable circumstances keep him or her from helping with or checking a child's homework.

Marlene Parmentier, Greenport Elementary, Hudson, NY

Name _____

Just in Time!

Write three synonyms for the adjective on each backpack. Then write a noun that all of the synonyms could describe. Use a thesaurus for help.

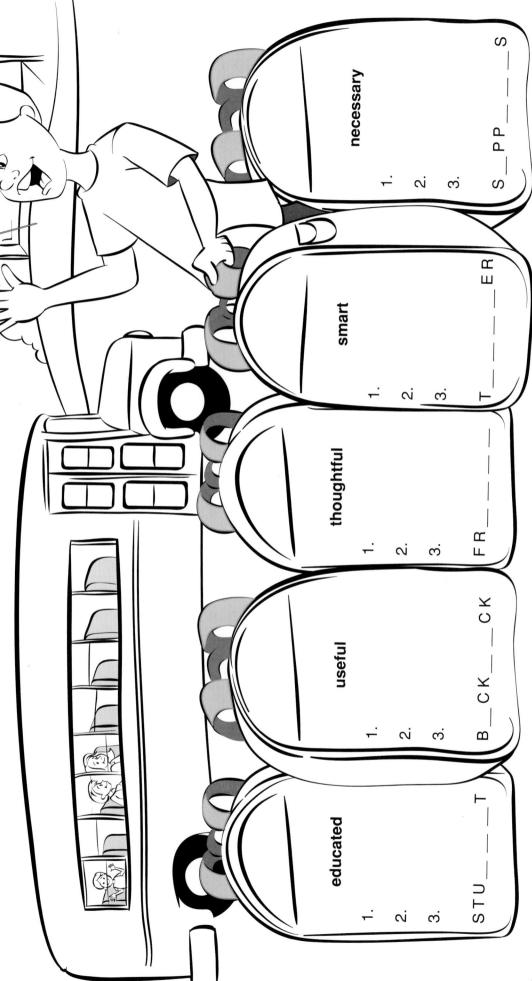

necessary

1.
2.
3.

S _ _ PP _ _ _ S

smart

1.
2.
3.

T _ _ _ _ ER

thoughtful

1.
2.
3.

FR _ _ _ _ _

useful

1.
2.
3.

B _ CK _ _ _ CK

educated

1.
2.
3.

STU _ _ _ _ T

9

Name _____

Keep 'em Sharp!

Write the contraction formed by the two words on each pencil.
Then write five sentences, using a different contraction in
each sentence.

1 (might have ⟩ _____

2 (who is ⟩ _____

3 (I am ⟩ _____

4 (you are ⟩ _____

5 (they would ⟩ _____

6 (could not ⟩ _____

7 (let us ⟩ _____

8 (have not ⟩ _____

9 (there is ⟩ _____

10 (he will ⟩ _____

11. _____

_____

12. _____

_____

13. _____

_____

14. _____

_____

15. _____

_____

©The Mailbox® • TEC44032 • Aug./Sept. 2007 • Key p. 308 • written by Kay Cowherd, Flowery Branch, GA

Name_____

Happy Grandparents Day!

Complete the chart. Then answer the questions.

Type of Transportation	Details	Length of Trip
passenger train	1. Nana and Pop Roberts leave Atlanta, Georgia, at 8:15 AM. They arrive in Nashville, Tennessee, at 1:50 PM. How long is their trip?	
airplane	2. Grandma and Grandpa Adams leave Bangor, Maine, at 3:05 PM. They arrive in Tampa, Florida, at 9:55 PM. How long is their trip?	
car	3. Grandmother and Grandfather Warren leave Detroit, Michigan, at 8:30 AM. They arrive in Savannah, Georgia, at 10:52 PM. How long is their trip?	
walking	4. Granny and Gramps Smith leave their house at 9:00 AM. They arrive at their grandkids' house at 9:22 AM. How long is their trip?	
boat	5. Nanny and Pappy Jones leave their dock at 1:10 PM and reach the dock at their grandkids' house at 2:35 PM. How long is their trip?	
bus	6. Nona and Grandpa Green leave Dallas, Texas, at 8:05 AM and arrive in Tulsa, Oklahoma, at 12:55 PM. How long is their trip?	
RV	7. Mimi and Grandpop Norwood leave Chicago, Illinois, at 5:30 AM. They arrive in Raleigh, North Carolina, at 8:50 PM. How long is their trip?	
subway	8. Grandmother and Grandfather Cox leave the station at 5:50 PM. They arrive at their granddaughter's house at 6:22 PM. How long is their trip?	

9. Who had the longest trip? _____

10. Who had the shortest trip? _____

©The Mailbox® • TEC44032 • Aug./Sept. 2007 • Key p. 308 • written by Kay Cowherd, Flowery Branch, GA

Name _____

Nutty!

Write the ordered pair for each letter. Notice that two letters (*E* and *L*) appear twice in the grid in different places.

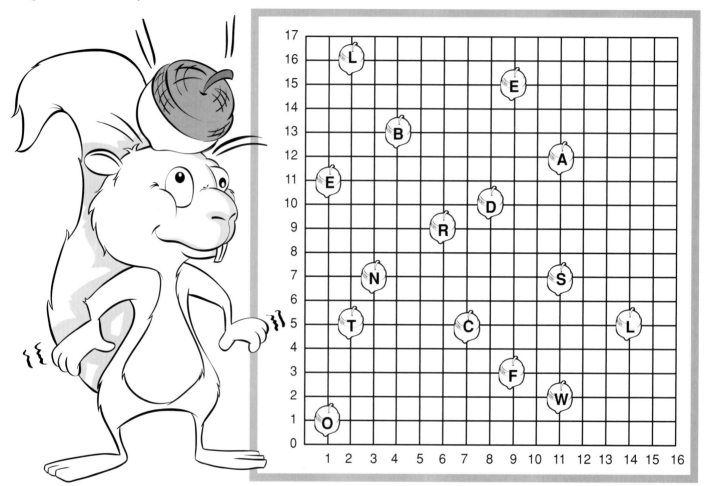

A = _____ L = _____

B = _____ L = _____

C = _____ N = _____

D = _____ O = _____

E = _____ R = _____

E = _____ S = _____

F = _____ T = _____

W = _____

To reveal a special message, write each letter at the left that matches an ordered pair below.

$\overline{\hspace{1cm}}$ $\overline{\hspace{1cm}}$ $\overline{\hspace{1cm}}$ $\overline{\hspace{1cm}}$
(11, 2) (9, 15) (14, 5) (2, 16)

$\overline{\hspace{1cm}}$ $\overline{\hspace{1cm}}$ $\overline{\hspace{1cm}}$ $\overline{\hspace{1cm}}$!
(8, 10) (1, 1) (3, 7) (1, 11)

©The Mailbox® • TEC44032 • Aug./Sept. 2007 • Key p. 308 • written by Kay Cowherd, Flowery Branch, GA

Math Monsters

Halloween

For a monstrously fun geometry activity, have each student label a sheet of drawing paper with the text shown at the bottom of the page. Then have her trace pattern blocks to create a monster, leaving room at the top for the monster's name. Direct the student to add other features and to color the monster to match the pattern blocks. Finally, have the student fill in the blanks at the bottom of her drawing and add her monster's name at the top. Mount the projects on construction paper before displaying them. If desired, extend the activity by using one of the writing prompts shown.

Leigh Anne Newsom, Cedar Road Elementary, Chesapeake, VA

Writing Prompts

Descriptive: Describe your monster.

Persuasive: Persuade the judges of the Most Marvelous Monster contest that your monster deserves to win.

Expository: Explain how you created your monster.

Narrative: Write a story telling how you first met your monster.

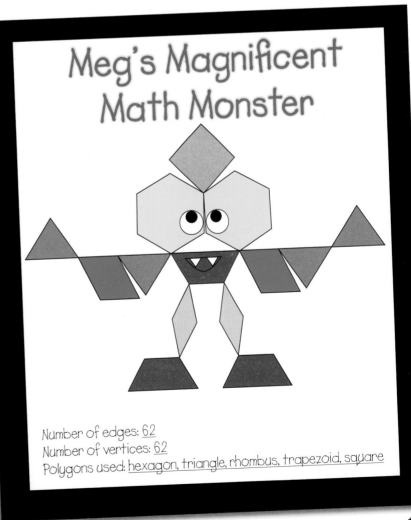

Meg's Magnificent Math Monster

Number of edges: <u>62</u>
Number of vertices: <u>62</u>
Polygons used: <u>hexagon, triangle, rhombus, trapezoid, square</u>

Creepy, Crawly Poetry
Halloween

To prepare for this kid-pleasing writing activity, purchase inexpensive bags of small plastic insects, bats, mice, and other creepy critters. After reviewing various forms of poetry, place a toy on each student's desk. Then have each child research facts about her creature and incorporate them into a poem about the animal. Post the poems on a bulletin board titled "Creepy, Crawly Poetry." If desired, use Sticky-Tac to attach each creature to its poem.

Lisa Kirby, Audrey Garrett Elementary, Mebane, NC

Spiders
Have fangs.
Spinning, paralyzing, trapping,
So amazing yet scary,
Arachnids.

near the picture
outside the house
beside the plant
underneath the pillows
in the drawer
in the doorway
beneath the covers
behind the desk
under the rug
among the toys

Hide the Monsters!
Prepositions and prepositional phrases

Begin this review by giving each student (or student pair) a large sheet of drawing paper. Challenge the child to draw a picture in which he has hidden ten monsters. Then have the student label each hiding place with a prepositional phrase, such as *behind the curtains, under the bed,* or *in the closet.* If desired, have small groups of students compare their drawings and vote on the best hiding place.

Kerry Christiano, Merritt Academy, Fairfax, VA

Horn-of-Plenty Paragraphs
Thanksgiving

Have each student write a paragraph using a prompt shown (or another that you provide). After she takes the paragraph through the writing process, have her copy the topic sentence onto a cornucopia cutout. Next, have the student draw and cut out construction paper fruits and vegetables and glue them to the cornucopia. Finally, have her write each supporting sentence on a piece of produce. Post the projects on a Thanksgiving display titled "Plenty of Paragraphs."

adapted from an idea by Juli Engel, Midland, TX

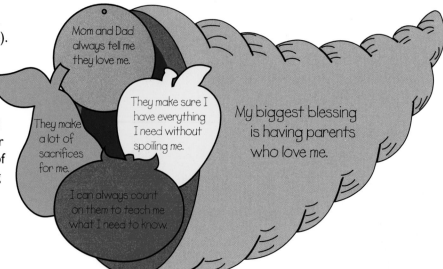

Mom and Dad always tell me they love me.

They make sure I have everything I need without spoiling me.

My biggest blessing is having parents who love me.

They make a lot of sacrifices for me.

I can always count on them to teach me what I need to know.

Thanksgiving Paragraph Prompts

I'll never forget the Thanksgiving when...
Life is easier when you are thankful.
My biggest blessing is...
If I could thank one person...

Boo-Boos

Circle the letter above each mistake. Then cross out the error and make the correction in the space provided.

1. We ~~our~~ going to have a huge party for halloween and invite all our friend's.
   are

   Ⓑ   S   O   C   O

2. Matt couldn't find a costume to where, but he came to the party anyway?

   A   O   B   E

3. all my friends where having a wonderful time at my party.

   R   Y   R   I

4. We played an game, but first we had to seperate the girls from the boy's.

   Y   P   N   I

5. The team that one recieved candy bars puzzle books and movie tickets.

   F   E   I   S

6. Haley said, "the party is great! Its the best one I have ever been too."

   C   R   M   E

7. Their were alot of laughs and great food for everyone.

   A   B   M   E

What food was served at the Halloween party?
To find out, write the circled letters from above in order on the lines below.

"B __ __ - __ __ __ __ __ __" __ __ __ and "__ __ __ __ __ __ __ __"

©The Mailbox® • TEC44033 • Oct./Nov. 2007 • written by Jacqueline Beaudry, Getzville, NY • Key p. 308

Voted Most Popular

Use the bar graph to answer each question.

1. How many girls voted in all?

   _____

2. How many boys voted in all?

   _____

3. What is the girls' favorite flavor?

   _____

4. How many more boys than girls like kettle corn best? _____

5. Which flavor has the largest difference in boy and girl votes? _____

6. Which flavor is liked almost equally well by the boys and girls?

   _____

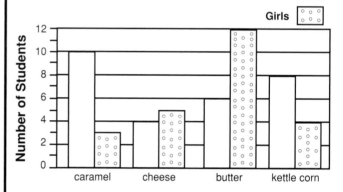

FAVORITE POPCORN FLAVORS

Boys ☐ Girls ⊡

Number of Students — Flavor: caramel, cheese, butter, kettle corn

Use the data below to create a bar graph.

title

_____

POPCORN SIZES SOLD AT THE MOVIES

Size	Number Sold
Small bag	22
Medium box	20
Large bucket	18
Belly Buster	15
Super Belly Buster	5

©The Mailbox® • TEC44033 • Oct./Nov. 2007 • written by Jacqueline Beaudry, Getzville, NY • Key p. 308

TURKEY IN THE KNOW

Label each part of the dictionary entry with its matching letter on the turkey.

☐ ☐ ☐ ☐

thanks•giv•ing (thăngks-**gĭv**´ ĭng) *n* **1.** an act of giving thanks; an expression of gratitude **2. Thanksgiving** a holiday for giving thanks, celebrated on the fourth Thursday of November in the United States and on the second Monday of October in Canada

Use each pronunciation below to write a common Thanksgiving word.

1. (māz) _____

2. (skwŏsh) _____

3. (**pĭl**´ grəm) _____

4. (**tûr**´ kē) _____

5. (**pŭmp**´ kĭn) _____

6. (**här**´ vĭst) _____

7. (**făm**´ ə-lē *or* **făm**´ lē) _____

8. (kärv) _____

9. (**krăn**´ bĕr´ē) _____

10. (pə-**tā**´ tō) _____

A. part of speech
B. pronunciation
C. definition
D. main entry

DICTIONARY

Use a dictionary to help you complete the entries below.

1. **feast** (fēst) *n.* _____
   Sentence: _____
   _____

2. **feast** (   ) *v.* to eat to one's delight: *I will feast on all this food until I am full.*

Pumpkin Pies Aplenty

Use the numbers to complete each equation.

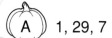 A) 1, 29, 7

(____ x 4) + ____ = ____

B) 2, 2, 6

(24 ÷ ____) − ____ = ____

C) 26, 6, 4

(____ x 5) + ____ = ____

D) 3, 8, 9

(____ + ____) − ____ = 14

E) 3, 16, 36

(____ ÷ ____) + 4 = ____

F) 11, 5, 2

(12 ÷ ____) + ____ = ____

G) 8, 60, 7

(____ + ____) x 4 = ____

H) 1, 14, 7

(____ ÷ ____) + ____ = 3

I) 10, 5, 25

(____ ÷ ____) + 5 = ____

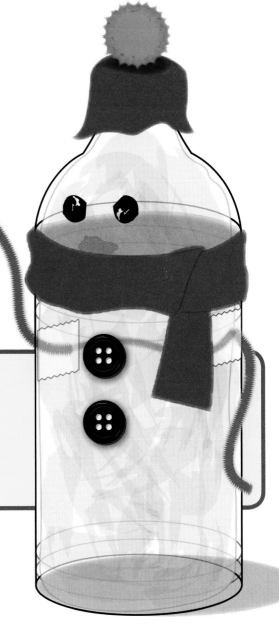

Snazzy Snowpals
Writing

These easy-to-make snowpals are the perfect inspiration for a cool writing activity! In advance, punch two small holes opposite each other on every bottle. When the projects are complete, have each student write a snowman story using one of the following prompts:

- There was a tapping at my window. To my surprise, it was the snowman I made yesterday!
- How did that snowman get inside our classroom?
- Imagine my shock when the snowman I just made said...

Mae Purrenhage, St. Ann School, Cadillac, MI

Materials for each student:

plastic water bottle (or liquid coffee creamer bottle) and cap, with label removed
white acrylic paint
paintbrush
black permanent marker
orange permanent marker
whiteout

1" x 12" strip of fleece fabric
3" circle of fleece fabric
pipe cleaner
2 to 3 buttons
glue
medium pom-pom
small wrapped candies, dried beans, or uncooked rice (optional)

Steps:

1. Paint the bottle white. When it's dry, draw eyes and a nose with the markers. Use the whiteout to make two small white dots on the eyes.
2. Tie the fabric strip around the snowman's neck to make a scarf. Glue the fabric circle around the bottle cap to make a hat.
3. Push the pipe cleaner through the hole on one side of the bottle and out the other to make arms. Bend the ends to create hands.
4. Glue the pom-pom and buttons to the bottle as shown.
5. If desired, stabilize the container by filling it with candies, beans, or rice.

St. Nick's Similes
Reading comprehension, writing

'Tis the season for this fun figurative language activity! Review the characteristics of a simile. Then read aloud Clement C. Moore's classic poem "A Visit From St. Nicholas" (also known as "'Twas the Night Before Christmas"). Challenge students to listen for the similes in the poem. As students identify each simile, write the line that includes it on the board. Then assign one simile to each student pair. Direct each duo to write a paragraph that identifies the two things being compared and explains how the simile helps readers visualize the poem. If desired, have the partners glue the paragraph to a large stocking cutout and write the simile at the top as shown.

Cathy Bruning, Rolling Hills Primary School, Vernon, NJ

"He had a broad face and a little round belly,
That shook when he laughed, like a bowlful of jelly."

The two things being compared in this simile are Santa's belly and a bowl of jelly. Jelly wiggles all over when you move it. This figure of speech helps us see how really chubby Santa is! It also helps us visualize how happy Santa is while doing his job of filling the stockings. When you laugh that hard while you're doing something, you must really be having fun!

Evan and Preston

In Austria, baked carp is served at Christmas dinner.

Around-the-World Ornaments
Research skills

To sharpen research skills this December, assign each student or student pair a country that celebrates Christmas. Have each pair research its country's holiday traditions and then create an ornament that illustrates or symbolizes one or more of the traditions. After students share their ornaments and researched facts, hang the projects from a classroom tree or bulletin board.

Dawn Rispinto, Ellsworth Elementary, Ellsworth, OH

Holiday Geopictures
Geometry

For an easy-to-implement math activity, post a list of geometric figures such as the one below. Have each child create on a sheet of drawing paper an original holiday picture or design that includes at least ten of the figures, each with a label. If desired, mount each picture on a slightly larger piece of gift wrap. Then post the pictures on a bulletin board titled "Our Geometry Skills Are Shaping Up!"

List of figures: right angle, acute angle, obtuse angle, ray, line segment, perpendicular lines, parallel lines, intersecting lines, equilateral triangle, isosceles triangle, scalene triangle, circle, semicircle, square, rectangle, pentagon, hexagon, octagon, decagon, parallelogram, rhombus, trapezoid

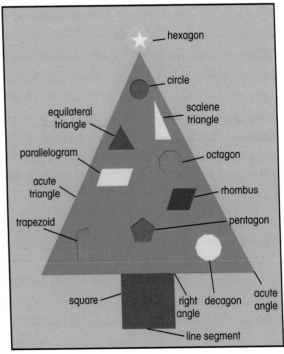

Name_____

Take a Spin!

Read each sentence. Color by the code to identify each underlined phrase.

Color Code
blue = complete subject
yellow = complete predicate

1.
The dreidel game <u>is played during Hanukkah</u>.
C

2.
<u>Any number of people</u> can play the dreidel game.
O

3.
<u>Each player</u> begins with the same number of game pieces.
T

4.
The dreidel <u>has four sides</u>.
O

5.
Each side of the dreidel <u>shows a different Hebrew letter</u>.
S

6.
Pennies <u>can be used as game pieces</u>.
N

7.
<u>Each player</u> puts one game piece in the center of the table.
L

8.
<u>The first player</u> spins the dreidel.
A

9.
The letter that is spun <u>determines how many game pieces a player wins or loses</u>.
I

10.
<u>The game</u> ends when one player has all the game pieces.
E

What tasty treats are sometimes used as game pieces for the dreidel game?

To answer the question, unscramble the boldface letters on the blue dreidels to spell the first word and the boldface letters on the yellow dreidels to spell the second word.

CH__ CO__ __ __ __ __   __ __ __ __ __ __

21

Sweet Dreams

Color each prime number red. Color each composite number green.
Then write each number's factors in the spaces of the candy cane next to it.

G. 18

F. 11

E. 2

D. 101

C. 97

L. 3

B. 12

J. 14

K. 70

A. 25

H. 59

I. 6

Bonus Box: What is the only prime number above that is also an even number?

Happy New Year!

Circle the adverb in each sentence. Then draw an arrow to the verb it describes.

1. I will arrive at school promptly at 8:30 AM.

2. I will wait patiently for the school bus.

3. I will dress for school quickly each morning.

4. I will play nicely with my classmates at recess.

5. I will write all my homework assignments correctly.

6. I will neatly organize the supplies in my desk.

7. I will listen attentively to the teacher.

8. I will carefully proofread all my written work.

9. I will always do my homework before watching TV.

10. I will regularly go to bed on time.

11. I will never leave my backpack at school.

12. I will study hard for all my tests.

Write two more resolutions for the New Year. Use one adverb in each sentence.

1. _____

_____

2. _____

_____

Downhill Data

Find the range, median, and mode for each set of data. Then write the mean on the matching sled.

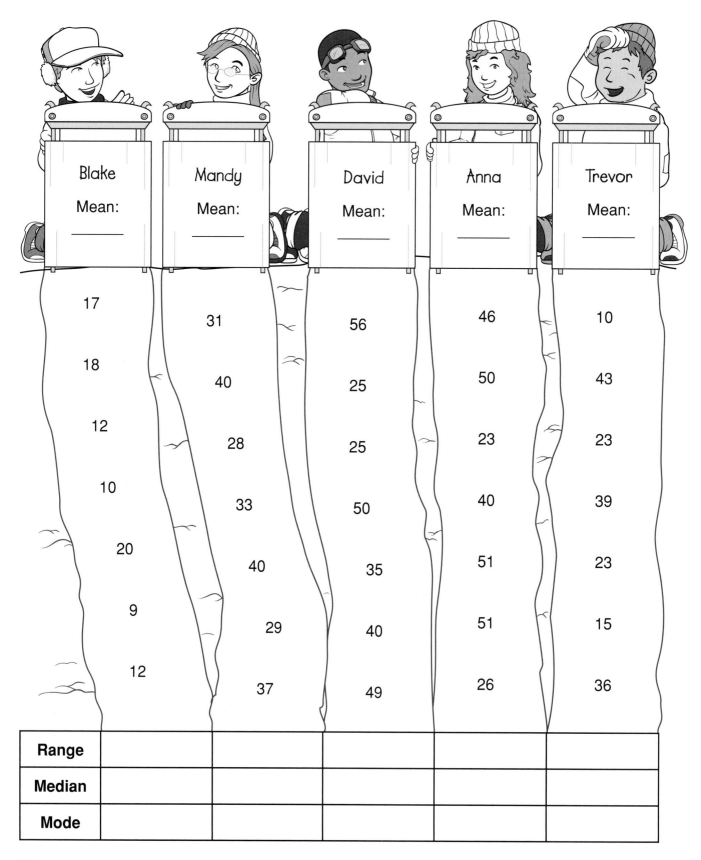

	Blake Mean: _____	Mandy Mean: _____	David Mean: _____	Anna Mean: _____	Trevor Mean: _____
	17	31	56	46	10
	18	40	25	50	43
	12	28	25	23	23
	10	33	50	40	39
	20	40	35	51	23
	9	29	40	51	15
	12	37	49	26	36

Range					
Median					
Mode					

©The Mailbox® • TEC44034 • Dec./Jan. 2007–8 • written by Heather Kime Markland, Springfield, PA • Key p. 309

Breezy Noun Poems
Writing poetry

When you flip the calendar to March, you'll want to pencil in this skill-packed poetry activity. Have each student choose a pair of opposing nouns and write his poem according to the framework shown below. After peer-editing, the student copies his poem onto a white kite cutout and glues the cutout onto colorful paper. He trims the paper as shown and, if desired, decorates the border. Finally, the student adds a yarn tail and cutout bows labeled to spell a one-word title. Post the kites on a bulletin board titled "Poetry Is Blowing in the Wind!"

Val R. Cheatham, Wichita, KS

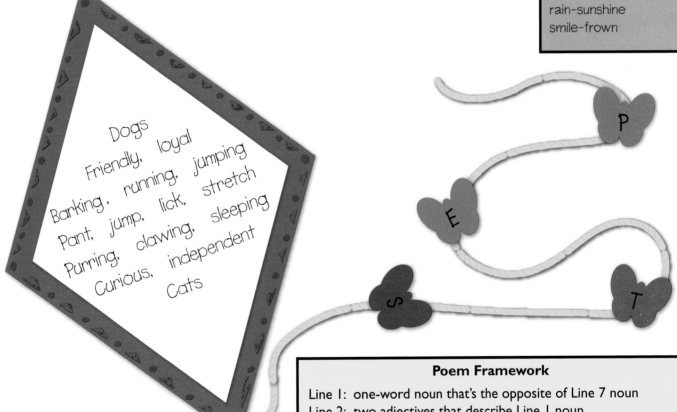

Dogs
Friendly, loyal
Barking, running, jumping
Pant, jump, lick, stretch
Purring, clawing, sleeping
Curious, independent
Cats

Suggested Opposing Nouns

night-day
young-old
war-peace
children-parents
fear-courage
enemy-friend
student-teacher
sadness-happiness
defeat-victory
dishonesty-honesty
yesterday-tomorrow
kids-adults
rain-sunshine
smile-frown

Poem Framework

Line 1: one-word noun that's the opposite of Line 7 noun
Line 2: two adjectives that describe Line 1 noun
Line 3: three -*ing* verbs or three adverbs related to Line 1 noun
Line 4: two verbs related to Line 1 noun, followed by two verbs related to Line 7 noun
Line 5: three -*ing* verbs or three adverbs related to Line 7 noun
Line 6: two adjectives that describe Line 7 noun
Line 7: one-word noun that's the opposite of Line 1 noun

Hearts for Justice
Black History Month

Improve students' nonfiction comprehension skills with an activity that's perfect for Black History Month. Ask your librarian for grade-appropriate books, Web site addresses, and other materials about famous Black Americans who worked for civil rights. Have each student research two civil rights pioneers and then organize her notes into a heart-shaped Venn diagram as shown. Provide time for students to share their diagrams before posting the projects on a display titled "They Had a Heart for Justice."

Debbie Berris, Poinciana Day School, West Palm Beach, FL

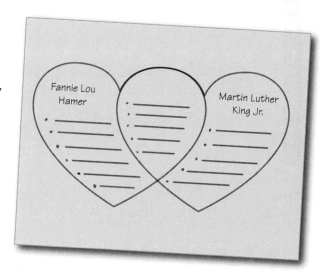

How Sweet It Is!
Valentine's Day

Celebrate the season of hearts and hugs with a fun cross-curricular group activity. Ask parents to donate a class supply of different full-size candy bars. (Be sure to have on hand a small selection of nonchocolate, no-nut candies for students with allergies.) Then have each group of four or five students complete the steps shown. After groups share their work, invite students to unwrap their candy bars and dig in!

Steps:
1. Without mentioning the candy's name, write a sentence that describes each candy bar's wrapper.
2. List the ingredients of each candy bar in your group. Circle any ingredient found in every bar.
3. Choose one group member to tally the other groups' candy bars. Add your group's information to the data. Then display the data in a circle or bar graph.
4. Write five math statements using the data in Step 3, such as Chocolate Yum Bar + Caramel Zap = Four Chocolateers – Peanut Crunch.
5. For each candy bar in your group, create a special award, such as "Most Crunchy" or "Best Wrapper."

Mary Korowin, Dogwood Elementary, Germantown, TN

March Madness Math
Fractions, decimals, and percents

For a math activity that's sure to be a slam dunk with students, place an empty trash can on a chair. Affix masking tape to the floor several feet from the chair to make a free-throw line. Also have each student label an index card with the headings shown. To play, each child attempts ten free throws with a medium-size ball and tallies his shots on the card. When he's finished, he writes a fraction for the number of successful shots and then converts the fraction to a decimal and a percent. Finally, have students swap cards and check each other's calculations.

Brooke Beverly, Dudley Elementary, Dudley, MA

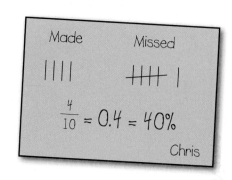

Name _____

HEART-O-METER

Unscramble each word and write it correctly on the line.

1. OLVE _____
2. DCPUI _____
3. CNAYD _____
4. ESSRO _____
5. RDSAC _____
6. LWROFES _____
7. SEKSIS _____
8. WLERJEY _____
9. GHUS _____
10. RTAHES _____
11. VLEOSRBDI _____
12. ERD _____
13. FGITS _____
14. LOHDYAI _____

15. ASNTI VLENTNAEI _____
16. WETHEASRSTE _____
17. RPPEA ACEL _____
18. HCOACOLET _____
19. OMARTNCI _____
20. LEVNATNISE' AYD _____

NUMBER CORRECT			
0–5	6–10	11–15	16–20
ASK A LOVED ONE FOR HELP.	YOUR HEART IS NOT IN IT.	SWEET	A CUPID IN THE MAKING.

©The Mailbox® · TEC44035 · Feb./Mar. 2008 · written by Dr. D. Jackson Maxwell, Memphis, TN · Key p. 309

Presidential Trivia

Solve.

A $(5.25 + 10.5) - 3.36 =$ _____

M $(24 ÷ 6) \times 7 + 9 =$ _____

I $(8 \times 3) ÷ 2 + 9 =$ _____

W $(24 \times 2) ÷ 6 =$ _____

L $45 - (4 \times 9) =$ _____

A $(18\frac{1}{4} + 17\frac{3}{4}) ÷ 9 =$ _____

I $(9\frac{5}{6} - 3\frac{1}{6}) + 5\frac{1}{3} =$ _____

T $5 \times (5 + 2) + (7\frac{1}{2} + 8) =$ _____

F $(2.9 + 27.1) ÷ 5 =$ _____

T $[(54.9 - 8.7) + (5 - 1.2)] ÷ 2 =$ _____

H $(4\frac{1}{5} + 5\frac{4}{5}) \times 0.5 =$ _____

L $(6.09 \times 3) ÷ 3 =$ _____

Which president started the tradition of throwing the first pitch of each baseball season?

To find out, write each letter from above on its matching numbered line below.

___ ___ ___ ___ ___ ___ ___   ___.
8   12   6.09   9   21   4   37   5.0

___ ___ ___ ___
25   12.39   6 $50\frac{1}{2}$

Name _____

Luck of the Irish

Add a suffix to each base word. Write the new word on the line. Use each suffix once.

1. success _____

2. back _____

3. pay _____

4. govern _____

5. courage _____

6. hero _____

7. music _____

8. fool _____

9. speech _____

10. child _____

11. quiet _____

12. friend _____

13. fast _____

14. good _____

15. duck _____

-ward

-en   -ly

-ous   -less

-like   -ness   -ic

-ish   -ful   -ling   -ship

-al

-ment   -or

Hot on the Trail

Solve. Write each answer in its simplest form.

A. $\frac{3}{8} + \frac{1}{4} =$

B. $\frac{1}{2} + \frac{3}{12} =$

C. $\frac{7}{8} - \frac{1}{3} =$

D. $\frac{1}{6} + \frac{1}{4} =$

E. $\frac{11}{12} - \frac{1}{3} =$

F. $\frac{1}{2} + \frac{1}{3} =$

G. $\frac{3}{9} + \frac{1}{6} =$

H. $\frac{7}{10} - \frac{2}{5} =$

I. $\frac{7}{14} - \frac{3}{7} =$

J. $\frac{1}{3} + \frac{1}{5} =$

K. $\frac{8}{9} - \frac{5}{9} =$

L. $\frac{2}{5} + \frac{1}{6} =$

M. $\frac{5}{6} - \frac{1}{8} =$

N. $\frac{2}{7} + \frac{1}{2} =$

O. $\frac{4}{6} + \frac{3}{12} =$

One Person's Junk

Earth Day

Celebrate Earth Day by focusing on an environmental challenge that's right inside your mailbox: junk mail. Share with students that junk mail is mailed advertising of some type, and that it's only "junk" if a person doesn't want to receive it. Then give each child a copy of the survey below. Have each student survey at least ten adults about whether they want to receive certain types of junk mail. After students help you compile their results, discuss the four questions at the right. For a math extension, have students find the percentage of respondents who do or do not want to receive each type of junk mail.

Why is junk mail considered harmful to the environment?

Were you surprised at the survey results? Why or why not?

What are some ways people can recycle junk mail?

Why did some respondents want to receive certain types of junk mail?

Name _____ Data collection

Junk Mail Survey

Ask at least ten adults (21 years old and older) whether they want to receive each type of junk mail in the chart.

Tally and then total their responses in the correct columns.

Keep a tally of the number of people you asked: _____

Junk?

CATALOG

Do you want to receive the following types of junk mail?

Types of Junk Mail	"Yes" Tallies	"Yes" Total	"No" Tallies	"No" Total
Catalogs				
Advertising flyers and supplements				
Preapproved offers of credit or credit cards				
Requests for donations from charitable or nonprofit organizations				
Sweepstakes and prize information				
Envelopes or card decks containing ads from different companies				
Ads that include discount coupons				
Consumer surveys				
Magazines (free ones with advertising to get you to buy a subscription)				

Note to the teacher: Use with "One Person's Junk" above.

Four Hours?
April Fools' Day

Sneak in persuasive-writing practice this April Fools' Day by announcing you've heard a rumor that a new law may require teachers to assign four hours of homework each night. When students protest (and they will!), explain that they might be able to persuade legislators to vote down the measure if there are letters that provide reasons against it. Display the outline shown. Then have each student use it to write a persuasive letter to one of your state's lawmakers. After students share their letters, proclaim that the homework law is an April Fools' hoax (whew!) and then treat the class to a small celebratory snack!

Sarah Shaw, Sunrise Elementary, Phoenix, AZ

Letter Outline
- Greeting
- Introduction: Tell who you are and why you are writing.
- Reason 1 for voting against the law
  - Supporting evidence/detail
  - Supporting evidence/detail
  - Supporting evidence/detail
- Reason 2 for voting against the law
  - Supporting evidence/detail
  - Supporting evidence/detail
  - Supporting evidence/detail
- Reason 3 for voting against the law
  - Supporting evidence/detail
  - Supporting evidence/detail
  - Supporting evidence/detail
- Conclusion
- Closing: Restate your position and respectfully request action.

Four hours?

Find the Fakes
Anniversary of the First Dictionary of American English

On April 14, 1828, Noah Webster published the first dictionary. To honor this anniversary and reinforce key dictionary skills, list on the board the words at the left. Have students rewrite the words in alphabetical order and then circle the ones they think are actual words, using dictionaries for help. (The fake words are *shibby, draven, namow,* and *laisten.*) To conclude, have each child make up her own illustrated definition for each fake word.

Ann Fisher, Toledo, OH

Find the fakes!

shibby	obelisk
draven	namow
lessee	brisket
clavichord	laisten
twang	quibble

Just for You, Mom!
Mother's Day

For a fun Mother's Day gift that cashes in on the popularity of TV musicals, have each student complete a copy of page 36. After he folds the completed page, have him place it in a business envelope, decorate the envelope, and then take it home to his mom.

adapted from an idea by Debby Sato, Jefferson Elementary, Honolulu, HI

Name_____

Cups of Advice

Write the correct prefixes to complete each sentence.

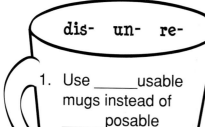
dis- un- re-

1. Use _____usable mugs instead of _____posable cups.

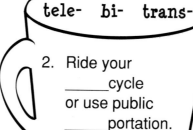
tele- bi- trans-

2. Ride your _____cycle or use public _____portation.

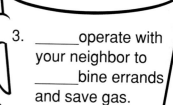
com- co- con-

3. _____operate with your neighbor to _____bine errands and save gas.

un- de- re-

4. _____frost frozen foods to _____duce cooking time.

pre- de- per-

5. _____form an energy audit to _____termine how much energy your family uses.

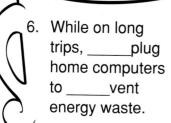
re- un- pre-

6. While on long trips, _____plug home computers to _____vent energy waste.

uni- un- re-

7. Avoid buying products that cannot be _____cycled or that have _____necessary packaging.

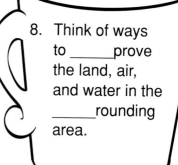
sur- dis- im-

8. Think of ways to _____prove the land, air, and water in the _____rounding area.

Name _____

In Bloom

Color each polygon by the code. Circle each object that contains at least one regular polygon.

Color Code

triangle = red   hexagon = yellow
quadrilateral = brown   octagon = purple
pentagon = orange

Bonus Box: On the back of this page, write the name of each type of quadrilateral pictured above.

Cinco de Mayo

Combine each pair of sentences on the matching lines below.

 In 1862, France was trying to take over Mexico.

 In 1862, France was trying to set up a new government in Mexico.

 Cinco de Mayo celebrates a Mexican victory on May 5, 1862, at the Battle of Puebla.

 Cinco de Mayo celebrates a Mexican victory over the French at the Battle of Puebla.

 The Mexican army won the battle even though the French army was better armed.

 The Mexican army won the battle even though the French army was larger.

 France withdrew its troops a few years later because of resistance by many Mexicans.

 France withdrew its troops a few years later because of pressure from the United States.

 Some Mexican towns celebrate Cinco de Mayo with parades.

 Some U.S. cities celebrate Cinco de Mayo with parades.

 In the United States, people often celebrate Cinco de Mayo with folk dancing.

 In the United States, people often celebrate Cinco de Mayo with Mexican music.

Mom: The Musical

Mom

A major television studio wants to produce a television musical about—of all people—your mom!

The studio wants your help coming up with titles for some of the musical's songs.

Finish each prompt.

My mom is a great mom because _____

_____

My mom and I have fun together when we _____

_____

My favorite memory with my mom is _____

_____

My mom is unique because _____

_____

My mom's best quality is _____

_____

Use the information above to create four titles for songs about your mom.

1. _____

2. _____

3. _____

4. _____

Okay, so your mom really isn't going to be the subject of a musical. But she's still a star to you, right? Write a message to your mom explaining why she's so special: _____

_____

_____

_____

_____

Name _____

ALWAYS REMEMBER

Solve. Then color by the code.

Color Code

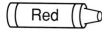

Red	Orange	Yellow	Purple	Pink	Green

1. 12,758
   3,694
   + 5,314

2.   10.82
   + 6.09

3.   73
   x 24

4. $2\frac{3}{8}$
   + $1\frac{1}{8}$

5. 525,617
   − 42,716

6. $8\overline{)9,176}$

  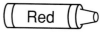 

Blue	Purple	Green	White	Red	Pink

7.   41.02
   x   9

8. $6\frac{5}{6}$
   − $4\frac{2}{6}$

9.   22.57
   − 13.14

10. $5\overline{)1.25}$

11. $12\frac{12}{16}$
   − $10\frac{2}{16}$

12. 123.05
   x   1.3

Wrapping Up the School Year

Memory-Sharing Stick

End of school

This year-end activity is a grand way for students to recall the year's fun events. In advance, cover a paper towel tube with construction paper and label it as shown. Punch a hole near one end of the tube. Then cut a long length of ribbon or yarn for each child. Thread the ribbons through the hole and knot them together.

Next, have the class sit in a circle. Invite each student to share his favorite memory from the school year. As he talks, have him wrap one length of ribbon around the tube. Then have him tape the end of the ribbon in place and pass the tube to the next child. Continue in this manner until every student has shared a memory and the tube is covered with ribbon.

adapted from an idea by Brooke Beverly, Dudley Elementary, Dudley, MA

Father's Day Favorites
Writing

For an unforgettable gift any father (or father figure) would love to receive, provide each student with a large envelope and construction paper. Have the student decorate the envelope to look like the packaging of her father's favorite snack. On the front and back, have her change the text to information about her father. Then, on a sheet of notebook paper, have the student write a poem or an essay about her father and his favorite snack. Place the writing in the envelope and send it home for the child to present to her dad on Father's Day.

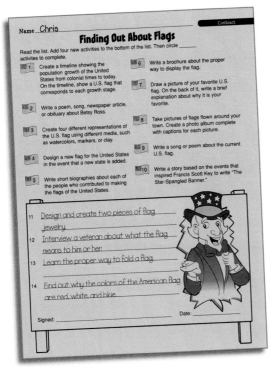

Focus on the Flag
Research contract

Celebrate Flag Day with this ongoing independent activity. To begin, program a copy of page 44 with the number of projects you wish students to do; then make a copy for each child to complete as directed. During free time or after finishing all other assignments, have the student work on his selected activities. At the end of the allotted time, invite each child to share one of his completed projects with the class.

Margery Stueve, New Bremen Elementary, New Bremen, OH

Summer Harvest
Problem-solving strategies

Reviewing different methods of solving word problems can be bushels of fun with this simple activity! Have each student write on the front of an index card a word problem about her favorite summer fruit or vegetable and record the solution on the back. If desired, have her add an illustration to the problem side of her card that might help a visual learner solve the problem. When everyone is finished, have each student trade cards (answer-side down) with a classmate and solve on notebook paper the problem he receives. Require that he identify the problem-solving strategy he uses to find the answer before turning the card over to check his work. Continue having students swap cards in this manner as time allows. Then, using a show of hands, poll the class to determine how many different problem-solving strategies students used.

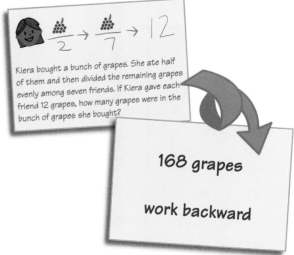

Name

It's Time for a Vacation!

Use the information on the sign to solve each set of problems.

Bluestone National Park

Sites to See	Time Needed
Dragon's Kettle	35 min.
Great Fount	48 min.
Scorching Springs Visitor's Center	1 hr. 25 min.
Woolly Hot Springs	2 hr. 30 min.
Daisy Pool	37 min.
Mudslide Volcano	40 min.
Black Glass Cliff	39 min.
Scorching Springs Museum	1 hr. 45 min.
Frothy Dome Geyser	51 min.

1. Dad wants to go through the visitor's center and then visit Daisy Pool. How long will it take him to do both activities?

   Dad also wants to visit Scorching Springs Museum. If it is scheduled to open in 2 hours and 55 minutes, how much time will Dad have to get to the museum after visiting Daisy Pool?

2. Mom wants to see Great Fount Geyser and Frothy Dome Geyser. How long will it take her to see both geysers?

   Mom also wants to watch a film at the visitor's center that starts in 2 hours and 15 minutes. After she sees the geysers, how much time will she have left to buy a snack and get seated for the film?

3. Rick wants to tour Woolly Hot Springs. Suzie wants to visit Black Glass Cliff. If Rick and Suzie must stay together, how long will it take them to see the springs and the cliff?

   Mom wants Rick and Suzie to be back in $2\frac{1}{2}$ hours for dinner. How late will Rick and Suzie be for dinner?

4. Ryan wants to see Mudslide Volcano and Dragon's Kettle. How long will it take him to see both sites?

   If the park closes in $1\frac{1}{2}$ hours, will Ryan have time to see both sites? Why or why not?

©The Mailbox® • TEC44037 • June/July 2008 • written by Jennifer Otter, Oak Ridge, NC • Key p. 310

Name _____

Camping Out

Estimate the measurement of each labeled angle.
Then find the actual measurement.
Write the measurements in the chart. Write the letter
of each angle inside the correct campfire flame.

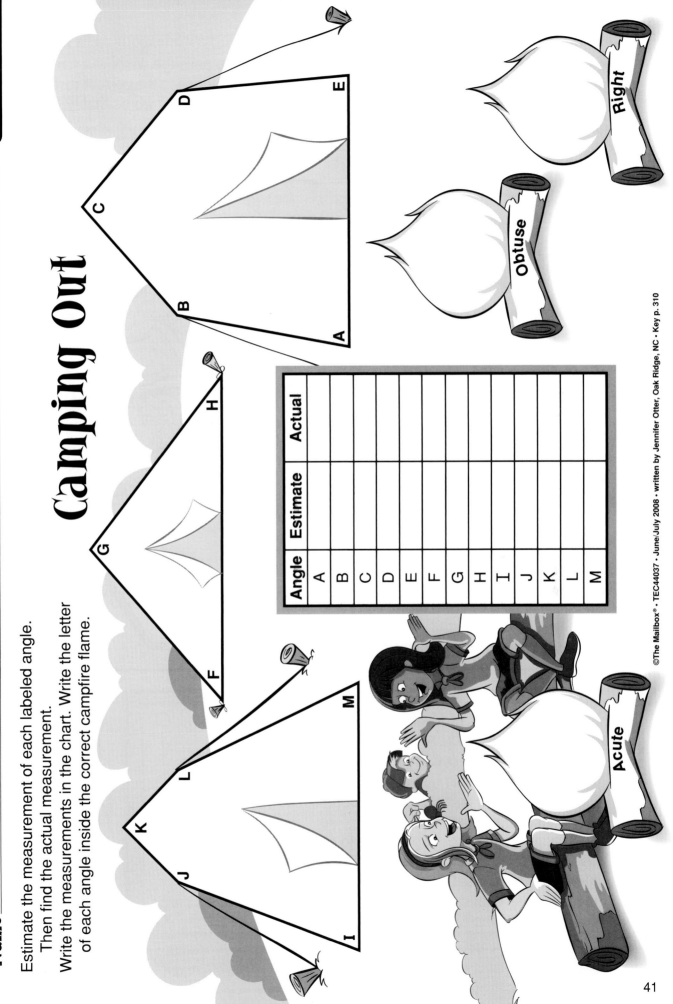

Angle	Estimate	Actual
A		
B		
C		
D		
E		
F		
G		
H		
I		
J		
K		
L		
M		

Obtuse

Right

Acute

How Cool Are Hot Dogs?

Read the passage. Write the number of each sentence in the correct cart section. Underline the key words that help you in each sentence.

Facts

_____

_____   _____

Opinions

_____

_____   _____

1. Hot dogs have been eaten in American baseball parks since 1893. 2. However, Americans adored hot dogs even before then. 3. The first Coney Island hot dog stand opened in 1871. 4. The stand sold nearly 4,000 hot dogs in its first year. 5. Customers went crazy for the delicious hot dogs. 6. Today, hot dogs are sold across the country.

7. There are many delicious ways to eat a hot dog. 8. The best New York hot dogs are covered in steamed onions and mustard. 9. A Kansas City–style hot dog has sauerkraut and melted Swiss cheese. 10. No matter what tops a hot dog, it's the coolest food in the nation.

©The Mailbox® • TEC44037 • June/July 2008 • written by Kim Minafo, Apex, NC • Key p. 310

FABULOUS FATHER

Read the card. Think about the father who will receive it. On the ribbon for each topic, write a sentence telling what you can infer about this dad.

HAPPY FATHER'S DAY!

F abulous father to Kevin, Karen, and Kyle
A lways has equipment ready for his team
T errific husband to Dana
H elps his students do well in math
E njoys the street noises he hears at his home
R ides bikes on faraway wooded trails

#1

You're the best, Dad!

Community

Career

Family

Hobby

Home

Finding Out About Flags

Read the list. Add four new activities to the bottom of the list. Then circle _____ activities to complete.

 1 Create a timeline showing the population growth of the United States from colonial times to today. On the timeline, show a U.S. flag that corresponds to each growth stage.

 2 Write a poem, song, newspaper article, or obituary about Betsy Ross.

 3 Create four different representations of the U.S. flag using different media, such as watercolors, markers, or clay.

 4 Design a new flag for the United States in the event that a new state is added.

 5 Write short biographies about each of the people who contributed to making the flags of the United States.

 6 Write a brochure about the proper way to display the flag.

 7 Draw a picture of your favorite U.S. flag. On the back of it, write a brief explanation about why it is your favorite.

 8 Take pictures of flags flown around your town. Create a photo album complete with captions for each picture.

 9 Write a song or poem about the current U.S. flag.

10 Write a story based on the events that inspired Francis Scott Key to write "The Star-Spangled Banner."

11. _____

_____

12. _____

_____

13. _____

_____

14. _____

_____

Signed: _____   Date: _____

CLASSROOM DISPLAYS

Classroom DISPLAYS

Positive Peas in Our Pod

Self-Discipline: Abby, Nate, Raoul
Helpfulness: Theo, Chris, Haley
Respect: Ashley, Meredith, Sam
Trustworthiness: Mitch, Maria, Matt

To recognize great behavior, label copies of the pea pod pattern on page 55 with positive character traits. Cut slits on the dotted lines and post the pods on the board. Write each student's name on a pea pattern. When a child demonstrates a specific trait, slip her pea cutout into the appropriate pod.

Natalie McGregor, Grenada Upper Elementary
Grenada, MS

JAMMIN' JOBS

Pledge Leader — Adam
Calendar — Maddie
Errands — Leah
Bookshelves — Nick
Papers — Brent
Lights — Scott
Line Leader — Tori
Board Cleaner — Alia
Plants — Travis
PE Equipment — Cam

For a one-of-a-kind jobs chart, label cutouts of jammer shorts with classroom jobs. Post the shorts on the board. Then have each student personalize, decorate, and cut out a copy of the shorts. Each Monday, pin the assigned helpers' cutouts atop the job shorts just below the job title.

Donna G. Pawloski, Springfield, PA

We're Exploring Verbs!

SS McGregor

This October display can be kept afloat all year long! Make it 3-D by twisting brown bulletin board paper tightly to make the mast. Around the ship, post student papers on a topic the class is currently studying. To change the display, simply post a new topic in the title and display different work samples. For added fun, have a student make a small cutout of the captain (that would be you!) to place on the deck.

Natalie McGregor, Grenada Upper Elementary, Grenada, MS

"EIFFEL" FOR THIS BOOK!

Celebrate National Children's Book Week in November (held annually the week before Thanksgiving) with a display that tips its hat to a famous French landmark! Post an enlarged copy of the Eiffel Tower pattern on page 56. Each student writes his name, the title of a favorite book, and the sentence starter shown on an index card. Then he lists three endings for the starter that give details about why he likes the book.

adapted from an idea by Colleen Dabney
Williamsburg, VA

Hatchet by Gary Paulsen
"Eiffel" for this book because

Ricky

FUNNY FRACTION FACES

What fraction of faces have blue eyes or a blue mouth?

A patch of pumpkins is the perfect place to practice fractions! Have each student cut out a pumpkin shape and decorate it with colorful cutout facial features. Post the pumpkins with a question such as the one shown. Change the question frequently, letting students make suggestions of their own.

Good Friends Are
GIFTS!

Honor the gift of friendship with this December writing display. If your class has younger reading buddies, have each child write a paragraph about his partner and their friendship. (No buddies? Then just pair your students and have them write about each other's interests and talents.) The student copies his paragraph on a square of lined paper and then staples atop it a piece of construction paper decorated as shown. Once you add a bow and a photo of the buddies cut into the shape of a gift tag, it's ready to display.

Jeri Gramil, Mother Seton School, Emmitsburg, MD

Classroom DISPLAYS

Set sail for a brand-new year with an activity that integrates writing with geometry. Give each student a sheet of polygons to review. Have the child use the polygons to create a picture of a unique ship. Then have her write a paragraph describing the steps she will take to guarantee a shipshape year. Post the pictures and paragraphs as shown.

adapted from an idea by Vickie Robertson, Whittier, CA

For a reading display that can stay up all winter long, have each student cut out a copy of the bear on page 57. After writing his name on the book and decorating the scarf, have the child label a 3" x 3" sticky note with the title and author of his book, followed by a brief review. Then have him stick the note on the cutout as shown. When he is ready to share a new review, he just replaces the old note with a new one!

adapted from an idea by Angelique Kwabenah, Potomac Landing Elementary, Fort Washington, MD

We ♥ Books!

Ernest Shackleton:
Gripped by the Antarctic
by Rebecca L. Johnson

A Wrinkle in Time
by Madeleine L'Engle

The Giver by Lois
Lowry

The Miraculous Journey of
Edward Tulane
by Kate DiCamillo

Diary of a Wimpy Kid
by Jeff Kinney

The Man Who Made Time
Travel by Kathryn Lasky

The Invention of Hugo
Cabret by Brian Selznick

Eldest by Christopher
Paolini

How the Amazon Queen
Fought the Prince of Egypt
by Tamara Bower

Patrick

Meredith

Nico

Stacey

Raven

Cushi

Tomas

Becca

Brad

Is there little time to put up a Valentine's Day display? Take heart—this one's a snap! Post a giant heart as shown. Place a small heart template, markers, scissors, and construction paper nearby. When a student finishes a book, he writes its title and author on the large heart. Then he signs a small cutout and adds it to the display. Challenge students to see how many books they can list on the heart by the last day of February!

adapted from an idea by Colleen Dabney, Williamsburg, VA

Classroom DISPLAYS

St. Patrick's Sentences

Brian
<u>Simple:</u> The dog ate the purple crayon.
<u>Compound:</u> The dog ate the purple crayon, and Mom screamed.
<u>Complex:</u> When I saw that my dog ate a purple crayon, I couldn't believe my eyes.

To review sentence types, have each student write three unrelated words on a shamrock cutout. Post the shamrocks. During free time, a student chooses a shamrock and labels an index card with simple, compound, and complex sentences using the words. After checking the sentences, display the card with its shamrock. Adapt this idea for math by having students label shamrocks with three sets of five numbers and retitling the board "St. Patrick's Averages." Then have students find the mean, median, mode, and range of each set.

adapted from an idea by Brooke Beverly, Dudley Elementary, Dudley, MA

When Do You Feel "Eggs-tra" Happy ?

I feel "eggs-tra" happy when I am reading a great book. The story can carry me away from anything that is bothering me. I love imagining what the characters are like and wondering what will happen next. When I read a great book, I'm totally relaxed and happy!

Meg

For a writing activity that's perfect for the weeks leading up to Easter, copy the egg card pattern on page 58 for each student. Post the title shown, writing the last word on a paper strip. Have each student decorate the front of a card to look like an Easter egg and then write on the inside a paragraph that answers the title question. Change the last word in the title each week (see the suggestions below) and have students repeat the activity.

Bored   Silly
          Angry   Grateful
Nervous
Loved   Content
        Lonely

52

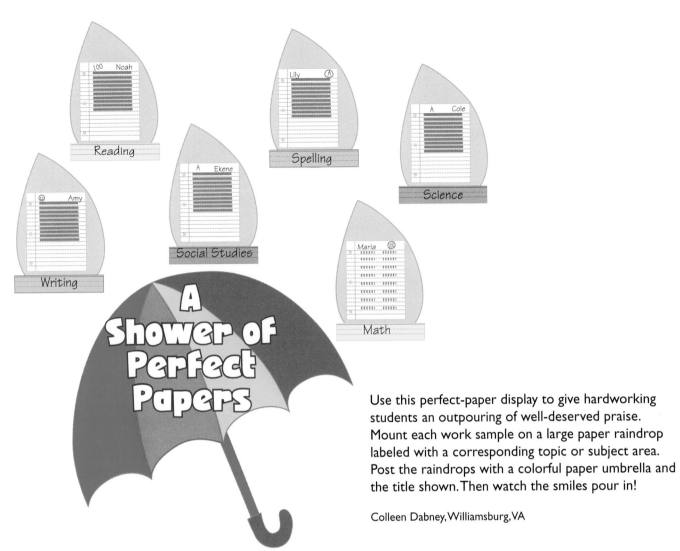

A Shower of Perfect Papers

Use this perfect-paper display to give hardworking students an outpouring of well-deserved praise. Mount each work sample on a large paper raindrop labeled with a corresponding topic or subject area. Post the raindrops with a colorful paper umbrella and the title shown. Then watch the smiles pour in!

Colleen Dabney, Williamsburg, VA

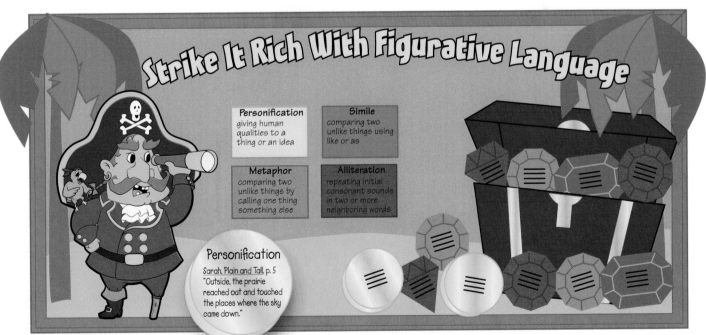

Strike It Rich With Figurative Language

Personification
giving human qualities to a thing or an idea

Simile
comparing two unlike things using like or as

Metaphor
comparing two unlike things by calling one thing something else

Alliteration
repeating initial consonant sounds in two or more neighboring words

Personification
Sarah, Plain and Tall, p. 5
"Outside, the prairie reached out and touched the places where the sky came down."

Post a paper treasure chest and an enlarged copy of the pirate pattern on page 59. Add colorful paper rectangles, each labeled with the definition of a different type of figurative language. When a student finds an example of figurative language in his reading, have him record the example and where it was found on a matching colorful gem or coin cutout; then have him add it to the display.

Amy Binette, Freeman Centennial School, Norfolk, MA

Classroom DISPLAYS

"Water" Your Plans for the Summer?

Discover students' summer plans with this display. Post an enlarged copy of the watering can pattern from page 60 with water droplet cutouts. Then have each child make a flower cutout and label its center with what he is looking forward to doing this summer. Mount the flowers below the watering can to create a garden of student writing.

Corrie Brubaker, Providence School, Chambersburg, PA

Look "Whoooo's" Wiser!

Chantal
- equivalent fractions
- the capitals of all 50 states
- prime and composite numbers
- how to write a persuasive paragraph
- how to add and subtract decimals

It's a hoot to make this display, which features students' learnings! Have each child list on an index card five things she learned during the school year. Mount the completed cards on colorful paper and post them with an enlarged copy of the owl pattern from page 60.

Colleen Dabney, Williamsburg, VA

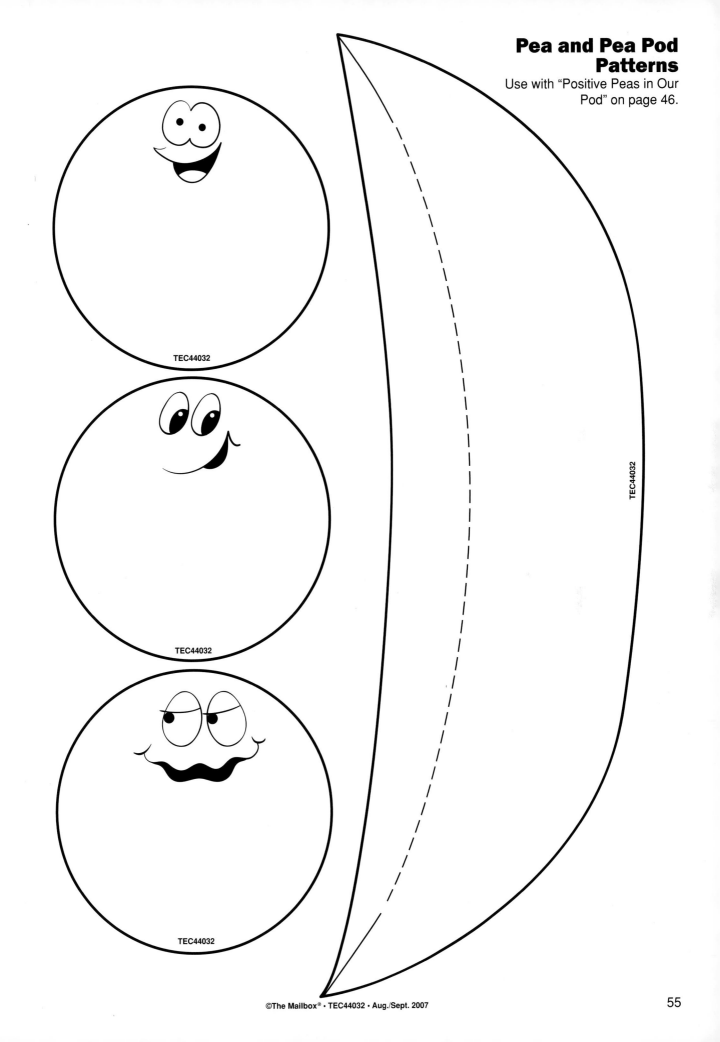

TEC44032

TEC44032

TEC44032

TEC44032

Eiffel Tower Pattern

Use with "'Eiffel' for This Book!" on page 48.

TEC44033

Reviewed
by

TEC44034

Egg Card Pattern

Use with "When Do You Feel 'Eggs-tra' Happy?" on page 52.

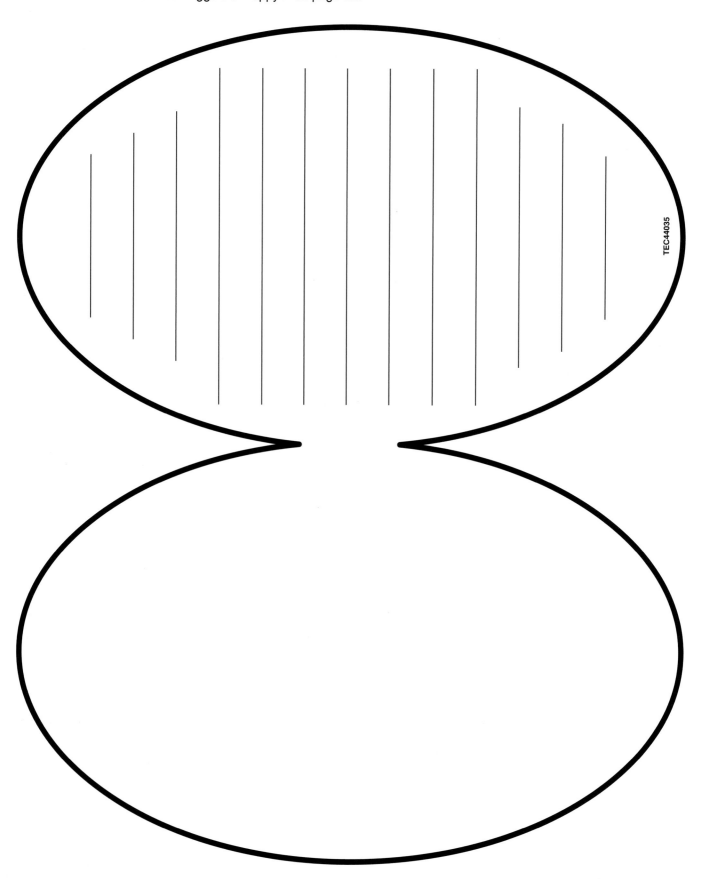

TEC44035

Watering Can Pattern

Use with "'Water' Your Plans for the Summer?" on page 54.

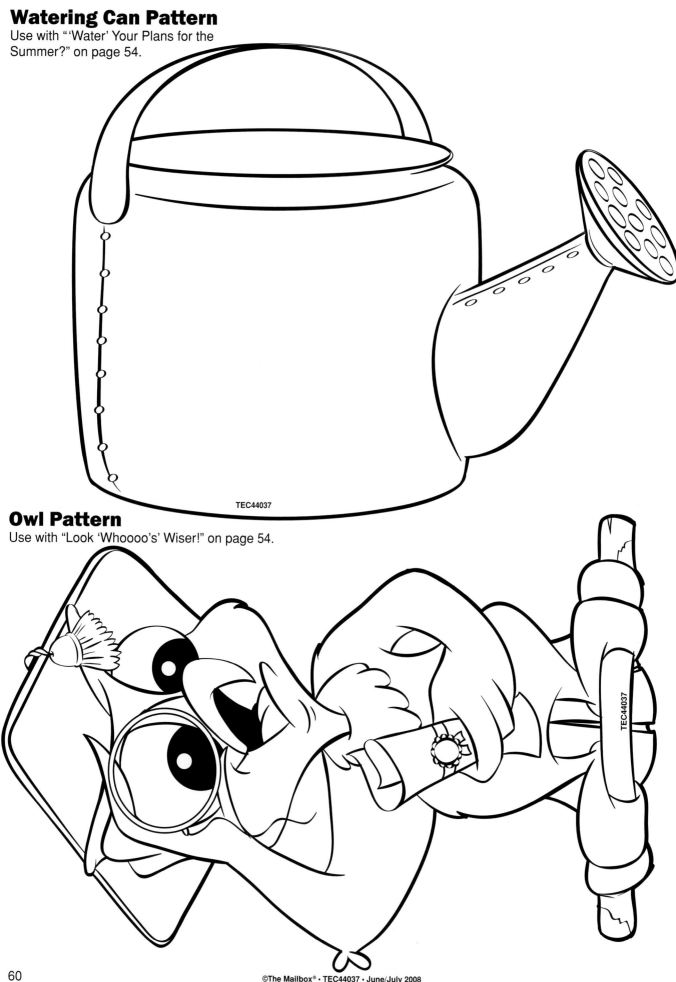

TEC44037

Owl Pattern

Use with "Look 'Whoooo's' Wiser!" on page 54.

TEC44037

LANGUAGE ARTS UNITS

On the Trail of Capitalization and Punctuation

with ideas by Farrah Milby, Weddington Hills Elementary, Concord, NC

CASE FILES
Student reference

Invite your students to create a special file so they'll have at their fingertips important usage rules that all good writers need. Provide each child with a file folder and a copy of the charts on page 64. Have the student complete the charts by writing an example for each rule. Then have her label the outside of her folder "Top Secret" or "Confidential" and glue the completed charts inside as shown. Allow students to keep their folders at their desks to help them solve any capitalization and punctuation mysteries that might arise.

COLLECT THE CLUES!
Editing sentences

This small-group activity is terrific for practicing capital-ization and punctuation skills. First, secretly select a book that's familiar to the entire class. Next, label each of several index cards with a different sentence from the book or about the book that hints at the book's identity but not its title. Write the sentences without the correct punctuation marks and capitalization (see the examples). Then display the cards around the room. Have each group of students work together as investigators from a detective agency to find all the clue cards, spot the mistakes on each card, and then write each sentence correctly on a sheet of paper. Once a group has corrected all of the sentences, have it write on scrap paper (using correct capi-talization and punctuation, of course!) its prediction of the mystery book's title. After discussing possible answers with the class, reveal the book's title.

HOLES

if you take a bad boy and make him dig a hole every day in the hot sun it will turn him into a good boy

the setting of this book is a camp for boys called camp green lake

Punctuation	Symbol	Point Value
period	.	1 point
question mark	?	1 point
exclamation point	!	1 point
quotation marks	" "	2 points
comma	,	2 points
apostrophe	'	2 points
colon	:	3 points
semicolon	;	3 points
hyphen	-	4 points
parentheses	( )	4 points
dash	—	5 points

POINTS FOR PUNCTUATION
Review game

To begin this partner game, list on the board the types of punctuation shown. Assign a point value to each type. Challenge the partners to search the classroom for as many examples of each type of punctuation as possible within a given amount of time. Have the duo record its findings in a detective log similar to the one shown. When time is up, have each twosome share its findings with the class and then total the number of points earned. If desired, post the completed logs along with a copy of the points chart on a display titled "Hot on the Trail of Punctuation."

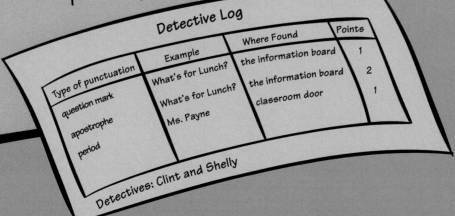

Detective Log

Type of punctuation	Example	Where Found	Points
question mark	What's for Lunch?	the information board	1
apostrophe	What's for Lunch?	the information board	2
period	Ms. Payne	classroom door	1

Detectives: Clint and Shelly

Capitalization and Punctuation Charts

Use with "Case Files" on page 62.

PUNCTUATION MARK	COMMON USE(S)	EXAMPLE
. period	• at the end of a declarative or an imperative sentence • after most initials • when writing the number form of a decimal • after most abbreviations	
? question mark	after a question	
! exclamation point	to express strong feeling	
" " quotation marks	• to show the exact words of a speaker • in titles of poems, short stories, songs, magazine articles, newspaper articles, and book chapters	
, comma	• to separate items in a series • in compound sentences • in dates and addresses • to separate three-digit periods in large numbers • before or after a direct quotation • after the greeting and closing in a friendly letter	
' apostrophe	• in contractions • in possessive nouns • when referring to the plural of letters and words	
: colon	• to introduce a list • to separate the hour and minutes when writing time • after the greeting in a business letter	
; semicolon	• to join two complete sentences that are not joined by a conjunction • to separate groups of items within a list that have commas	
– hyphen	• to divide a word between syllables at the end of a line • when writing the word form of fractions and two-part numbers from 21 to 99 • in some compound words	

©The Mailbox® · TEC44032 · Aug./Sept. 2007

WHAT TO CAPITALIZE	EXAMPLE
first word in a sentence	
pronoun I	
first, last, and all important words in titles	
proper nouns and adjectives	
first word in the greeting and closing of a friendly letter	

©The Mailbox® · TEC44032 · Aug./Sept. 2007

THE BOOK BANDIT

Rewrite each sentence using correct capitalization and punctuation.

1. books are being stolen from the library every saturday stated the librarian

_____

_____

SUSPECT 1

2. detective smith wrote the information on his pad and started to question more people

_____

_____

3. after asking all the right questions i still dont know who the bandit is declared the detective

_____

_____

SUSPECT 2

4. suddenly he spotted a book that looked out of place

_____

_____

5. right next to the book was the clue hed been looking for

_____

_____

6. it was a poem titled im the book bandit

_____

_____

SUSPECT 3

7. the detective used the clues and now he knows who the bandit is

_____

_____

When you look left,
I go right.
You search hard,
But I stay out of sight.

Here's one last clue
For you to think about:
You get around on two,
But I need three, without a doubt!

Read the poem. Use its clues to tell who the bandit is.

The book bandit is Suspect _____.

Getting
Sentence Skills
in Shape

Nutty-O cereal

tastes good.

This crunchy cereal is made from whole-grain oats.

SOMETHING'S MISSING
Fragments

To help students spot groups of words that do not make complete sentences, collect empty cereal or cereal-bar boxes. Give groups of students several boxes. Instruct each group to search its boxes for sentence fragments and record them on a sheet of paper. Have the group decide whether each recorded fragment is missing a subject or a predicate and then write a sentence that includes the missing part. Next, have students cut cereal shapes from light-colored paper, copy each of their sentences onto a separate cutout, and highlight the part of the sentence that was the original fragment. Display the completed cutouts on a board titled "We're 'Cereal-ous' About Fixing Fragments!"

Colleen Dabney, Williamsburg-JCC Schools, Williamsburg, VA

PUT YOUR HAND ON THE *AND*
Compound sentences

For this fun review, write on separate sentence strips several simple, compound, and complex sentences that each include one of the following conjunctions: *and, but,* or *or.* Omit the comma in front of the conjunction in each compound sentence. In addition, cut out a large comma from black paper. Next, invite two students to hold up one of the sentence strips. Have another student read aloud the sentence on the strip. Then have him stand behind the strip and cover the conjunction with his hand. Instruct the class to tell whether the words on each side of the child's hand make a complete sentence. If they do, have him attach the comma cutout to the sentence strip in front of the conjunction. If they do not, have students explain why the comma is not needed. Then remove the comma and select two new students to hold up the next strip.

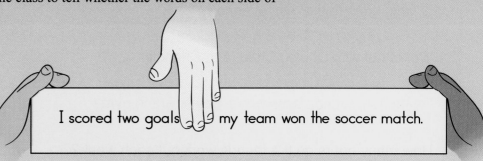

I scored two goals my team won the soccer match.

Kristi Titus, Leesburg Elementary, Leesburg, VA

LET'S HEAR THE SOUND EFFECTS
Declarative, interrogative, imperative, and exclamatory sentences

After reviewing the four kinds of sentences, have students agree on an appropriate sound to distinguish each type of sentence from the others, such as a click made with the tongue for a declarative sentence, a fist hitting an open palm of the hand for an imperative sentence, a whistle followed by a click for an exclamatory sentence, and a "woo-oo-oo" sound followed by a click for an interrogative sentence. Next, read aloud one sample sentence at a time from a textbook. Then either call on individual students to make the matching sound(s) or have the entire class respond in unison. This activity will be on your students' minds when they are asked at home, "What did you do in school today?" To follow up, have each child complete a copy of page 68 as directed.

Amy Evans, Grace Christian School, Blacklick, OH

IT'S ALL ABOUT STRUCTURE
Simple, compound, and complex sentences

To provide practice with the three types of sentence structure, divide students into groups of three. Inform the groups that they will be writing conversations that take place among three cartoon superhero characters: Simple Simon (who speaks only in simple sentences), Connie Compound (who speaks only in compound sentences), and Complex Rex (who speaks only in complex sentences). Next, give each threesome a different strip cut from a copy of the conversation topic strips on page 69. Have the trio write a conversation that the three characters might have about the strip's topic, with each character speaking at least three times using its designated sentence structure. After students finish writing, allow each group to practice reading its conversation aloud, with each child reading a different character's part. Then invite each group to perform for the class. For more practice, have each student complete a copy of page 70 as directed.

The mayor is missing!

His car is parked at city hall, but he is not there.

Although we've searched everywhere, he has not been found.

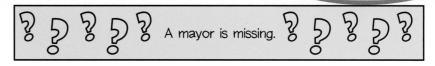

A mayor is missing.

Julia Ring Alarie, Williston, VT

Getting Stronger!

Decide whether each group of words is a fragment or a complete sentence. If the words are a complete sentence, tell which type of sentence it is. Use the code.

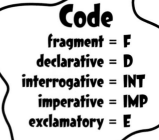

Code
fragment = **F**
declarative = **D**
interrogative = **INT**
imperative = **IMP**
exclamatory = **E**

1. Charlie goes to the gym every day. _____

2. Works out with Chuck, Chad, and Chandler. _____

3. Do the four friends work with a trainer at the gym? _____

4. How many hours do the friends work out each week? _____

5. Are really tired when they leave the gym. _____

6. Exercise to stay in shape. _____

7. Chad did 100 sit-ups! _____

8. Eat healthy foods every day. _____

9. Chuck lifted ten pounds more than the trainer did! _____

10. Chandler is getting stronger every week. _____

11. Arrives at the gym at 8 AM. _____

12. At what time does the gym close? _____

13. Meet them there early. _____

14. Charlie lifted 250 pounds. _____

15. Chad won the weight lifting contest! _____

Sentence Skills

©The Mailbox® • TEC44032 • Aug./Sept. 2007 • Key p. 310

Conversation Topic Strips

Use with "It's All About Structure" on page 67.

A mysterious illness is sweeping the town.

TEC44032

Pets are acting very strangely.

TEC44032

A mayor is missing.

TEC44032

Tap water throughout the town is an eerie shade of green.

TEC44032

Puzzling messages are being left in people's mailboxes.

TEC44032

Parents are allowing children to eat whatever they want.

TEC44032

Grandparents are talking and acting like teenagers.

TEC44032

Video games, DVDs, and CDs are suddenly disappearing from all stores.

TEC44032

A meteor has landed in the middle of town.

TEC44032

There are weird lights in the sky.

TEC44032

Weighty Matters

Tell whether each sentence is simple, compound, or complex by writing its number on a corresponding disk below. If your answers are correct, the sum of the numbers on the disks will equal the number on the bar for each dumbbell.

1. Dumbbells can be bought one at a time, or they can be bought in sets.

2. A dumbbell is a short bar with a heavy ball or one or more disks at each end.

3. A dumbbell is a weight that a person lifts for exercise.

4. Dumbbells come in many sizes and shapes.

5. Since many people use dumbbells that range in weight from five to 50 pounds, sets with those weights are popular.

6. Some dumbbells are chrome, but others have parts coated with rubber.

7. Weights much smaller than dumbbells can be worn around a person's wrists, or they can be strapped around the ankles.

8. Some people use hand weights.

9. Some weight lifters lie on benches that they can adjust.

10. Many weight lifters sit on benches for support during their workouts.

11. People should not use a heavy weight unless a light weight is too easy for them.

12. Some dumbbell sets have standard handles, but others have Olympic handles.

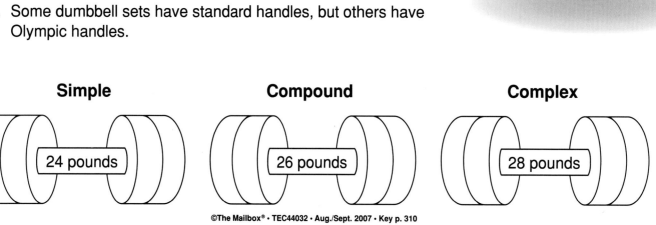

Simple	Compound	Complex
24 pounds	26 pounds	28 pounds

A **Noun and Pronoun** Hoedown

with ideas by Amber Barbee, Wharton, TX

A BALE OF NOUNS
Study aid

To help students remember different types of nouns, have them create a special tool in which to record examples. Give each child a white construction paper copy of the hay bale pattern on page 73. Have her write on the pattern a different noun and sample sentence for each category. Next, instruct her to cut out the pattern and also cut along the short dotted line on Section B and then glue the two cutouts together where indicated. Then have her fold the left and right sections of her project along the thin lines and use crayons or markers to decorate the front and back so the shape resembles a hay bale. Finally, have her insert the tab into the slit as shown. Allow students to keep their completed projects at their desks to refer to the next time they're not sure how to classify a particular noun.

Collective noun: flock

A <u>flock</u> of hens clucked along with the music.

Concrete noun: fiddle

A <u>fiddle</u> is a violin.

Common noun: rooster

The <u>rooster</u> crowed.

Proper noun: Old Red

<u>Old Red</u> crowed at the end of the song.

Singular noun: pig

A <u>pig</u> grunted to the music.

Plural noun: bandanas

The animals wore <u>bandanas</u>.

Abstract noun: happiness

Happiness ... barn.

Compound noun: square dance

Common noun: rooster

Concrete noun: fiddle

Nouns

Lauren

Waldo was sitting at the kitchen table eating a bowl of cereal and
reading the morning newspaper when ~~he~~ [Waldo] spotted an article about a
series of burglaries. ~~He~~ [Waldo] decided to finish up ~~his~~ [Waldo's] breakfast and head
into work to see what ~~he~~ [Waldo] could do to help with the case. Waldo drove
downtown and parked next to the police station. Once Waldo was in
the building, ~~his~~ [Waldo's] boss assigned ~~him~~ [Waldo] to go on a stakeout that evening.
The chief had decided to put officers in front of all stores that the
burglar might target in hopes that the officers would capture a suspect.
Waldo and ~~his~~ [Waldo's] partner were assigned to watch a jewelry store.

THE LOWDOWN ON PRONOUNS
Antecedents, fluency

Just how important are pronouns? Do they help with
fluency? This simple activity will help students answer
these questions. Photocopy an excerpt of a story students
have recently read. Cross out each pronoun and replace
it with its antecedent noun; then read the selection aloud.
Ask students to comment on its style and clarity. Have
them also discuss whether a writer could ever use too
many pronouns, and if so, what might happen as a result.
Follow up by having students mimic your demonstration. Have them work alone or with a partner to select
a paragraph from a different reading selection, replace
all pronouns with their noun antecedents, and then trade
papers and rewrite that paragraph using pronouns where
appropriate.

Julia Ring Alarie, Williston, VT

USE YOUR NOODLE!
Review game

Students will be able to review more than pronouns when they use this game's foldable mat!
Laminate the game mat on page 74 and the game cards and answer key on page 75. Cut out
the cards and place them in a manila envelope along with several game markers, a die, and the
key. Fold the game mat, as shown, and tape the envelope to the back. To play, simply have two
to three students at a time follow the game mat's directions. To review other grammar or math
skills, just replace the game cards!

USE YOUR NOODLE!

USE YOUR NOODLE!

Directions:
1. Place the game markers on Start. Stack the cards.
2. Roll the die. Move your marker ahead the number of spaces rolled.
3. Follow the directions on the space. If you answer a question correctly, leave your marker where it is. If you answer incorrectly, return to Start.
4. The first player to reach Finish wins.

You're getting closer! Draw a card.

Oops! Your mind went blank. Go back one space.

Hang in there! Draw a card.

You're still in the running! Draw a card.

What brain power! Move ahead two spaces.

Your mind got boggled! Trade places with another player.

Finish

What a great thinker you are! Draw a card.

You're a whiz at this! Draw a card.

Only one space left! Draw a card.

Wow, you're smart! Move ahead one space.

You're almost there! Draw a card.

Uh-oh! Your head hurts from thinking so hard. Move back two spaces.

Way to go! Draw a card.

Start

Put your thinking cap on! Draw a card.

Now you're thinking! Draw a card.

Stay focused! Draw a card.

You're so brainy! Move ahead one space.

Directions:
1. Place the game markers on Start. Stack the cards.
2. Roll the die. Move your marker ahead the number of spaces rolled.
3. Follow the directions on the space. If you answer a question correctly, leave your marker where it is. If you answer incorrectly, return to Start.
4. The first player to reach Finish wins.

② What's the subject pronoun?
She likes to write letters to him.

⑥ What's the possessive pronoun?
It was time for our favorite TV show.

⑮ What's the object pronoun?
They want me to bake cookies.

Answer Key for "Use Your Noodle!"
1. you
2. She
3. his
4. It
5. us
6. our
7. I
8. me
9. His
10. them
11. Their
12. we
13. him
14. her
15. me
16. You
17. His

Hay Bale Pattern

Use with “A Bale of Nouns” on page 71.

section A

section B

tab
Collective noun:
Compound noun:
Concrete noun:
Abstract noun:
Glue to section A.
Common noun:
Proper noun:
Singular noun:
Plural noun:
TEC44033

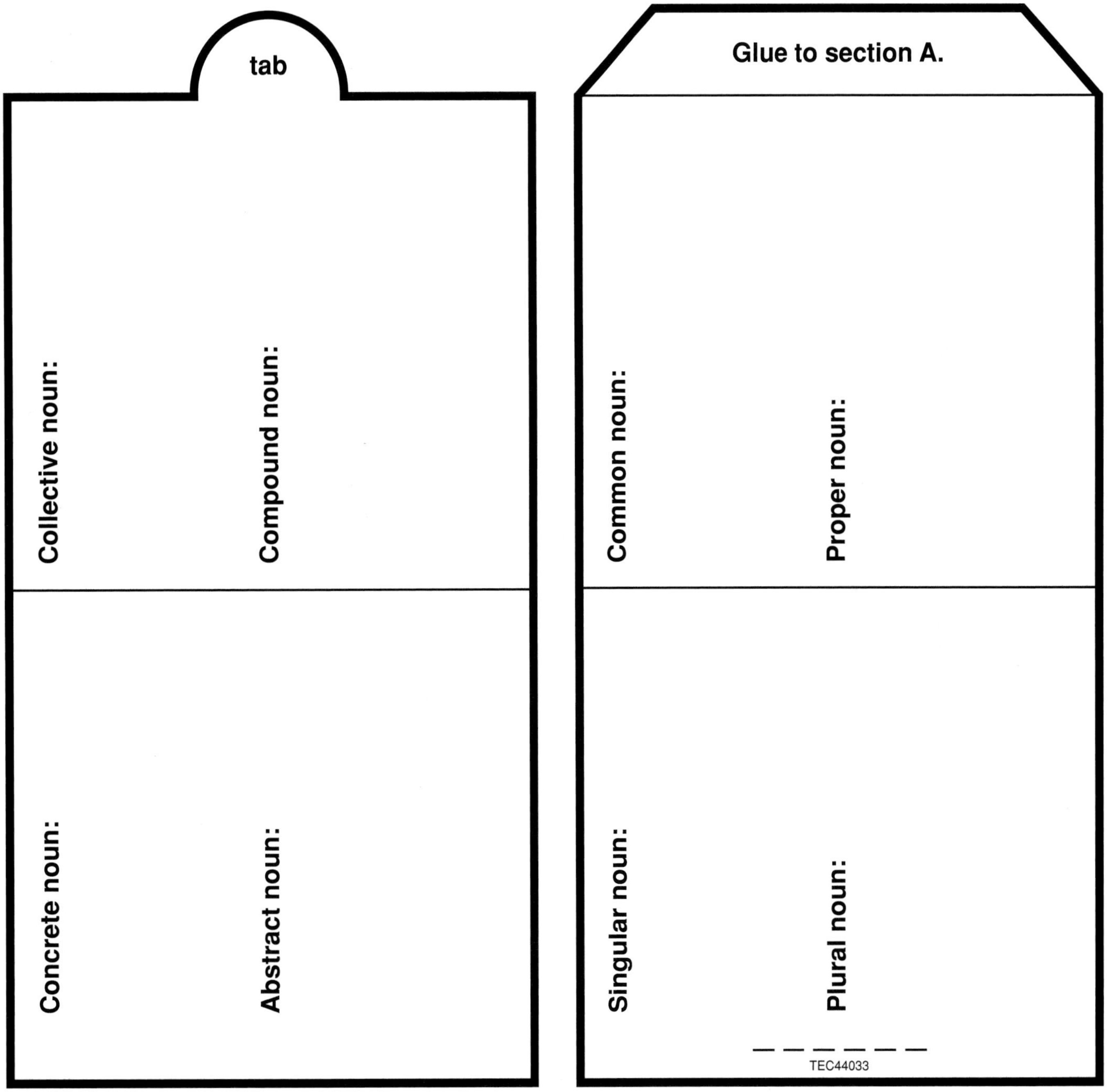

Use Your Noodle!

You're getting closer! Draw a card.

Oops! Your mind went blank. Go back one space.

Hang in there! Draw a card.

You're still in the running! Draw a card.

Your mind got boggled! Trade places with another player.

What brain power! Move ahead two spaces.

Finish

You're a whiz at this! Draw a card.

What a great thinker you are! Draw a card.

Only one space left! Draw a card.

You're almost there! Draw a card.

Uh-oh! Your head hurts from thinking so hard. Move back two spaces.

Wow, you're smart! Move ahead one space.

Way to go! Draw a card.

Start

Put your thinking cap on! Draw a card.

Now you're thinking! Draw a card.

Stay focused! Draw a card.

You're so brainy! Move ahead one space.

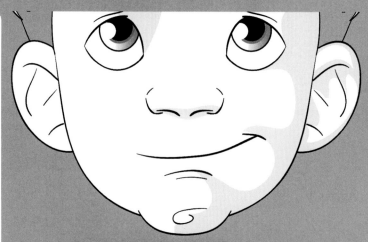

Directions:
1. Place the game markers on Start. Stack the cards.
2. Roll the die. Move your marker ahead the number of spaces rolled.
3. Follow the directions on the space. If you answer a question correctly, leave your marker where it is. If you answer incorrectly, return to Start.
4. The first player to reach Finish wins.

74

① What's the object pronoun?

I called you yesterday.

TEC44033

② What's the subject pronoun?

She likes to write letters to him.

TEC44033

③ What's the possessive pronoun?

If he doesn't want his burger, I'll eat it.

TEC44033

④ What's the subject pronoun?

It was a great day for us to go hiking.

TEC44033

⑤ What's the object pronoun?

They saw us at the ticket booth.

TEC44033

⑥ What's the possessive pronoun?

It was time for our favorite TV show.

TEC44033

⑦ What's the subject pronoun?

I am tired of her excuses.

TEC44033

⑧ What's the object pronoun?

It was a present for me.

TEC44033

⑨ What's the possessive pronoun?

His mom picked him up at noon.

TEC44033

⑩ What's the object pronoun?

We gave them a ride home.

TEC44033

⑪ What's the possessive pronoun?

Their house is right next to it.

TEC44033

⑫ What's the subject pronoun?

When will we get to see it?

TEC44033

⑬ What's the object pronoun?

She gave him the keys.

TEC44033

⑭ What's the possessive pronoun?

Will she get to her appointment on time?

TEC44033

⑮ What's the object pronoun?

They gave the cookies to me.

TEC44033

⑯ What's the subject pronoun?

You must not miss seeing it.

TEC44033

⑰ What's the possessive pronoun?

His dog barked at her.

TEC44033

Answer Key for "Use Your Noodle!"

1. you	6. our	11. Their	16. You
2. She	7. I	12. we	17. His
3. his	8. me	13. him	
4. It	9. His	14. her	
5. us	10. them	15. me	

TEC44033

Barnyard Gossip

Write the correct possessive form of each noun in parentheses.

1. Bernard was happy that none of his _____ crops were destroyed by the storm.
   (parents)

2. The old _____ repair bill was less than _____ parents thought
   (tractor)   (Bernard)
   it would be.

3. _____ cat caught five mice in the _____ granary last week.
   (Miss Lizzy)   (barn)

4. Someone stole one of _____ apple pies, which were cooling on a windowsill.
   (Mrs. Jones)

5. Jasper, the _____ dog, tracked down the thief and found him hiding in a
   (family)
   cornfield behind a _____ barn, eating the _____ last piece.
   (neighbor)   (pie)

6. This year, the scarecrow in the _____ strawberry patch will be wearing
   (children)
   overalls and a plaid shirt from their _____ closet.
   (grandpa)

7. Squawks from the chicken coop and

   squeals from the pigpen brought

   _____ afternoon nap to a
   (Miss Lizzy)
   quick end today.

8. If all the _____ words are
   (farmhands)
   true, _____ dinner menu will
   (tonight)
   include both ham and chicken!

©The Mailbox® • TEC44033 • Oct./Nov. 2007 • Key p. 310

Scaredy-Cat Scarecrow

Decide whether the pronoun in each sentence is used correctly. Circle the letter in the matching column. If you are correct, the circled letters will spell what scared the scarecrow.

	Correct	Incorrect
1. Him and Grandpa love to play the banjo.	G	A
2. Dad is teaching Sam and me to play the fiddle.	H	L
3. Aunt Hannah took Sam and me to a hoedown.	O	T
4. My cousins, Joe and Jessie, love to square dance.	R	P
5. Joe and Jessie asked us to dance too.	R	A
6. Me and Sam decided to watch instead.	N	O
7. We thought beginners shouldn't perform.	R	G
8. Sam and myself sat on hay bales to watch.	T	M
9. Prissy the cat curled up between Sam and I.	C	O
10. Behind us was a scarecrow.	V	S
11. Sam recognized it clothes.	K	I
12. They belonged to Dad and Grandpa!	E	B

Comprehension
Tune-Up

I'M FLAGGING THE CONFUSING PARTS.

AUTO REPAIR MANUAL

Flag places where you had to reread the text to understand it.

Flag the main idea of the text.

Flag difficult words.

Flag examples of figurative language.

Flag examples of strong imagery.

Flag words or phrases that describe the setting (or a character's traits or motives).

Flag your favorite part of the text.

Flag sections that you would like to read aloud and discuss.

FLAGGED!
Reading for a purpose

Comprehension involves many different reading skills. Use this simple activity to target specific skills your students need to practice. Provide each child with small sticky notes that have been cut into strips. Then announce the skill(s) you want students to focus on as they read a particular selection of text (see the sample list). When a child comes to a portion of text representing that skill, have her flag it with a sticky strip. After ten minutes, have small groups of students meet to discuss the examples they flagged and the reasons for their choices. Then repeat the procedure, varying the directions so students are reading for a different purpose than before. Regardless of the genre used, this page-flagging method can help your readers understand more of what they read.

Kim Minafo, Dillard Drive Elementary, Raleigh, NC

TIME-OUT!
Recalling facts and details

Help students visualize what they are reading with this simple activity. Divide a reading selection into sections. After reading aloud the first section, give the listeners a five-minute time-out to quickly draw what that section of text was about. When time is up, allow a student or two to share her sketch with the class. Repeat the process with the remaining sections. Once the reading is completed, have each child use her pictures to retell the reading selection in her own words to a partner.

Cheryl Farris, College Park Elementary, La Porte, TX

INSPECTION STATION
Question-and-answer relationships

Boost comprehension skills by occasionally turning the tables and allowing your students to become teachers! Give each child a copy of the form on page 80 and have her complete it by listing vocabulary words, questions, and activities that will help another student understand an assigned reading selection. Once she has completed the form, have her trade papers with a classmate and complete her partner's review page.

Dee Demyan, Atwater, OH

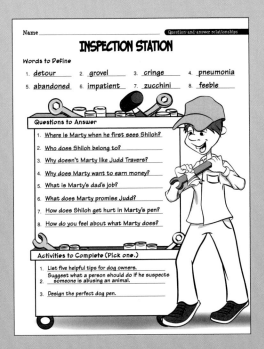

FUNNY PAPER FINISHERS
Drawing conclusions

Include the Sunday comics in your next comprehension lesson. Photocopy a comic strip onto an overhead transparency. Then use a sticky note to cover one of the strip's frames or a speech bubble belonging to one of its characters. Challenge each child to write what she thinks the character said or what happens next. Encourage the student to use details from the previous frame(s) for help. If desired, have her illustrate her thoughts by drawing the missing scene on unlined paper. Then display the completed drawings on a board next to the original comic strip.

Kimberly Snipes, Woodhill Elementary Gastonia, NC

INSPECTION STATION

Words to Define

1. _____ 2. _____ 3. _____ 4. _____

5. _____ 6. _____ 7. _____ 8. _____

Questions to Answer

1. _____

2. _____

3. _____

4. _____

5. _____

6. _____

7. _____

8. _____

Activities to Complete (Pick one.)

1. _____

2. _____

3. _____

©The Mailbox® · TEC44033 · Oct./Nov. 2007

80   **Note to the teacher:** Use with "Inspection Station" on page 79.

Write the title or page numbers of your assigned reading selection on a top tire. On the tires below it, write in your own words what the reading selection was about.

RETREADS

Title or Pages

Title or Pages

Title or Pages

Note to the teacher: Have students complete this page after reading a chapter or portion of fiction or nonfiction text.

Launching Literary Elements

Rob's Reading Rocket

Plot
Caroline Malloy is seeking revenge against Wally Hatford. She plans to compliment Wally at least once each day so that he will accept a disgusting Christmas gift from her.

Resolution
The crazy pranks pulled by each family on the other actually help the kids become friends.

Ending
The content of the letters that the brothers and sisters exchange gives the reader a hint that there will be more pranks played in the future.

Style
conversational

Point of View
third person

Tone
humorous

Theme
Things don't always go as planned.

READING ROCKET
Specific literary elements

When your students need more practice with identifying particular parts of a story, launch this project, which becomes an out-of-this-world display! After a child reads a fictional selection, give him a copy of the rocket pattern on page 85. Have him label the cone with the selection's title and author and the rocket's remaining parts with the story elements you specify. After he fills in the sections, have him cut out his rocket and trace it onto white construction paper. Then have him decorate and cut out the tracing, place the decorated cutout on top of his labeled cutout, and tape the tips together as shown. Display the completed projects along with cutouts of stars and asteroids.

Natalie McGregor, Grenada Upper Elementary, Grenada, MS

SYMBOLIC BUSINESS CARDS
Characterization, setting, and theme

What real-world services could fictional characters provide the general public? To find out, and to assess students' understanding of three key literary elements as well, have your readers complete this project. Give each child a 2" x 3½" piece of tagboard to create a business card for a character of his choice. Have him decorate the front of the card with lettering and symbols that not only represent the character's strongest traits, but also hint at the selection's setting and theme. Then have him use the back of the card to explain what the illustrations mean.

Darla Miles
Brawner Intermediate School
Granbury, TX

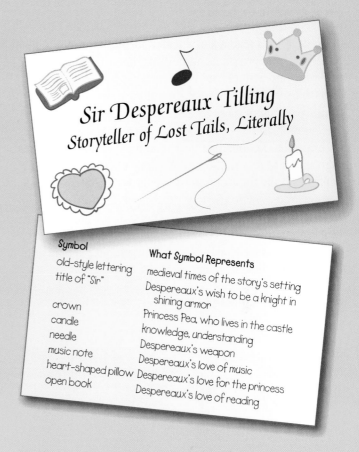

Sir Despereaux Tilling
Storyteller of Lost Tails, Literally

Symbol	What Symbol Represents
old-style lettering title of "Sir"	medieval times of the story's setting Despereaux's wish to be a knight in shining armor
crown	Princess Pea, who lives in the castle
candle	knowledge, understanding
needle	Despereaux's weapon
music note	Despereaux's love of music
heart-shaped pillow	Despereaux's love for the princess
open book	Despereaux's love of reading

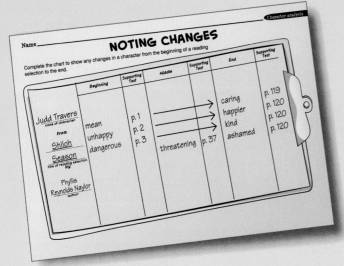

Name_____

NOTING CHANGES
Complete the chart to show any changes in a character from the beginning of a reading selection to the end.

	Beginning	Supporting Text	Middle	Supporting Text	End	Supporting Text
Judd Travers *name of character* From Shiloh Season *title of reading selection* By Phyllis Reynolds Naylor *author*	mean unhappy dangerous	p. 1 p. 2 p. 3	threatening	p. 37	caring happier kind ashamed	p. 119 p. 120 p. 120 p. 120

TRAIT TRACKER
Character analysis

To chart progressive changes in a character's attitudes and actions throughout a reading selection, give each child a copy of page 86. Instruct students to record in the columns specific traits a character exhibits at the beginning, middle, and end of a tale, as well as the page numbers of the supporting text. If a trait does not change from one story part to another, direct students to indicate it by drawing a horizontal line as shown. When students are finished, have them discuss their findings in small groups.

VaReane Heese, Springfield Elementary, Springfield, NE

MAP IT OUT
Plot, graphic organizer

When students read a story, it's important for them to be able to identify the problems and events that affect a character's thoughts and actions and to understand how those problems are resolved. Completing a story map can help. Display a transparency of page 87 and discuss the significance of the symbols in the key. Next, using a recent read-aloud as an example, demonstrate how to draw symbols along the map's path to record the sample story's setting, its main characters, and the progression of events and problems. Also demonstrate how to use key words and descriptive phrases as labels. Then give each child a copy of the page and have him complete it using a story he has read independently. If he needs more space to write, have him cut out his map and glue it to a larger sheet of paper.

Simone Lepine, Fayetteville, NY

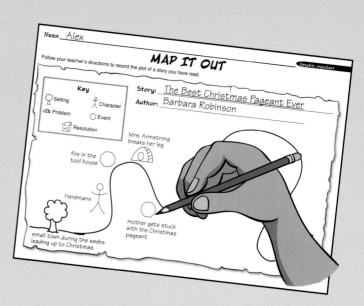

OPEN THE SHUTTERS!
Assessment project

This enlightening book report project can help you assess your students' understanding of literary elements. Each child folds the edges of a sheet of construction paper toward the center and labels the left flap with the book's title and the right flap with the author's name. She then decorates the flaps to make them look like closed window shutters. Next, she opens the shutters and cuts and folds in half the same number of pieces of white paper as the number of story elements you assign. She glues four pieces in the center section so that they resemble windowpanes and glues the remaining pieces inside the outer flaps. After she labels the top of each piece, she lifts each flap and records the appropriate information underneath. Then she places a matching strip of construction paper over each outer flap, decorates the strip so that it looks like the inside of a shutter, and tapes it to the top of the outer flap. To complete the project, she writes a book summary on the back.

Kimberly Akers, Sul Ross Middle School, San Antonio, TX

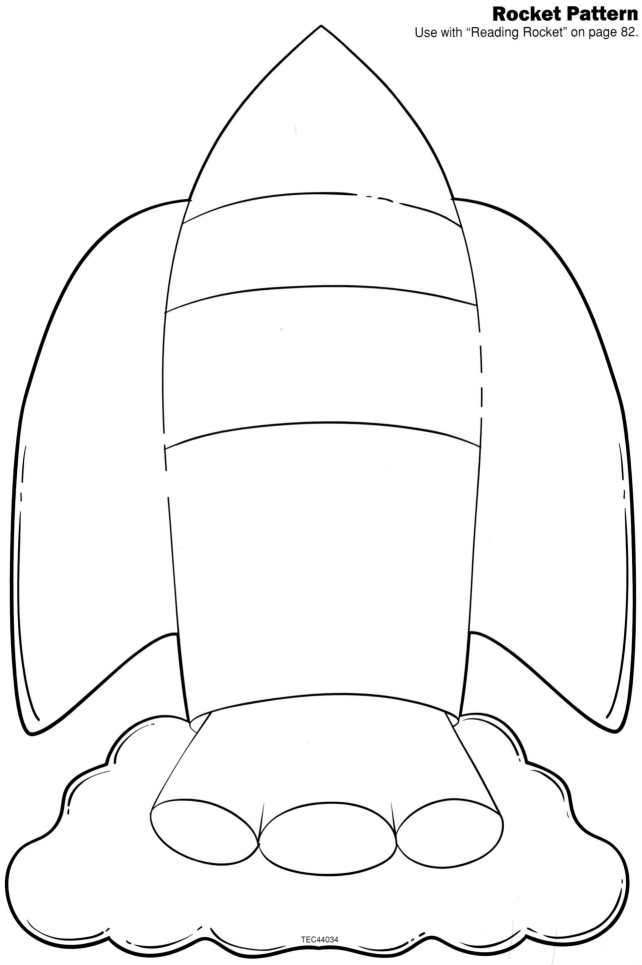

TEC44034

NOTING CHANGES

Complete the chart to show any changes in a character from the beginning of a reading selection to the end.

Beginning	Supporting Text	Middle	Supporting Text	End	Supporting Text

From _____
name of character

_____
title of reading selection

by _____
author

Note to the teacher: Use with "Trait Tracker" on page 83.

Name _____

MAP IT OUT

Follow your teacher's directions to record the plot of a story you have read.

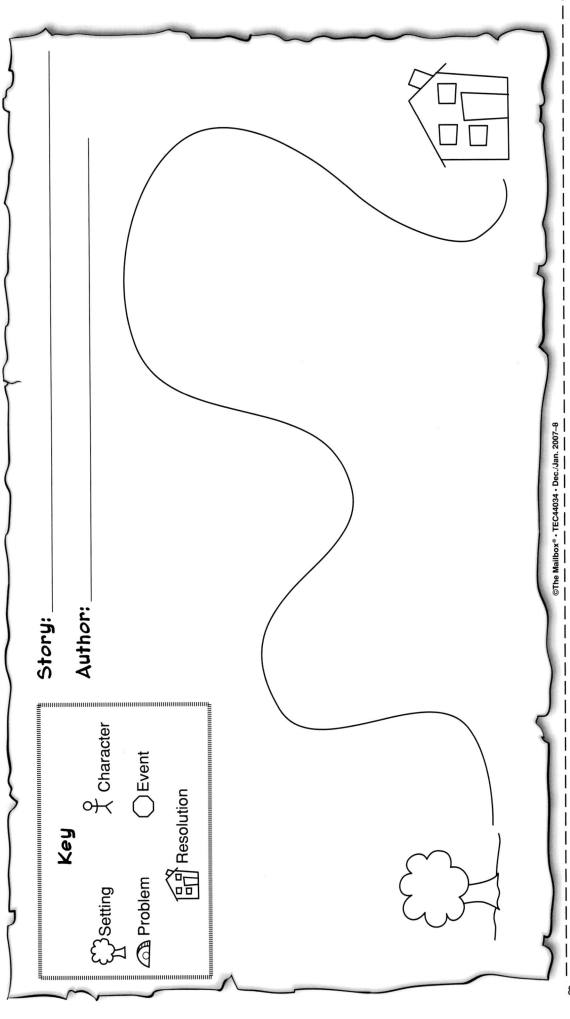

Story: _____

Author: _____

Key

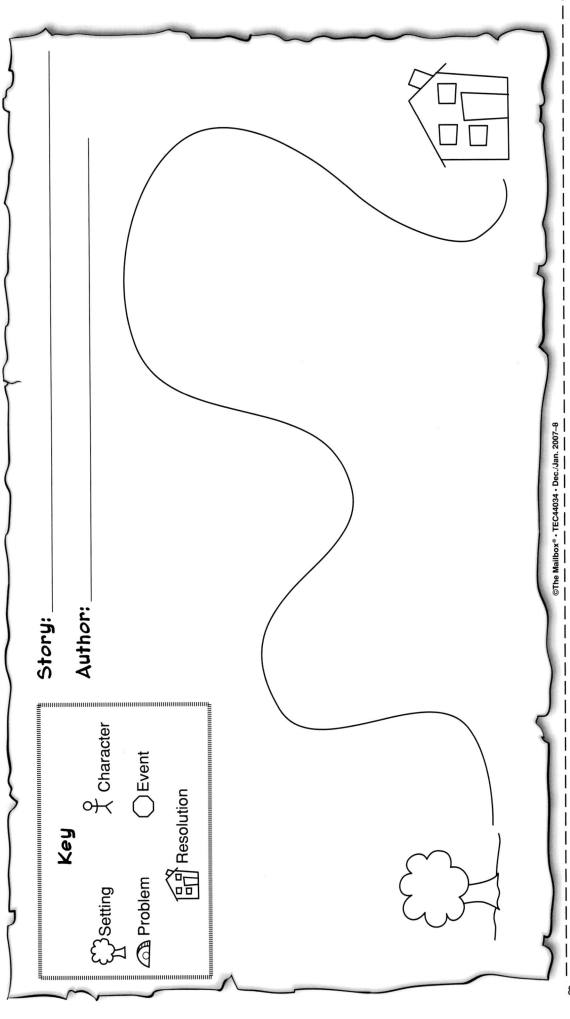 Setting

 Character

 Problem

 Event

 Resolution

Note to the teacher: Use with "Map It Out" on page 84. Or give each child a copy of the page to use as a prewriting activity to help him plan an original story.

Delicious Descriptions

with ideas by Kim Minafo, Apex, NC

Describe a delicious new doughnut that pastry shops should sell at this time of year.

Wheel labels:
- **Topic** — new doughnut
- **Sight** — thick and round with creamy icing and colorful toppings
- **Sound** — toppings crunch as they're chewed
- **Taste** — sweet and yummy
- **Touch** — soft and sticky
- **Smell** — pumpkin pie spices
- **Similar to** — birthday cakes with white icing
- **Different from** — a pie or other goodies at a bakery

Details

I CAN ALMOST TASTE IT!
Adding details

Post a mouthwatering writing topic, such as the one at the left, on the front board. Have each child complete a two-minute quick write on the topic. Ask one or two students each to share their quick writes with the class. Discuss whether adding sensory details to the examples would make the described treats easier to visualize. Next, provide each child with a copy of the graphic organizer on page 90. Have the student record on the organizer specific details he can incorporate into his writing as he revises and edits his description. If desired, have each child trim his organizer and use various craft materials to decorate it to represent the food he described. Then post the cutouts on a display next to their tasty descriptions.

SNAPSHOT DETAILS
Who, what, when, where, and why

For this partner project, have each student bring in a photo of himself involved in an activity. Instruct the child to tape his photo near the top of a sheet of paper, list the five questions shown, and then trade papers with a partner without saying a word. Have each student study his partner's photo and answer the questions. Then have him write an elaborative paragraph that describes the experience captured in the picture. When students are finished, have the partners take turns reading their paragraphs to each other and rating the description on a scale of 1 to 10 (1 = "It's like you were there" and 10 = "That's not at all what it was like"). Repeat the activity as time allows, pairing students with different partners.

Who? Craig and a woman
What? Craig touching a baby alligator
When? during warm weather
Where? in a room at a nature museum
Why? to learn more about reptiles

On a day warm enough to wear a T-shirt, Craig visited a nature museum. While he was in one particular room, a blond lady wearing a blue apron walked in. She was holding a baby alligator. Keeping his eyes on the gator's head, Craig carefully reached out and felt the animal's leg and tail.

Ms. Becker was one of my favorite teachers. She was always smiling. Her short blond hair framed her small, round face. Her bright blue eyes seemed to twinkle even more when she laughed.

PAINTING WITH WORDS
Character sketch, visualization

Invite students to write about something they all have in common—teachers! Have each child write a detailed description of either a favorite teacher she has had in the past or a zany one she'd like to have in the future. When she is finished, have her paint a picture of the teacher that represents only what is literally written on the paper. Students will quickly understand how important it is to include specific details in their writing!

Cara Christensen, Keeny Street School, Manchester, CT

A LOOK INTO THE FUTURE
Vivid descriptions, voice

Have each student close his eyes and imagine that it is 25 years in the future. He has graduated from college and is very successful. Now the elementary school he attended wants to recognize him for an outstanding achievement, and he must give a speech at the school. Provide each child with a copy of the organizer on page 91 to complete as directed. After all the organizers have been completed, have each student use his completed organizer to help him write an interesting and entertaining speech that vividly describes his accomplishment. If desired, present each child with a construction paper medal after he has given his speech.

Graphic Organizer

Use with "I Can Almost Taste It!" on page 88.

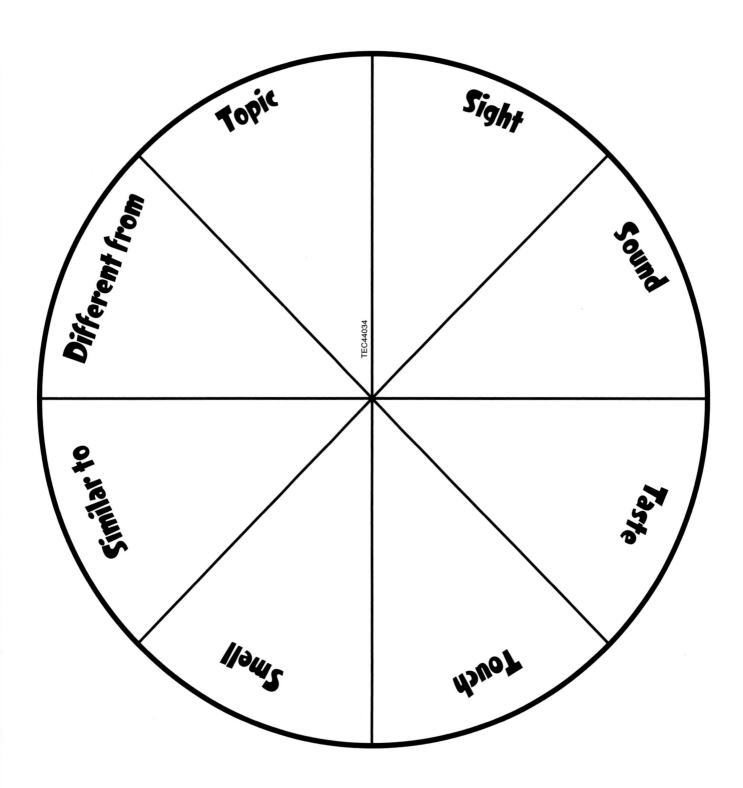

FAST FORWARD TO THE FUTURE

Imagine that it is 25 years in the future and you are being recognized by the school for an outstanding accomplishment. Complete the organizer to help you write a speech for the award ceremony.

Why are you being honored with an award? Describe what you did to earn this recognition. Be specific.

What can you do to make your speech more interesting for your audience? Use vivid words to describe what you will do.

How will you keep your audience's attention? Describe the type of voice and tone you should use.

Now write your speech on another sheet of paper. Use lots of descriptive details!

Note to the teacher: Use with "A Look Into the Future" on page 89.

It's in the Mail?

Oh, no! You mailed a special gift to someone, but it never arrived! Complete the form below so the lost package can be found as soon as possible.

Lost Package Form

Sender's Name: _____

Receiver's Name: _____

Package Details
Describe the package. Include its size, weight, color, texture, and sound.

Value of Gift
Tell how much you paid for the gift. Then describe what the gift will mean to the receiver.

Other Details
Describe how you will feel if the package is not found.

SPEEDY
Delivery Company

Getting the Scoop on Multiple-Meaning Words

with ideas by Teri Nielsen, Tracey's Elementary
Tracey's Landing, MD

garment for a woman or girl consisting of a one-piece bodice and skirt

to put clothes on

dress

MEANINGFUL FLAVORS
Bulletin board or center

Give each child (or pair of students) a copy of the ice cream cone and scoop patterns on page 95. Also assign each child a different multiple-meaning word to write on her cone. Then have her use a dictionary to find two meanings for her assigned word: one for a noun and one for a verb. Instruct her to label one ice cream scoop with the noun meaning and the other scoop with the verb meaning. Have students color their cutouts so that all noun scoops are one color and all verb scoops are a different color. Mount the cutouts on a board with the corresponding scoops atop their matching cones. To make this a self-checking center, have each student also write her assigned word on the backs of her ice cream scoops. Each child using the center then arranges two scoops atop each cone and turns the scoops over to check.

NAME AND EXPLAIN GAME
Small-group activity

Students can play their way to a stronger understanding of multiple-meaning words with this fun card game. Give each group of students a copy of the cards on page 96 to cut apart and stack facedown. Have one child draw a card and read its sentence aloud. Instruct him to identify which word in the sentence has multiple meanings and to explain the word's meaning in that sentence. If his group agrees with his answer, he earns a point. He earns an extra point if he also provides a sentence in which the identified word has a different correct meaning. The next person then takes a turn. If the group agrees that his answer is incorrect, the next person can try to earn the point plus an additional point before drawing a card and taking a turn. Play continues until the cards are gone and each player has taken the same number of turns. Follow up by having each child complete a copy of page 97 as directed.

Mario's cat had a litter of kittens yesterday.

WORDS ON THE LOOSE
Whole-class activity

Bring out the dictionaries for this detective-style vocabulary activity. In advance, label individual index cards (one for each student) each with a different multiple-meaning word from selections students will be reading. Include the page number where the word can be found. Also label separate index cards each with a corresponding meaning. While students are out of the room, tape the definition cards in different places around the room. When students return, announce that fugitives (important vocabulary words) are loose in the room and must be captured. Then hand each detective a word card and a copy of page 98. Have her follow the steps on the recording sheet to find and arrest a suspect (card labeled with matching definition). Once all the detectives have located a suspect, have each sleuth share her word and its suspected definition with the detective agency (the class). Have students signal thumbs-up if they agree that the detective arrested the correct suspect and thumbs-down if they disagree.

Dawn Reilly, Bridgewater Middle School and Evergreen Elementary Stirling, NJ

VOCABULARY NECKLACES
Study aid

If multiple-meaning words are troublesome for your students, have them make this nifty accessory. Direct each child to cut five colorful shapes from poster board and hole-punch each one. Instruct him to label the front of each cutout with a word you assign and the back with at least two definitions for the word (one noun, one verb). Then have him thread the cutouts onto a length of yarn to make a necklace to wear while he's in class. When he has those multiple meanings memorized, assign him five new words and have him add more shapes to his necklace. Continue in this manner until he has learned all the words you assign. By the time standardized testing rolls around, his confidence will be soaring!

Chris Ward, Atkinson Elementary, Fremont, OH

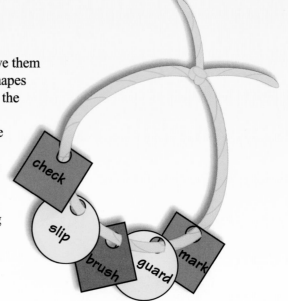

TEC44035

Sentence Cards

Use with "Name and Explain Game" on page 94.

My family vacations in the same season each year.

TEC44035

The president will address the nation at six o'clock.

TEC44035

Laura's lucky number is seven.

TEC44035

My sister's voice has a higher pitch than mine.

TEC44035

The bird's bill was bright orange.

TEC44035

Joey didn't mind that I borrowed his video game.

TEC44035

Mario's cat had a litter of kittens yesterday.

TEC44035

The mean of the numbers 7, 8, and 12 is 9.

TEC44035

The workers agreed to end the strike at noon.

TEC44035

Jake watched his dad light the charcoal.

TEC44035

What kind of milk shake would you like?

TEC44035

The video store is just a mile from here.

TEC44035

Name

Seeing Twins!

Circle the letter of the sentence whose underlined word has the same meaning as the one in the numbered sentence.

1. A pentagon is a <u>shape</u>.
   A. Grandma tried to <u>shape</u> the dough into a circle.
   B. The boxes all had the same <u>shape</u>.
   C. Mom told my brother to <u>shape</u> up.

2. The sun <u>rose</u> at 6:10 AM this morning.
   A. Aunt Marge is proud of her <u>rose</u> bushes.
   B. That lady has <u>rose</u> petals in her basket.
   C. The people <u>rose</u> to their feet when the judge entered.

3. Don't <u>trip</u> over the toys scattered on the floor.
   A. Our family won a <u>trip</u> to Disney World!
   B. The rumpled rug caused the old man to <u>trip</u>.
   C. Buy some milk on your next <u>trip</u> to the store.

4. Mandy's hair <u>band</u> fell on the floor.
   A. Greg was mad when the rubber <u>band</u> broke.
   B. The <u>band</u> competition will be this weekend.
   C. We watched the <u>band</u> march by in the parade.

5. Greg performed in the school <u>play</u>.
   A. My black lab wanted me to <u>play</u> ball with her.
   B. Mrs. Anderson took her twins to the park to <u>play</u>.
   C. The actress won a part in a new Broadway <u>play</u>.

6. Workers loaded heavy boxes onto the <u>ship</u>.
   A. At what time will the cruise <u>ship</u> arrive in the port?
   B. The company promises to <u>ship</u> the computer by Friday.
   C. Uncle Bob paid $28.00 to <u>ship</u> the tool back to the factory.

7. The office manager will <u>screen</u> a lot of people for the job.
   A. Dad put a new <u>screen</u> in the window after the cat ripped a hole in it.
   B. When the computer <u>screen</u> went blank, Amy's report disappeared.
   C. The Smiths <u>screen</u> the movies they allow their children to watch.

8. A giant <u>wave</u> knocked the surfer off his surfboard.
   A. The queen began to <u>wave</u> from the balcony.
   B. Mom felt a <u>wave</u> of relief once she knew we were safe.
   C. Erin smiled when she saw her mom <u>wave</u> at her.

©The Mailbox® • TEC44035 • Feb./Mar. 2008 • Key p. 310

Note to the teacher: Use alone or after "Name and Explain Game" on page 94.

MOST-WANTED WORDS

FUGITIVE WORD: _____

All Points Bulletin

CLUE 1   Last seen on page _____

CLUE 2   Copy the sentence containing that word on the lines below. Underline the word.

_____

_____

_____

I think the underlined word means _____

_____

_____

CLUE 3   Find the underlined word in a dictionary. Write a definition for each part of speech listed. Circle the one that matches the meaning of the underlined word in the sentence above.

Verb: _____

_____

Noun: _____

_____

MAKE AN ARREST

Find a suspect card in the room that has a definition matching the one circled above. Tape that card in the box at the right.

Tape Suspect Definition here.

On Track With Expository Writing

with ideas by Teri Nielsen, Tracey's Elementary
Tracey's Landing, MD

Team finishing first = 10 points
Team finishing second = 5 points
Team finishing third = 3 points

Best paragraph = 15 points
Second-best paragraph = 10 points
Third-best paragraph = 5 points

Topics
Why Kids Like to Talk on the Phone
Why _____ Is a Favorite Day of the Week
Why Dogs (or Cats) Make Great Pets
Why _____ Is a Fun Month
Why Our State (or Town) Is a Great Place to Visit

February is a fun month for many reasons. On Groundhog Day, it's fun to predict whether spring will arrive early or whether there will be six more weeks of winter. On Valentine's Day, it's fun to eat candy and give and receive cards from friends and family members. On Presidents' Day, it's interesting to learn about George Washington, Abraham Lincoln, and other men who have served as our country's president. February is a short month with lots of holidays and special days.

TRIAL LAPS
Paragraph structure

Make winning writers of your students with this whole-class activity. Form relay teams of five students each and post chart paper on the board for each team. Instruct each team to line up an equal distance away from its assigned chart paper. Next, announce a topic (see the list above). Explain that each team will be trying to be the first to finish writing on its paper a paragraph like the one modeled. Give each team two minutes to brain-storm ideas; then hand the first person in each line a marker. At your signal, have each student with a marker go to his team's chart paper, quickly compose a strong topic sentence, and then pass the marker to the next student in his line. Continue in this manner until each team finishes its paragraph. Then use the point system on the flags above to determine the winning team.

TEAMWORK
Five-paragraph essay

To help your writers better understand how sentences and paragraphs within an essay are related, divide students into teams of three. Give each student a copy of the introductory paragraph shown. Read the paragraph aloud; then explain that it will be the first paragraph of a five-paragraph essay each team will work together to write. Have individual teams decide what the next three paragraphs should be about and which team member will write each one (a paragraph supporting sentence 2 of the introductory paragraph, a paragraph supporting sentence 3, and a paragraph supporting sentence 4). Next, give each student a copy of page 101 on which to compose her assigned paragraph. After each writer finishes her work and shares it with her team, have the trio compose a concluding paragraph together on a separate sheet of paper. Then have each team tape its five paragraphs together to create a vertical flowchart of the completed essay's format. For a nifty follow-up activity, see "The Work of the Pit Crew" on this page.

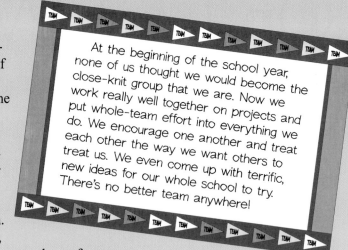

At the beginning of the school year, none of us thought we would become the close-knit group that we are. Now we work really well together on projects and put whole-team effort into everything we do. We encourage one another and treat each other the way we want others to treat us. We even come up with terrific, new ideas for our whole school to try. There's no better team anywhere!

no doubt

another

as a result

furthermore

THE WORK OF THE PIT CREW
Transitional words and phrases

This activity makes linking paragraphs together easier for your writers to do. In advance, type a simple, three-paragraph essay without transition words, adding a line space between each paragraph. Or use paragraphs from the "Teamwork" activity above. Make a copy of the essay and a copy of the writing reference on page 102 for each pair of students. Next, explain that just as a racer wants his re-entry into a race from a pit stop to be smooth, a reader likes each paragraph of text to transition smoothly into the next. Ask students to think of the breaks between the essay's paragraphs as pit stops and then decide how to make smooth transitions between them by incorporating words or phrases from the reference sheet into the essay's text. Invite students to share and discuss their decisions with the class to determine the most popular word choices.

GOING FOR THE CHECKERED FLAG!
Organizing and writing an essay

Motivate students to write expository essays with the help of a handy organizer. Have each child complete a copy of page 103 based on a topic of his choice (see the suggestions), writing the paragraphs of the body (Laps 1–3) first if desired. When he is finished, have him edit his work with a partner to be sure he followed the correct format and used appropriate transition words. If desired, have him mount his final copy on colorful paper and border it with checkered flags. Before collecting or displaying the final copies, group the writers by topic and have them share their essays with classmates who wrote about the same topic.

Topics

How to Be a Friend
How to Stop Hiccups
Why _____ Is My Favorite Cartoon
    Character
Why My Family Is the Greatest
What Makes a Perfect Day
Competition Is a Good/Bad Thing

Name _____

REV UP YOUR PARAGRAPHS!

Start Your Engine: Write a topic sentence. _____
_____

Complete Lap 1: Write a sentence that supports the topic sentence. _____
_____

Complete Lap 2: Write a second supportive sentence. _____
_____

Complete Lap 3: Write a third supportive sentence. _____
_____

Cross the Finish Line: Write a concluding sentence. _____
_____

©The Mailbox® • TEC44035 • Feb./Mar. 2008

Note to the teacher: Use alone or with "Teamwork" on page 100.

Transition Words and Phrases

Contrasting

although	on the other hand
but	otherwise
even though	still
however	yet

Sequencing

after
afterward
also
at first
at last
before
before long
finally
first
furthermore
generally
in the first place
in the meantime
lastly
meanwhile
next
second
soon
then
third

Comparing

also	likewise
as	similarly
in the same way	while
like	

Adding or Clarifying Information

again	as well
along with	besides
also	for example
and	for instance
another	next

Introducing

certainly
in general
no doubt
obviously
of course
to be sure

Concluding or Summarizing

as a result
finally
in conclusion
to sum up
lastly
therefore

Note to the teacher: Use with "The Work of the Pit Crew" on page 100. Or have each student keep a copy of the page in his writing folder to use as a reference.

Going for the Checkered Flag!

topic _____

Start Your Engine: Write an introductory paragraph that has a topic sentence, three sentences that support the topic sentence, and a concluding sentence that leads into the next paragraph.

Complete Lap 1: Write a similar paragraph that fully supports sentence two of paragraph one.

Complete Lap 2: Write a similar paragraph that fully supports sentence three of paragraph one.

Complete Lap 3: Write a similar paragraph that fully supports sentence four of paragraph one.

Cross the Finish Line: Write a similar concluding paragraph that summarizes paragraphs two through four and ends with a sentence that makes the reader think or smile.

©The Mailbox® • TEC44035 • Feb./Mar. 2008

Note to the teacher: Use to guide students in writing a five-paragraph essay or with "Going for the Checkered Flag!" on page 100.

Diving Into **Poetry**

Splash around in these cool activities! They'll help your students understand different elements of poetry and practice important reading skills too.

with ideas by Kim Minafo, Apex, NC

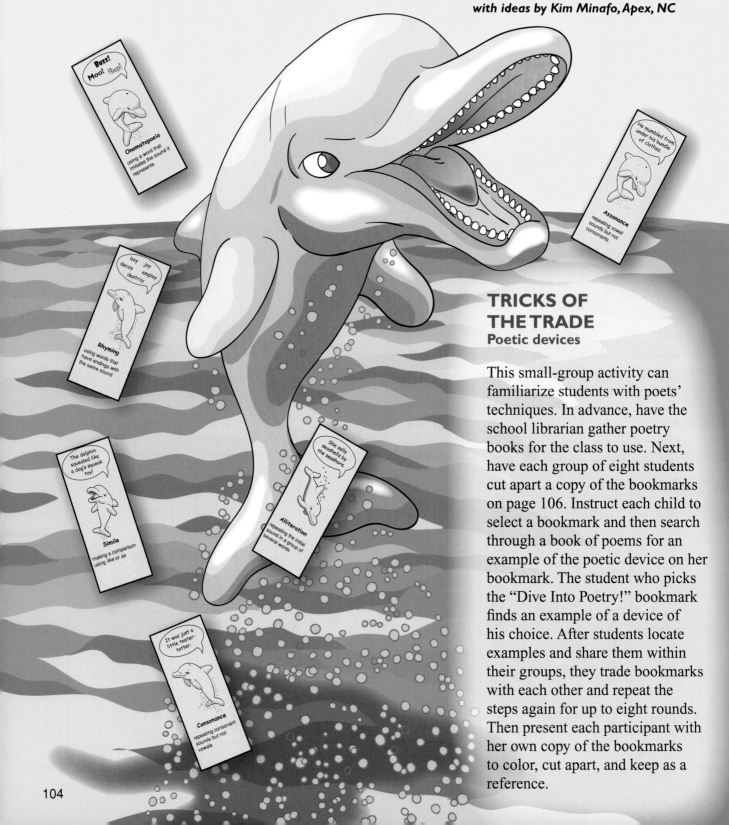

Buzz!
Moo! Peep!

Onomatopoeia
using a word that imitates the sound it represents

He mumbled from under his bundle of clothes.

Assonance
repeating vowel sounds but not consonants

boy joy
decoy employ
destroy

Rhyming
using words that have endings with the same sound

The dolphin squealed like a dog's squeak toy!

Simile
making a comparison using like or as

She sells seashells by the seashore.

Alliteration
repeating the initial sound in a group of several words

It was just a little teeter-totter.

Consonance
repeating consonant sounds but not vowels

TRICKS OF THE TRADE
Poetic devices

This small-group activity can familiarize students with poets' techniques. In advance, have the school librarian gather poetry books for the class to use. Next, have each group of eight students cut apart a copy of the bookmarks on page 106. Instruct each child to select a bookmark and then search through a book of poems for an example of the poetic device on her bookmark. The student who picks the "Dive Into Poetry!" bookmark finds an example of a device of his choice. After students locate examples and share them within their groups, they trade bookmarks with each other and repeat the steps again for up to eight rounds. Then present each participant with her own copy of the bookmarks to color, cut apart, and keep as a reference.

COMIC CREATIONS
Rhyme schemes

Expect giggles as students complete this nifty poetry-writing activity! Begin by having students brainstorm things they did not like to do when they were younger, such as brush their teeth or eat green vegetables. On a transparency of the organizer on page 107, use an *aabb* or *abab* rhyme scheme while modeling how to write a humorous poem about one of the brainstormed ideas. Then have each child complete a copy of page 107 and share his resulting poem with the class or a partner.

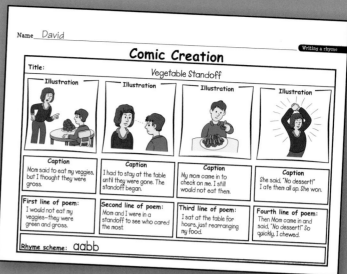

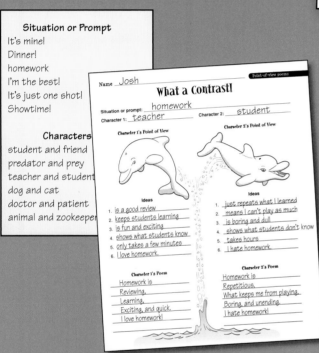

POETIC PERSPECTIVES
Point of view

Begin this activity by posting a chart like the one at the left. Next, pick one of the situations or prompts and discuss with students the contrasting emotions that might be felt by the corresponding pair of characters. If desired, have two students role-play the selected situation to clarify each character's perspective. Afterward, demonstrate how to write two poems about the chosen situation: one from character 1's viewpoint and one from character 2's viewpoint. Follow up by having each student complete a copy of page 108 to write a similar duo of poems using a different situation or prompt from the chart.

GUESS THE GOAL
Author's purpose

What is a poet's reason for writing a poem? This activity can help students answer that question. Gather six to eight different poetry anthologies from the library. In addition, post sheets of paper labeled with the purposes at the right. Next, read aloud two poems. Have students identify the author's purpose in each poem and affix to the appropriate poster a sticky note labeled with each poem's title and author. Then give several sticky notes and an anthology to each small group of students. Have the groups read aloud several poems, discuss each author's purpose, and attach sticky notes to the matching posters. After an appropriate amount of time, discuss the findings. Encourage students to add to the display during free time by placing the anthologies and sticky notes in an accessible area.

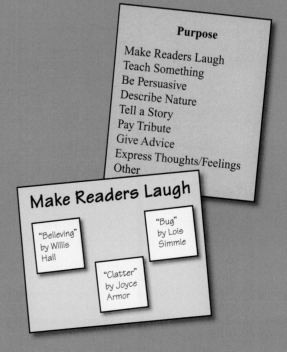

Bookmarks

Use with "Tricks of the Trade" on page 104.

Onomatopoeia

using a word that imitates the sound it represents

TEC44036

Rhyming

using words that have endings with the same sound

TEC44036

Simile

making a comparison using *like* or *as*

TEC44036

Metaphor

making a comparison by calling one thing something else

TEC44036

Alliteration

repeating the initial sound in a group of several words

TEC44036

Assonance

repeating vowel sounds but not consonants

TEC44036

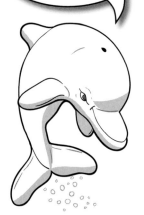

Consonance

repeating consonant sounds but not vowels

TEC44036

Dive Into Poetry!

A Sea of Techniques
- Onomatopoeia
- Rhyming
- Simile
- Metaphor
- Alliteration
- Assonance
- Consonance

TEC44036

Comic Creation

Title:

Illustration | **Illustration** | **Illustration** | **Illustration**

Caption | Caption | Caption | Caption

First line of poem: | Second line of poem: | Third line of poem: | Fourth line of poem:

Rhyme scheme:

©The Mailbox® • TEC44036 • April/May 2008

Note to the teacher: Use with "Comic Creations" on page 105.

What a Contrast!

Situation or prompt: _____

Character 1: _____   Character 2: _____

Character 1's Point of View

Character 2's Point of View

Ideas

1. _____
2. _____
3. _____
4. _____
5. _____
6. _____

Ideas

1. _____
2. _____
3. _____
4. _____
5. _____
6. _____

Character 1's Poem

_____

_____

_____

_____

_____

_____

Character 2's Poem

_____

_____

_____

_____

_____

_____

Digging Up Text Features and Structures

with ideas by Dee Demyan, Atwater, OH
and Diane Marshall, Salem, AL

Keys to Understanding Nonfiction Text

Look at

1. the selection's title.
2. subtitles and headings.
3. charts, tables, and graphs.
4. pictures, maps, and diagrams. Read the captions.
5. highlighted text and words in italics or bold print.
6. bulleted points.
7. labels.

HIDDEN TREASURES
Features of nonfiction text

To improve students' comprehension of fact-based material, give them each a tool labeled with tips that are sure to help. Provide each child with a laminated copy of a bookmark from page 111 to keep as a reference. Then have students skim their textbooks for examples of each feature listed on their bookmarks and discuss the benefits of paying attention to such features as they preview and read nonfiction text. To have students practice identifying and using these helpful features, see the reproducible on page 112.

WHAT PART OF A CELL CONTROLS ITS ACTIVITIES?

The Nucleus, page 128!

USE THE TREASURE MAP!
Using an index

All you need to play this whole-class game are students' textbooks. Announce which subject's textbook students are to use; then divide the class into teams of three or four students. Ask the teams a question that can be answered using the index in each student's textbook. Then have each team's members search their books' indexes to find the answer. Award a point to the first team that provides both the correct answer and the page number on which the answer is found. Continue playing in this manner until one team reaches a predetermined number of points.

SPOTTING THE STRUCTURE
Using signal words

Give each child a copy of page 113. Explain that the six categories on the handout correspond to common nonfiction text structures. Refer to each appropriate set of words as you discuss with students one such structure at a time. Next, give each child a copy of the form below. Have her complete it as directed as she reads from a textbook an assigned chapter that has one of the text structures just discussed. When everyone is finished, have students share their answers and discuss why they think the author chose that particular organizational structure to convey the content. Periodically repeat this activity, focusing on a different text structure each time.

Text Structure Signal Words

Cause and Effect

as a result of	leads/led to
because	may be due to
consequently	so that
for this reason	therefore
if...then	thus
in order to	when...then
is caused by	

Sequence or Time Order

after	next!
afterward	not long after
as soon as	now
before	on (date)
during	second
finally	soon
first	then
following	third
immediately	today
later	when
meanwhile	

Compare and Contrast

although	in common
as well as	in comparison
as opposed to	instead of
both	on the other hand
but	otherwise
by contrast	similar to
compared with	similarly
different from	unlike
either...or	whereas
even though	yet
however	

Description

appears to be	in front of
as in	looks like
behind	near
below	on top of
beside	onto
between	outside
down	over
for example	such as
for instance	under
in back of	

Problem and Solution

conflict	possibly
could be	recommendations include
despite that	resolved
in efforts to	result
mishap	a solution
perhaps	trouble
possible	

Question and Answer

How...?
One answer is...
The question is...
What...?
When...?
Where...?
Who...?

Name _____

Identifying nonfiction text structure

Spying for Clues!

Read the assigned selection. As you read, list the words that signal the selection's structure. Then circle the correct structure.

Clue words: _____

_____

_____

_____

Circle the structure: Cause and effect   Compare and contrast   Description

Problem and solution   Question and answer   Sequence or time order

Keys to Understanding
Nonfiction Text

Look at

 1 the selection's title.

 2 subtitles and headings.

 3 charts, tables, and graphs.

 4 pictures, maps, and diagrams. Read the captions.

 5 highlighted text and words in italics or bold print.

 6 bulleted points.

 7 labels.

TEC44036

Keys to Understanding
Nonfiction Text

Look at

 1 the selection's title.

 2 subtitles and headings.

 3 charts, tables, and graphs.

 4 pictures, maps, and diagrams. Read the captions.

 5 highlighted text and words in italics or bold print.

 6 bulleted points.

 7 labels.

TEC44036

Dig for Answers!

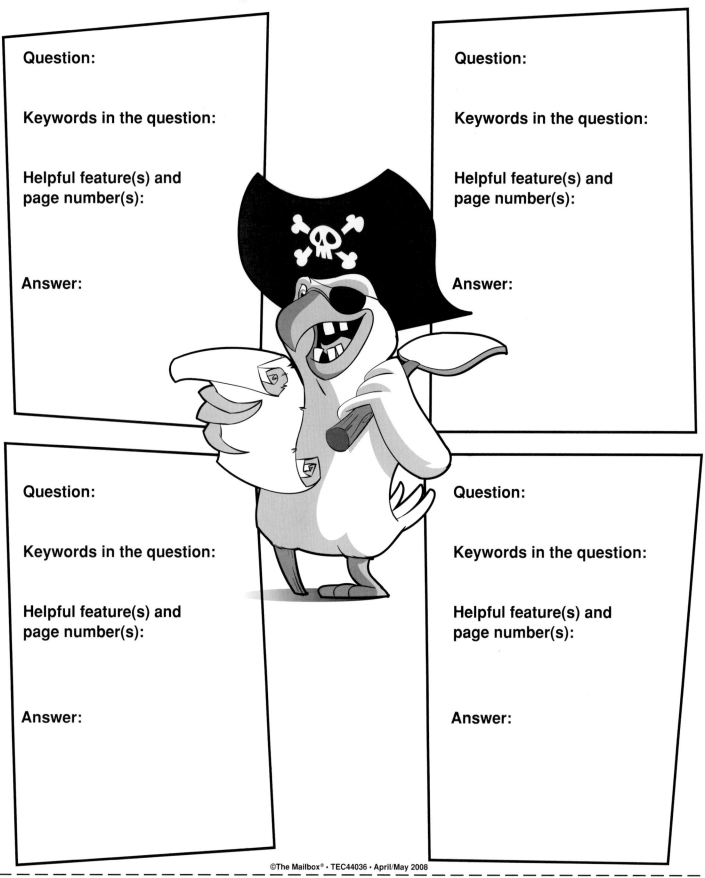

Question:

Keywords in the question:

Helpful feature(s) and page number(s):

Answer:

Question:

Keywords in the question:

Helpful feature(s) and page number(s):

Answer:

Question:

Keywords in the question:

Helpful feature(s) and page number(s):

Answer:

Question:

Keywords in the question:

Helpful feature(s) and page number(s):

Answer:

Note to the teacher: Use with "Hidden Treasures" on page 109. Have each child read a chapter of a textbook. Then have him complete this organizer to help him answer the review questions for that chapter.

Text Structure Signal Words

Cause and Effect

as a result of   leads/led to
because   may be due to
consequently   so that
for this reason   therefore
if…then   thus
in order to   when…then
is caused by

Sequence or Time Order

after   next
afterward   not long after
as soon as   now
before   on (date)
during   second
finally   soon
first   then
following   third
immediately   today
later   when
meanwhile

Compare and Contrast

although   in common
as well as   in comparison
as opposed to   instead of
both   on the other hand
but   otherwise
by contrast   similar to
compared with   similarly
different from   unlike
either…or   whereas
even though   yet
however

Description

appears to be   in front of
as in   looks like
behind   near
below   on top of
beside   onto
between   outside
down   over
for example   such as
for instance   under
in back of

Problem and Solution

conflict   possibly
could be   recommendations include
despite that   resolved
in efforts to   result
mishap   a solution
perhaps   trouble
possible

Question and Answer

How…?
One answer is…
The question is…
What…?
When…?
Where…?
Who…?

©The Mailbox® • TEC44036 • April/May 2008

Note to the teacher: Use with "Spotting the Structure" on page 110.

Reference Materials
Are Cool!

Make it easier for students to know when to use a dictionary, an encyclopedia, an atlas, and a thesaurus by creating this eye-catching reminder. Provide each child with a copy of page 117 and access to the four reference books. Instruct students to peruse the books to determine the type(s) of information each reference provides. Afterward, have each child use the patterns to cut out four different colors of ice cream scoops and one cone. Have him label each scoop cutout with a different reference and examples of what that reference can help him with and then glue the scoops atop the cone.

Kim Minafo, Apex, NC

Dictionary
- spelling
- capital letters
- syllable division
- pronunciation
- part of speech
- multiple meanings
- sample sentence
- word history
- synonyms and antonyms

Encyclopedia
- basic facts
- details
- related topics

Atlas
- maps
- tables
- charts

Thesaurus
- definitions
- synonyms
- part of speech

Distinguishing primary and secondary resources

Here's a concrete way to help students remember the differences between the two major categories of reference materials. Create on the board a web for each classification that includes a brief definition and several examples. Next, have each student make two flash cards by copying the web for primary resources onto a half sheet of yellow construction paper and the web for secondary resources onto a half sheet of orange paper. Then read aloud selections from various resource books. Instruct students to hold up the corresponding card to identify the source as primary or secondary. If desired, have the student record the title and author of each shared example on the back of the appropriate card.

Starin Lewis, Phoenix, AZ

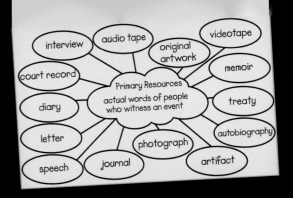

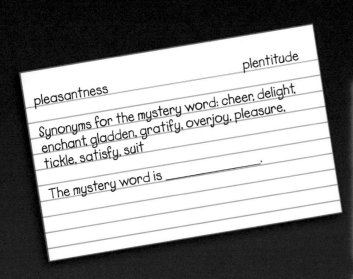

MYSTERY WORD
Using a thesaurus

To begin this partner activity, have each student open a thesaurus to a two-page spread and pick one of the pages. Instruct the child to record that page's first guide word in the top left corner of an index card and the second guide word in the card's top right corner. Next, have each student select any entry from the page and list the selected word's synonyms on her card. Then have the partners exchange cards. Challenge each student to use the thesaurus and the information on her partner's card to identify which word he chose.

adapted from an idea by Ann Fisher, Toledo, OH

PAGE WALK
Dictionary skills

This fun scavenger hunt is the perfect vehicle for students to discover what a valuable resource a dictionary really is! Just place at a table a couple of dictionaries and student copies of page 118. Whether a child completes the page alone, with a partner, or with a small group of his classmates, he'll realize just how much information this sometimes-underappreciated resource contains. If desired, challenge each student to create a new dictionary hunt after he completes the page.

Virginia Land, Tennessee Temple Academy, Chattanooga, TN

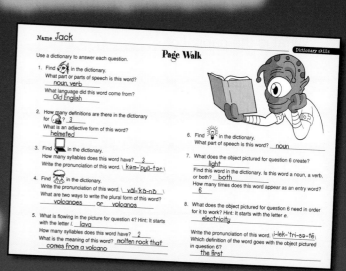

For periodic practice with secondary resources, place a phone book, a magazine, a newspaper, an atlas, a dictionary, and a thesaurus at a center along with preprogrammed copies of the form below. Instruct each student visiting the center to complete the form as directed. If time allows, invite her to write on another sheet of paper a new question that can be answered using one of the materials and then leave it at the center for the next child to answer.

Kathy Thomas, Saints Joseph and John School, Strongsville, OH

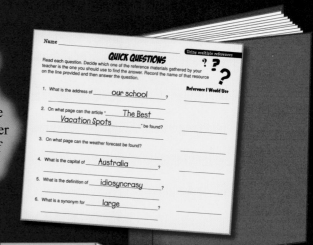

Name _____

QUICK QUESTIONS

Using multiple references

Read each question. Decide which one of the reference materials gathered by your teacher is the one you should use to find the answer. Record the name of that resource on the line provided and then answer the question.

Reference I Would Use

1. What is the address of _____ ?

   _____

2. On what page can the article " _____

   _____ " be found?

   _____

3. On what page can the weather forecast be found?

   _____

4. What is the capital of _____ ?

   _____

5. What is the definition of _____ ?

   _____

6. What is a synonym for _____ ?

   _____

Note to the teacher: Use with "Quick Questions" on this page. Before making copies of the form, program questions 1, 2, 4, 5, and 6 with information that can be found in the collection of reference materials you will provide.

TEC44037

Page Walk

Name _____

118

Use a dictionary to answer each question.

1. Find 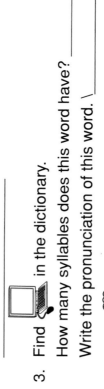 in the dictionary.
   What part or parts of speech is this word? _____

   What language did this word come from? _____

2. How many definitions are there in the dictionary
   for 🐟? _____
   What is an adjective form of this word? _____

3. Find 💻 in the dictionary.
   How many syllables does this word have? _____

   Write the pronunciation of this word. _____

4. Find 🧁 in the dictionary.
   Write the pronunciation of this word. _____

   What are two ways to write the plural form of this word? _____

5. What is flowing in the picture for question 4? Hint: It starts
   with the letter *l*. _____

   How many syllables does this word have? _____

   What is the meaning of this word? _____

6. Find 💡 in the dictionary.
   What part of speech is this word? _____

7. What does the object pictured for question 6 create? _____

   Find this word in the dictionary. Is this word a noun, a verb,
   or both? _____
   How many times does this word appear as an entry word? _____

8. What does the object pictured for question 6 need in order
   for it to work? Hint: It starts with the letter *e*. _____

   Write the pronunciation of this word. _____
   Which definition of the word goes with the object pictured
   in question 6? _____

©The Mailbox® • TEC44037 • June/July 2008 • Key p. 310

Note to the teacher: Use with "Page Walk" on page 115.

Sticking With Prepositions and Conjunctions

with ideas by Carol Lawrence, Madera, CA

with   his best   buddy

"CHEW-SING" FLAVORFUL COMBINATIONS
Forming prepositional phrases

Laminate the gum cards on page 121 and cut them apart. Give each child one card (pack of gum), making sure all packs of cinnamon-flavored gum ( ) are distributed and any extra packs of lemon-flavored ( ) and mint-flavored ( ) gum are in an accessible area. Then have all students with cinnamon gum stand. Instruct each child with lemon or mint gum to join a child with cinnamon gum so that when the packs are in cinnamon-lemon-mint order, the words form a sensible prepositional phrase. Explain that some students with lemon or mint gum may need to change groups or trade their gum for one of the extra packs in order to form a phrase that makes sense. If any group lacks enough members to complete a phrase, have the class suggest appropriate words. Once all the matches are made, have each child write five prepositional phrases of his own and use each one in a sentence. If desired, treat each child to a stick of flavorful gum when he's finished!

Look on page 122 for a fun practice page!

MIX-AND-MATCH STORY STARTERS
Using prepositions in writing

Here's a way to generate preposition-rich sentences that are perfect inspiration for students who have trouble jump-starting a story. Divide a half sheet of unlined paper into three sections, as shown, and make a copy for each child. Instruct students to complete each section according to the framework shown and then illustrate the sections. Assemble the completed pages into a flipbook so that the individual sections turn freely, creating multiple combinations of phrases for story-starting sentences.

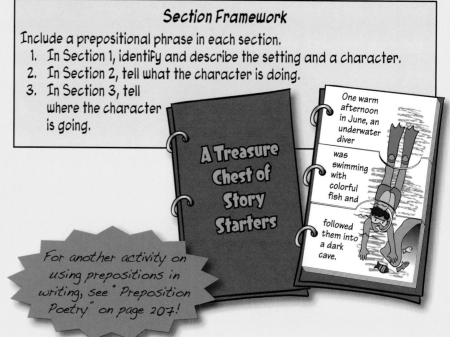

Section Framework
Include a prepositional phrase in each section.
1. In Section 1, identify and describe the setting and a character.
2. In Section 2, tell what the character is doing.
3. In Section 3, tell where the character is going.

A Treasure Chest of Story Starters

One warm afternoon in June, an underwater diver

was swimming with colorful fish and

followed them into a dark cave.

For another activity on using prepositions in writing, see "Preposition Poetry" on page 207!

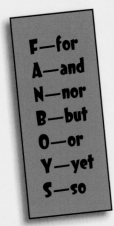

F—for
A—and
N—nor
B—but
O—or
Y—yet
S—so

CONNECTOR-WORD REMINDER
Coordinating conjunctions

To help your students recall the seven important words that join equal words, phrases, and sentences together, teach them the acronym FANBOYS as shown. Then have each child practice using the acronym by completing a copy of page 122 as directed.

STICK 'EM TOGETHER
Prepositions-and-conjunctions game

First, have students label each card in a supply of index cards with one of the phrases at the right. Collect the cards and then write on the board the point code shown below and the following conjunctions: *and, nor, but, for, yet, so,* and *or.* Next, divide students into three teams and hand two facedown cards to the first player on each team. On your signal, have the players turn their cards over. Give them 30 seconds to form a sentence that includes a coordinating conjunction from the board and both phrases on their cards. Instruct players to raise their hands as soon as they have a sentence. When time is up, have each player share her sentence; then award points accordingly. The team with the most points after all players have had a turn wins.

Prepositional Phrases

around the elephant	off the skateboard
for a tiny man	after sunrise
near a butterfly	aboard the spacecraft
under a log	below the window
among the seashells	by four o'clock
over her head	behind the water fountain
to the candy store	until noon
up the tree	about spiders
through the fog	down the pole
across the bridge	from Australia
beside a wooden fence	into the mailbox
on a roller coaster	out the door
during dinner	against the huge ship
past the driveway	of 26 men
between the rocks	till 2018

of 26 men

from Australia

A group of 26 men wanted a ticket, but the only man who got one was from Australia.

Points
First player to raise hand	=	3 points
Second player to raise hand	=	2 points
Third player to raise hand	=	1 point
Forming a simple sentence	=	5 points
Forming a compound sentence	=	10 points

under	over	between	above
TEC44037	TEC44037	TEC44037	TEC44037
around	behind	by	beside
TEC44037	TEC44037	TEC44037	TEC44037
with	below	on	in
TEC44037	TEC44037	TEC44037	TEC44037
the deep blue	a tall	two	a green
TEC44037	TEC44037	TEC44037	TEC44037
the revolving	a wooden	the famous	the popular
TEC44037	TEC44037	TEC44037	TEC44037
his best	the ground's	the back of a	a kettle of
TEC44037	TEC44037	TEC44037	TEC44037
sea	mountain peak	towers	valley
TEC44037	TEC44037	TEC44037	TEC44037
globe	fence	Statue of Liberty	movie star
TEC44037	TEC44037	TEC44037	TEC44037
buddy	surface	flying dragon	hot water
TEC44037	TEC44037	TEC44037	TEC44037

TO THE RESCUE!

Write a coordinating conjunction in each blank.
Use each of the following conjunctions at least once:
and, but, for, nor, or, so, and *yet.*

Andy _____ his best friend, Joe, were walking to school when they spotted

the Guminator. Neither Andy _____ Joe thought they were in danger, _____

as they turned a corner, Andy yelled, "Watch out, Joe! The Guminator is aiming his

atomic gumball chewer at us, _____ I don't think we can outrun it!"

"Maybe we should duck _____ run _____ something...oh, I don't know

what to do!" blubbered Joe.

"Those who hesitate are toast!" bellowed the Guminator as he blasted the boys

with wads of sticky gum. Soon their hair _____ clothes were covered with

colorful splotches. They were worried, _____ they knew better than to go to

class with gum all over them. _____ if they didn't, they'd be late for school!

All of a sudden, a dazzling pink figure appeared. "It's Super Bubbleman! He's

come to our rescue!" exclaimed Joe.

The Guminator froze in his tracks,

_____ he saw that Super Bubbleman

had not one _____ two things that

could spoil his fun: ice cubes _____

a jar of peanut butter. The Guminator

knew he was really in trouble if Super

Bubbleman had some gum removers

with him, _____ he left in a hurry.

"Oh, thank you, Super Bubbleman,"

chorused Andy _____ Joe. "You'll be

our hero forever!"

Note to the teacher: Use with "Connector-Word Reminder" on page 120.

MATH UNITS

Estimation Excursions

with ideas by Ann Fisher, Toledo, OH

50	300	7,000
60	400 ✗	8,000
70		9,000

Situations

A shelf in a bookstore holds 57 books. (60)

Last year, a toy store placed 8,136 special orders for video games. (8,000)

A popular candy store has 386 packages of gummy worms on sale. (400)

A customer at a music store bought 72 CDs last month! (70)

A new carpet store just ordered 9,362 square yards of carpeting. (9,000)

REALITY TIC-TAC-TOE
Rounding to the nearest whole number

The object of this game is to give students an opportunity to estimate numbers in real-life situations. Draw a tic-tac-toe grid and label it with multiples of ten, 100, and 1,000. Then divide students into two teams: X and O. Announce a situation (see the list and the italicized answers). Then have the first player on Team X go to the grid and mark an X below the most reasonable estimate for that situation. If Team O agrees, read a different situation to the first player on Team O. If Team O disagrees, allow one of its players to mark an O below a different number in the grid. Then provide the correct answer and erase the incorrect mark. If both answers are incorrect, erase both marks and continue with Team X. Play in this manner until one team has three marks in a row, column, or diagonal. If all numbers are marked before there is a winner, the team with more marks wins. Play more rounds as time allows.

STAND UP, SIT DOWN
Deciding when to round and why

When is an exact answer required instead of an estimate? Making that decision is tough for some students.
To provide practice with this skill, have everyone stand.
Read aloud one of the situations shown (not the italicized answer). If a child thinks the situation needs an
exact answer, she should continue to stand. If she thinks
an estimate is appropriate, she should sit. After allowing
students a few seconds to make their decisions, call on a
standing student and then on a seated student to explain
their choices. Then share the correct answer and help the
class understand why rounding is or is not appropriate
for that situation. Continue until each situation has been
discussed.

Situations

- A carpenter building a display case is measuring to see how long each shelf should be. (*exact*)

- The manager of a beauty salon wants to know about how much is spent each year on magazines. (*estimate*)

- A clerk is figuring out how much change to give a customer from a $20.00 bill. (*exact*)

- A sales clerk worked 15 hours in one week at $7.25 per hour. She wants to know about how much her paycheck will be. (*estimate*)

- A store manager is arranging six stacks of sales brochures on each foot of shelf space. About how many brochures can he stack on 19 shelves? (*estimate*)

- A toy store cashier must charge sales tax on each sale. How much tax should he add to a sale of $48.50? (*exact*)

- A bookstore buys pencils from a supplier for $0.12 each and sells them for a quarter. About how much profit will the store make on a case of 1,000 pencils? (*estimate*)

- In July, a bookstore sold 49 children's books. It sold 83 books in August. It sold 67 books in September. What was the approximate average number of books sold for those three months? (*estimate*)

- Workers at a party store are building a window display that calls for 200 balloons. If a dozen balloons come in one package, how many packages are needed for the display? (*exact*)

- A snack bar sells bottled water for $1.29, which includes tax. How much will a customer pay for eight bottles of water? (*exact*)

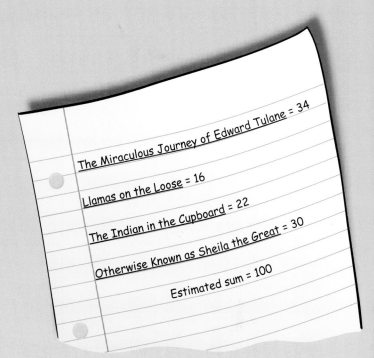

The Miraculous Journey of Edward Tulane = 34

Llamas on the Loose = 16

The Indian in the Cupboard = 22

Otherwise Known as Sheila the Great = 30

Estimated sum = 100

"SUM" AMAZING TITLES
Finding exact and estimated sums and differences

For this partner activity, have each student list the titles
of four favorite books, songs, movies, or games. When
he's finished, instruct him to count the number of letters
in each title, record the number next to the title, and then
estimate the numbers' sum. Have him also find the exact
sum of his numbers. Declare the child with the higher
sum the winner. Repeat the activity using different titles,
this time declaring the child with the lower sum the
winner. To have students estimate differences, have each
partner list four titles whose letters he thinks will have a
sum close to 150. Instruct him to count the letters in his
titles, find estimated and exact sums, and then subtract
each sum from 150. Declare the child whose sum is closer
to zero the winner.

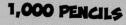

1,000 PENCILS

$ 0.12

WHERE DID THEY SHOP?

Round each number in the boxes below to the nearest ten.
Then subtract. To find the path, shade each box whose
answer contains a 7.

813 − 72	1,391 − 224	652 − 49	8,346 − 6,942
4,361 − 1,343	591 − 221	1,704 − 139	284 − 19
862 − 123	4,444 − 777	909 − 381	1,234 − 567
2,602 − 1,111	9,124 − 2,009	389 − 216	569 − 98

Pets Galore   Music 'n' More   Jewelry Boutique   Shoe Colony

Round each number in the boxes below to the nearest hundred.
Then add. To find the path, shade each box whose answer
contains a 4.

144 + 281	3,245 + 2,719	6,236 + 2,409	541 + 177
1,219 + 1,187	679 + 238	925 + 480	32,142 + 4,890
4,066 + 879	8,762 + 5,411	838 + 468	12,237 + 7,199
777 + 333	2,670 + 926	934 + 567	3,422 + 986

Shoe Colony   Sports Scene   Pets Galore   Music 'n' More

Mall Math

Write an estimate for each answer.

1. The Bookworm Bookstore ordered 32 boxes of children's books. Each box contains 22 books. About how many books will the store receive?

   _____

2. Saturday was a busy day at Movie Lovers Videos. The workers rented 585 DVDs to 200 customers. About how many DVDs did each customer rent?

   _____

3. A shipment of flour to the Cookie Nook weighs 330 pounds. The shipment contains eight large bags. About how much does each bag weigh?

   _____

4. Serena is putting 175 bags of chips, nuts, and cookies on displays at the Snack Shack. If there are six different displays, about how many bags will go on each display?

   _____

5. Each year, Readers Express orders 32 different magazines. If each magazine comes 12 times a year, about how many issues will the store receive?

   _____

6. A wall display at Shoe Scene holds 454 boxes of shoes on nine shelves. About how many boxes are on each shelf?

   _____

7. The Candy Castle has seven gumball machines. Each machine contains 578 gumballs. About how many gumballs are in all the machines?

   _____

8. The owner of Jill's Jewelry Box is placing a special order that will weigh 223 pounds. If shipping costs $0.48 per pound, about how much will it cost to ship the order?

   _____

9. Each month, workers at Totally Toys empty an average of 74 cartons of toys. About how many cartons do they empty in six months? _____

10. Eight clerks at Everything Sports worked a total of 317 hours last week. About how many hours did each person work?

    _____

Building
Perimeter, Area, and Volume Skills

with ideas by Vickie Robertson, Meadow Green Elementary, Whittier, CA

Make a copy of the game mat and cards on pages 130 and 131. Laminate the cards and answer key on page 131, cut them out, and place them in a large plastic bag along with the game mat. Have a small group of students play the game according to the directions on the mat.

FENCE IT IN!
Perimeter

To begin this hands-on activity, have each child cover an empty box with light-colored construction paper and color the box's top so that it resembles his dream backyard. Next, instruct the student to measure the perimeter of his yard, build a construction paper fence equal to the box's perimeter, and then glue the fence around the outside of his box as shown. Have him also insert a craft stick signpost labeled with his box's perimeter. Then place several boxes at a time at a center along with a cup to hold the matching perimeter sticks. Challenge students using the center to decide which stick goes with which box.

TINKERING WITH TILES
Area

Turn your students into busy builders who design pet store floors! First, have each child color the squares on a sheet of one-inch graph paper three different colors. Next, instruct her to cut out the squares, arrange them on a sheet of construction paper in a regular or an irregular shape, and then glue the squares in place. When she's finished, have her use the scale shown to find the area of the resulting design and write it on the project as shown. To follow up, have each child complete a copy of page 132 as directed.

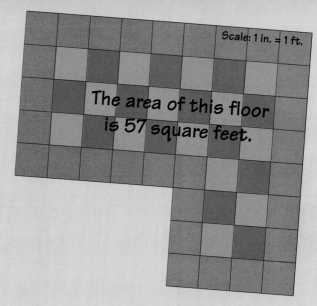

Scale: 1 in. = 1 ft.

The area of this floor is 57 square feet.

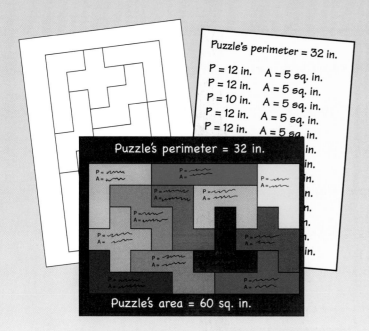

Puzzle's perimeter = 32 in.

P = 12 in.   A = 5 sq. in.
P = 12 in.   A = 5 sq. in.
P = 10 in.   A = 5 sq. in.
P = 12 in.   A = 5 sq. in.
P = 12 in.   A = 5 sq. in.

Puzzle's perimeter = 32 in.

Puzzle's area = 60 sq. in.

PIECING IT TOGETHER
Perimeter and area

For this skill-reinforcing activity, provide each child with a copy of a pentominoes puzzle. Have the student color the puzzle pieces, cut them out, place them in a resealable plastic bag, and then trade bags with a classmate. Next, instruct students to use a ruler to find the area and perimeter of each of the 12 puzzle pieces, label each piece with both measurements, and then arrange the pieces to form a rectangle. Afterward, have each child glue his assembled puzzle to black paper, find the puzzle's area and perimeter, and write both measurements on the paper. Discuss with students the differences between area and perimeter. Then display the completed puzzles on a board titled "Piecing Together Area and Perimeter."

FILL 'ER UP!
Estimating volume

Try using paper lunch sacks and Unifix cubes to teach pairs of students about volume. Have each duo trim a sack to any height. Afterward, have the pair guess about how many cubes it will take to fill the sack and record the guess on the sack's bottom. Next, instruct partners to fit rows or columns of connected cubes in the sack until it is full. Then have students remove the cubes, count them, and record the actual number as the sack's approximate volume, writing both pieces of information on the bottom of the sack just below the guess. Discuss why the actual number of cubes in each sack represents only an approximate volume. Then place a tub of cubes and sacks of various heights at a center for more practice.

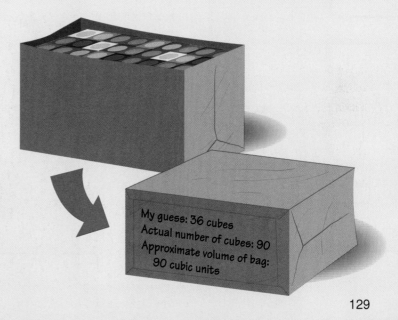

My guess: 36 cubes
Actual number of cubes: 90
Approximate volume of bag: 90 cubic units

Hard Hat Construction

Volume (in.)

Area (in.)

Perimeter (in.)

Directions:
1. Stack the cards in a pile.
2. Decide whether the large number on each card is the area, volume, or perimeter of the shape shown.
3. Place the card under the matching hat.
4. When all the cards have been placed, check your answers with the key.

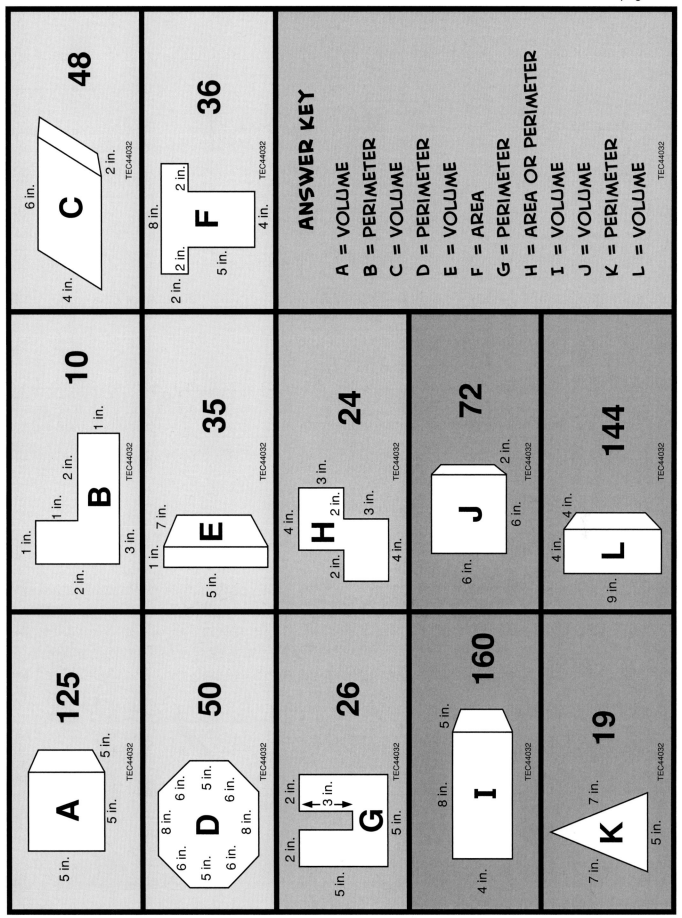

ANSWER KEY

A = VOLUME
B = PERIMETER
C = VOLUME
D = PERIMETER
E = VOLUME
F = AREA
G = PERIMETER
H = AREA OR PERIMETER
I = VOLUME
J = VOLUME
K = PERIMETER
L = VOLUME

Name _____

Mow, Joe!

Find the area.

Ⓐ

9 yd.
20 yd.

A = _____

Ⓑ

30 yd.
30 yd.

A = _____

Ⓒ

40 yd.
15 yd.

A = _____

Ⓓ

33 yd.
60 yd.

A = _____

Ⓔ

125 yd.
50 yd.

A = _____

Ⓕ

70 yd.
72 yd.

A = _____

Ⓖ

36 yd.
84 yd.

A = _____

Ⓗ

100 yd.
80 yd.

A = _____

Ⓘ

62 yd.
90 yd.

A = _____

Ⓙ

20 yd.
20 yd.
40 yd.
40 yd.

A = _____

Note to the teacher: Use alone or with "Tinkering With Tiles" on page 129.

On the Midway With
Factors and Multiples

with ideas by Jennifer Otter, Oak Ridge, NC

ROLL THOSE FACTORS!
Factors of two-digit numbers

This partner game provides lots of factoring practice! Give each duo a pair of dice and each partner a copy of the recording sheet at the top of page 135. To begin, one partner rolls the dice, forms a two-digit number from the numbers rolled, and records the number on his sheet. Next, he lists all the factors of his number and tallies his score using the guide on his sheet. His partner then takes a turn, following the same instructions. The partner with more points after five rounds is the winner.

FOOL THE GUESSERS
Factors and multiples, logical reasoning

This fun activity allows students to see whether they can identify a secret number using a series of questions. Divide the class into groups of four; then pair the students in each group. Give each duo a copy of the recording sheet on page 135 and instruct the twosome to secretly choose one of the numbers at the top. Each pair then tries to guess the other team's secret number by writing one question on the page at a time for the opposing team, trading papers, and having the opponents answer by checking the appropriate box and then returning the paper. The teams use each subsequent response to ask the next question up to a maximum of ten questions, attempting to narrow the field of numbers and correctly guess the secret number before exhausting their opportunities. If a team fails to guess the secret number after ten questions, the opposing team reveals it.

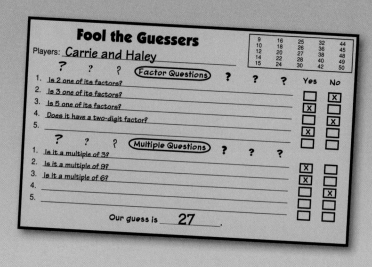

"A-MAZE-ING" MULTIPLES
Multiples up to 100

Challenge students to practice multiples by creating mazes their partners can solve. Give each child a copy of page 136. Have her plot the multiples of a one- or two-digit number that are 100 or less on the grid in a path from Start to Finish. Explain that the multiples do not have to be written in consecutive order and that skipping multiples is allowed. Then have her fill the remaining boxes with random numbers from 1 to 100 that are not multiples of her chosen number and decorate the page with appropriate art. When she's finished, have her trade mazes with a classmate, cover her partner's maze with a transparency, and then trace the correct path using a wipe-off marker. To get more mileage out of the mazes, periodically place several laminated mazes at a center for additional practice by individual students or small groups.

Roll Those Factors!

Player: _____

	Factors	Points
Roll 1: ☐ ☐	_____	_____
Roll 2: ☐ ☐	_____	_____
Roll 3: ☐ ☐	_____	_____
Roll 4: ☐ ☐	_____	_____
Roll 5: ☐ ☐	_____	_____
	Total	_____

2 factors
3 factors
4 factors
5 factors
6+ factors
25 points
20 points
15 points
10 points
5 points

ROLL!

©The Mailbox® • TEC44033 • Oct./Nov. 2007

Fool the Guessers

Players: _____

9	16	25	32	44
10	18	26	36	45
12	20	27	38	48
14	22	28	40	49
15	24	30	42	50

? ? ? (Factor Questions) ? ? ?   Yes   No

1. _____ ☐ ☐
2. _____ ☐ ☐
3. _____ ☐ ☐
4. _____ ☐ ☐
5. _____ ☐ ☐

? ? ? (Multiple Questions) ? ? ?

1. _____ ☐ ☐
2. _____ ☐ ☐
3. _____ ☐ ☐
4. _____ ☐ ☐
5. _____ ☐ ☐

Our guess is _____.

©The Mailbox® • TEC44033 • Oct./Nov. 2007

Multiples Maze

| Start | Find the path for the multiples of _____. |

©The Mailbox® • TEC44033 • Oct./Nov. 2007

136 **Note to the teacher:** Use with "'A-maze-ing' Multiples" on page 134.

Finish

Name _____

Blue-Ribbon Multiples

Color the multiples in each quilt section by the code. Hint: "Blue = 3" means to color all multiples of 3 in that section blue.

Color Code

A1	A2	A3	B1	B2	B3	C1	C2	C3
blue = 3	black = 7	black = 2	purple = 2	green = 5	black = 5	black = 2	purple = 4	black = 7
orange = 4	purple = 8	yellow = 3	orange = 7	yellow = 6	orange = 6	orange = 3	orange = 6	red = 8
black = 5	red = 9	purple = 5	black = 11	blue = 7	green = 8	yellow = 5	green = 15	blue = 11
yellow = 7	orange = 10	orange = 7	red = 15		blue = 9	blue = 7	black = 10	yellow = 15
green = 11	green = 12	red = 11	green = 25		purple = 11	red = 11		green = 20

1st PRIZE

	1	2	3
A	50 / 25 9 6 8 / 65 / 10 / 85	14 / 20 12 12 27 / 21 / 35 / 77	34 / 11 25 65 2 / 8 / 38 / 62
	95 / 50 5 14 49 / 11 / 7 / 42	32 / 88 10 30 16 / 50 / 64 / 60	9 / 51 39 4 26 / 27 / 16 / 49
B	25 / 11 33 52 63 / 32 / 4 / 7	75 / 20 12 36 40 / 14 / 10 / 77	33 / 78 11 5 15 / 6 / 12 / 16
	8 / 33 11 6 21 / 45 / 35 / 10	21 / 55 48 24 80 / 15 / 7 / 5	12 / 42 77 10 15 / 22 / 64 / 27
C	11 / 16 8 5 65 / 46 / 85 / 25	66 / 8 6 66 32 / 44 / 42 / 16	90 / 30 45 49 14 / 15 / 22 / 28
	26 / 62 49 7 39 / 34 / 4 / 32	10 / 18 28 4 45 / 50 / 50 / 70	21 / 100 64 16 63 / 42 / 35 / 7

Bumpin' Into Factors

Complete the chart. Then write the number of factors for each number on the bumper car with the matching letter. If your answers are correct, the sum of each row, column, and diagonal of car numbers will be the same.

	Number	Factors	Number of Factors
A.	15		
B.	36		
C.	7		
D.	25		
E.	16		
F.	64		
G.	30		
H.	1		
I.	20		

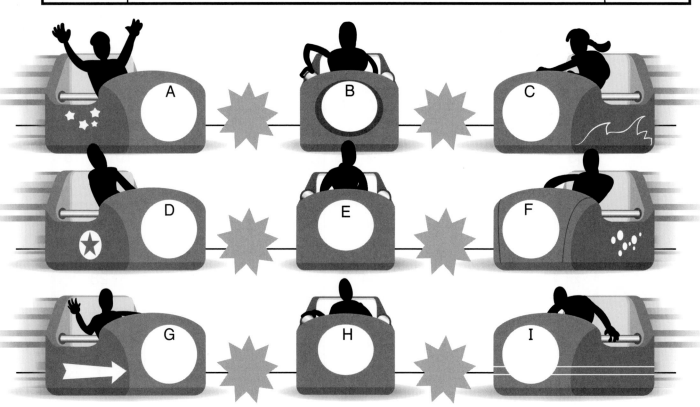

Hats Off to Measurement

CONVERSION BOOKLET
Capacity

To create this useful math tool, have each child make a flip booklet by stacking seven half sheets of different-colored construction paper between a folded sheet of construction paper and stapling the booklet across the top. After the student decorates the cover, instruct him to label the first booklet page "gallon." Then have him equally divide and label the sections of the next five pages, in order, to represent the following units: two half gallons, four quarts, eight pints, and 16 cups. Leave the back cover blank. Finally, direct him to carefully cut apart the strips on each page as shown. If desired, have him use his booklet to complete a copy of page 141.

Brenda Brought, Bradley Elementary
Ft. Leavenworth, KS

MAP AND MEASURE
Length

Practice linear measurement skills with this map-scale activity. Provide each child with small sticky notes that have been cut into narrow strips and a copy of a state, country, or world map. Then read aloud a picture book, such as *The Armadillo From Amarillo* by Lynne Cherry, or appropriate parts of a picture book in which a character travels to several locations. (Or create your own travel itinerary for students to map and measure.) As the character goes from one place to another in the story, have each student mark the locations on his map with sticky strips as shown. At the end of the story, have students work in small groups and use rulers to measure the distance in inches or centimeters between each place on the map and the next. Once the members of each group agree on the ruler measurements, have them use the map's scale to find the real distance between the places.

Erin Ward, Cape Fear Center for Inquiry
Wilmington, NC

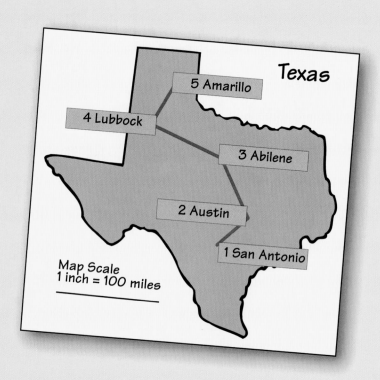

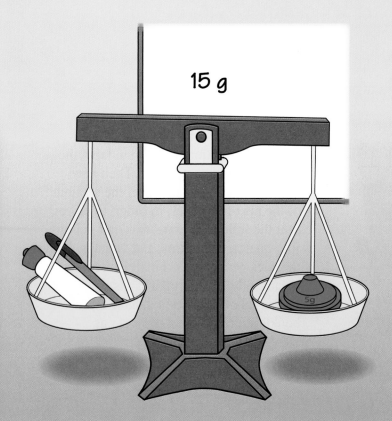

MEASUREMENT MADNESS
Weight

To play this quick game, obtain a scale. Then divide the class into teams of three or four students. Write a specific measurement on the front board. Then challenge one person from each team to find within a specified amount of time one or more classroom items she thinks might have the same total weight as the measurement on the board. Weigh the object or objects on the scale. Award five points to the team whose item's or items' total weight is closest to the one on the board. Continue in the same manner until all team members have had a turn. Then declare the team with the most points the winner.

John Hughes, Book Cliff Elementary, Green River, UT

The Ten-Gallon Hat

Complete the charts. Then convert each measurement to the unit shown.

Metric Conversion Chart

1 liter (L) = _____ milliliters (mL)

Customary Conversion Chart

_____ cup (c.) = 8 fluid ounces (fl. oz.)

1 pint (pt.) = _____ cups

1 _____ (qt.) = 2 pints

1 gallon (gal.) = _____ quarts

A. 12 c. = _____ pt.

B. 1 gal. = _____ c.

C. _____ fl. oz. = 4 pt.

D. 10 pt. = _____ c.

E. _____ pt. = 4 qt.

F. 24 qt. = _____ gal.

G. 5 gal. = _____ c.

H. 10 L = _____ mL

I. _____ L = 3,000 mL

J. 25,000 mL = _____ L

CATTLE DRIVE

Convert each weight to the unit of measure shown.

(1) 20,800 oz. horse = _____ lb.

(2) 2 lb. horseshoe = _____ oz.

(3) 2,400 oz. cowboy = _____ lb.

(4) 1,200 lb. bull = _____ oz.

(5) 2 tn. horse trailer = _____ lb.

(6) 2,000 lb. bale of hay = _____ tn.

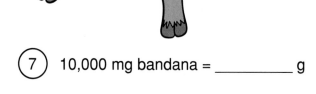

(7) 10,000 mg bandana = _____ g

(8) 1,000 g lasso = _____ mg

(9) 9,000 g saddle = _____ kg

(10) 544 kg cow = _____ mg

(11) 227 kg trough = _____ g

(12) 800,000 mg cactus = _____ g

Name _____

Rope 'em!

Circle the letter of the answer that completes each statement.

1. If a boot is 1 foot long, then it is also _____ long.
   - E. 16 inches
   - R. 1 yard
   - T. 12 inches

2. If tumbleweed is 24 inches long, then it is also _____ long.
   - A. 2 yards
   - S. 1 mile
   - Y. 2 feet

3. If the distance traveled on a cattle trail in one day is 8,800 yards long, then it is also _____ long.
   - J. 3,000 feet
   - R. 5 miles
   - T. 88 yards

4. If a cowboy rides for 7 miles, then he also rides for _____.
   - B. 10,500 yards
   - N. 44,060 inches
   - U. 36,960 feet

5. If a fence is 1,440 inches long, then it is also _____ long.
   - H. 120 feet
   - S. 120 yards
   - V. 12 miles

6. If a branding iron is 3 feet long, then it is also _____ long.
   - C. 24 inches
   - E. 1 yard
   - M. 3 yards

7. If a coyote's tail is 350 millimeters long, then it is also _____ long.
   - A. 35 centimeters
   - F. 3 centimeters
   - N. 1 meter

8. If a trough is 1 meter wide, then it is also _____ wide.
   - G. 10 centimeters
   - W. 10 decimeters
   - U. 100 millimeters

9. If a horse's stall is 3,000 millimeters high, then it is also _____ high.
   - M. 3 decimeters
   - R. 30 centimeters
   - S. 3 meters

10. If a calf is 1 meter high, then it is also _____ high.
    - N. 100 centimeters
    - R. 100 decimeters
    - S. 100 millimeters

11. If a lasso is 200 centimeters long, then it is also _____ long.
    - C. 2 decimeters
    - P. 2,000 millimeters
    - T. 20 meters

12. If a cactus is 7 decimeters high, then it is also _____ high.
    - E. 1 meter
    - G. 700 millimeters
    - H. 200 centimeters

Why do cowboys have trouble in math?

To solve the riddle, write each circled letter from above on the matching numbered line or lines below.

___ ___ ___ ___   ___ ___ ___   __L__ ___ ___ ___   __O__ ___ __DI__ ___   ___ ___ __I__ ___ ___   ___ __!__
 1   5   6   2   7   3   6   7   8   7   2   9   3   4   10   10 12   1   5   10 12 9   4   11

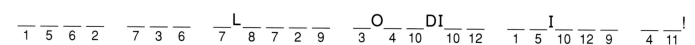

Delivering Equivalent Numbers

with ideas by Vickie Robertson, Meadow Green Elementary, Whittier, CA, and Renee Silliman, Spring Shadows Elementary, Houston, TX

$$\frac{51}{100} = 0.51 = 51\%$$

$$\frac{51}{100} = 0.51 = 51\%$$

PICTURE IT!
Fractions, decimals, and percents

Get this activity under way by providing each child with several copies of a hundredths chart. Next, call out a fraction that has a denominator of 10 or 100. Challenge each student to draw a design or an object on the chart as quickly as possible, shading only the number of squares that are equivalent to the announced fraction. Once the picture is complete, have the student label it with the fraction and its decimal and percent equivalents. Then have students hold up their work so everyone can see the different ways a particular fraction can be represented. Repeat as time allows, calling out a different fraction each time.

ALL SQUARED AWAY
Whole numbers

Begin this creative-thinking activity by having each child fold and cut a sheet of paper to create four flaps as shown. On the back, have the student write a whole number of her choice. Next, instruct her to label each of the four flaps with a different mathematical expression equivalent to the number she wrote. Under the flaps, have her write the question shown. Allow students to decorate the booklets if desired. Then have each child trade booklets with a partner, figure out her partner's equivalent number, and flip the booklet over to check the answer. For more practice with this skill, see page 148.

DRIVE THE ROUTE
Fractions

To prepare for this great center review game, mount the gameboard on page 146 and the key on page 147 on construction paper and laminate them for durability. Then store the key at a center in a resealable plastic bag along with the gameboard, game markers, and a die. To play the game, simply have pairs of students follow the directions on the gameboard.

HAND-TOSSED
Fractions, decimals, and percents

For this small-group or whole-class game, each child colors a paper plate to look like a pizza pan and three six-inch construction paper circles to look like whole pizzas. After he labels his pan as shown, he cuts one pizza in half, labeling one piece "½" and the other "0.5, 50%" and then arranges the halves on the pan to form a complete pizza. He repeats the process for the two remaining pizzas, cutting and labeling each one as shown. Then he stacks each assembled pizza in order on the pan, with the eighths on top.

To play, call out one of the following fractions: ½, ¼, or ⅛. Players then remove from their pans any combination of slices equivalent to the announced fraction unless any part of them is covered by another piece of pizza. Continue playing in this manner until one child has removed all the pizza slices from his pan.

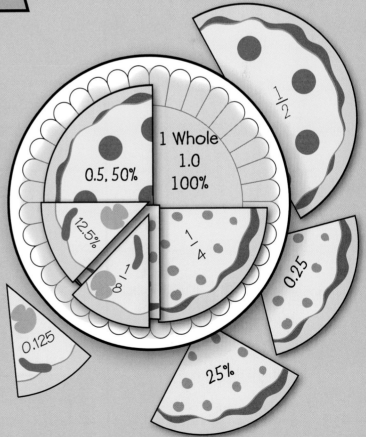

Drive the Route

Start

Finish

$\frac{1}{2}$ $\frac{3}{9}$ $\frac{1}{9}$

$\frac{1}{10}$

$\frac{4}{8}$

$\frac{2}{10}$

$\frac{2}{3}$

$\frac{5}{8}$

$\frac{1}{11}$

$\frac{3}{5}$

$\frac{1}{4}$

$\frac{3}{4}$

$\frac{2}{8}$

$\frac{4}{6}$

$\frac{5}{10}$ $\frac{6}{8}$

Directions:
1. Place your game markers at Start.
2. Player A rolls the die and moves forward that number of spaces. If he lands on a fraction, he must state two equivalent fractions. Player B checks the answers with the key.
3. If Player A is correct, he stays in the same spot. If he is incorrect, he returns to Start.
4. Player B then rolls the die and plays in the same manner.
5. The winner is the first person to reach Finish.

Answer Key for "Drive the Route"

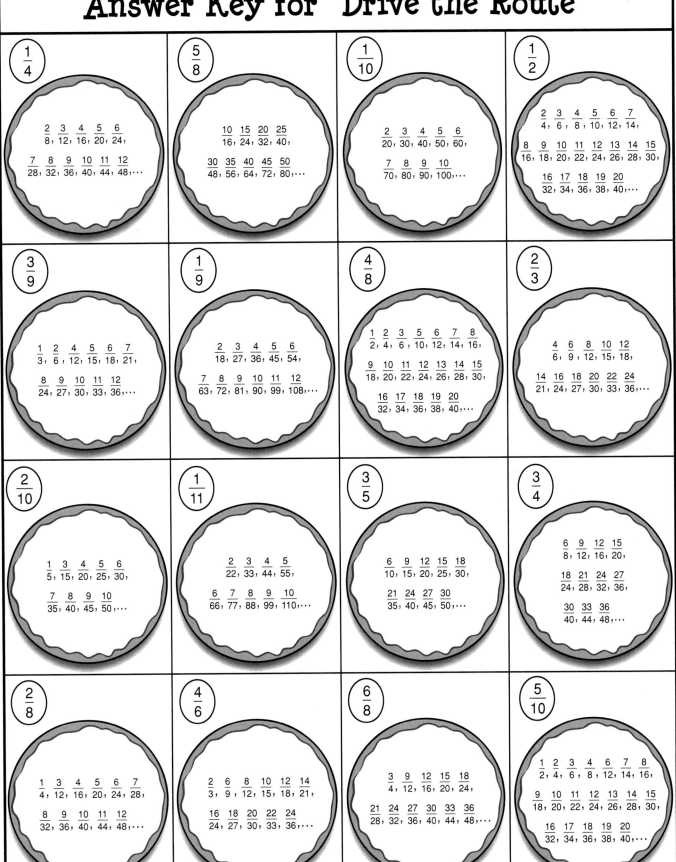

$\frac{1}{4}$

$\frac{2}{8}, \frac{3}{12}, \frac{4}{16}, \frac{5}{20}, \frac{6}{24},$

$\frac{7}{28}, \frac{8}{32}, \frac{9}{36}, \frac{10}{40}, \frac{11}{44}, \frac{12}{48}, \cdots$

$\frac{5}{8}$

$\frac{10}{16}, \frac{15}{24}, \frac{20}{32}, \frac{25}{40},$

$\frac{30}{48}, \frac{35}{56}, \frac{40}{64}, \frac{45}{72}, \frac{50}{80}, \cdots$

$\frac{1}{10}$

$\frac{2}{20}, \frac{3}{30}, \frac{4}{40}, \frac{5}{50}, \frac{6}{60},$

$\frac{7}{70}, \frac{8}{80}, \frac{9}{90}, \frac{10}{100}, \cdots$

$\frac{1}{2}$

$\frac{2}{4}, \frac{3}{6}, \frac{4}{8}, \frac{5}{10}, \frac{6}{12}, \frac{7}{14},$

$\frac{8}{16}, \frac{9}{18}, \frac{10}{20}, \frac{11}{22}, \frac{12}{24}, \frac{13}{26}, \frac{14}{28}, \frac{15}{30},$

$\frac{16}{32}, \frac{17}{34}, \frac{18}{36}, \frac{19}{38}, \frac{20}{40}, \cdots$

$\frac{3}{9}$

$\frac{1}{3}, \frac{2}{6}, \frac{4}{12}, \frac{5}{15}, \frac{6}{18}, \frac{7}{21},$

$\frac{8}{24}, \frac{9}{27}, \frac{10}{30}, \frac{11}{33}, \frac{12}{36}, \cdots$

$\frac{1}{9}$

$\frac{2}{18}, \frac{3}{27}, \frac{4}{36}, \frac{5}{45}, \frac{6}{54},$

$\frac{7}{63}, \frac{8}{72}, \frac{9}{81}, \frac{10}{90}, \frac{11}{99}, \frac{12}{108}, \cdots$

$\frac{4}{8}$

$\frac{1}{2}, \frac{2}{4}, \frac{3}{6}, \frac{5}{10}, \frac{6}{12}, \frac{7}{14}, \frac{8}{16},$

$\frac{9}{18}, \frac{10}{20}, \frac{11}{22}, \frac{12}{24}, \frac{13}{26}, \frac{14}{28}, \frac{15}{30},$

$\frac{16}{32}, \frac{17}{34}, \frac{18}{36}, \frac{19}{38}, \frac{20}{40}, \cdots$

$\frac{2}{3}$

$\frac{4}{6}, \frac{6}{9}, \frac{8}{12}, \frac{10}{15}, \frac{12}{18},$

$\frac{14}{21}, \frac{16}{24}, \frac{18}{27}, \frac{20}{30}, \frac{22}{33}, \frac{24}{36}, \cdots$

$\frac{2}{10}$

$\frac{1}{5}, \frac{3}{15}, \frac{4}{20}, \frac{5}{25}, \frac{6}{30},$

$\frac{7}{35}, \frac{8}{40}, \frac{9}{45}, \frac{10}{50}, \cdots$

$\frac{1}{11}$

$\frac{2}{22}, \frac{3}{33}, \frac{4}{44}, \frac{5}{55},$

$\frac{6}{66}, \frac{7}{77}, \frac{8}{88}, \frac{9}{99}, \frac{10}{110}, \cdots$

$\frac{3}{5}$

$\frac{6}{10}, \frac{9}{15}, \frac{12}{20}, \frac{15}{25}, \frac{18}{30},$

$\frac{21}{35}, \frac{24}{40}, \frac{27}{45}, \frac{30}{50}, \cdots$

$\frac{3}{4}$

$\frac{6}{8}, \frac{9}{12}, \frac{12}{16}, \frac{15}{20},$

$\frac{18}{24}, \frac{21}{28}, \frac{24}{32}, \frac{27}{36},$

$\frac{30}{40}, \frac{33}{44}, \frac{36}{48}, \cdots$

$\frac{2}{8}$

$\frac{1}{4}, \frac{3}{12}, \frac{4}{16}, \frac{5}{20}, \frac{6}{24}, \frac{7}{28},$

$\frac{8}{32}, \frac{9}{36}, \frac{10}{40}, \frac{11}{44}, \frac{12}{48}, \cdots$

$\frac{4}{6}$

$\frac{2}{3}, \frac{6}{9}, \frac{8}{12}, \frac{10}{15}, \frac{12}{18}, \frac{14}{21},$

$\frac{16}{24}, \frac{18}{27}, \frac{20}{30}, \frac{22}{33}, \frac{24}{36}, \cdots$

$\frac{6}{8}$

$\frac{3}{4}, \frac{9}{12}, \frac{12}{16}, \frac{15}{20}, \frac{18}{24},$

$\frac{21}{28}, \frac{24}{32}, \frac{27}{36}, \frac{30}{40}, \frac{33}{44}, \frac{36}{48}, \cdots$

$\frac{5}{10}$

$\frac{1}{2}, \frac{2}{4}, \frac{3}{6}, \frac{4}{8}, \frac{6}{12}, \frac{7}{14}, \frac{8}{16},$

$\frac{9}{18}, \frac{10}{20}, \frac{11}{22}, \frac{12}{24}, \frac{13}{26}, \frac{14}{28}, \frac{15}{30},$

$\frac{16}{32}, \frac{17}{34}, \frac{18}{36}, \frac{19}{38}, \frac{20}{40}, \cdots$

The Domino Effect

Solve the equations in each box. Next, cut out the boxes. Match each box to the next with an equivalent math equation. Then glue the boxes in order on a large sheet of construction paper.

Row 1

Box 1 — top: 18 + 6 =; left: (8 x 7) + 4 =; right: (16 + 16) + 10 =; bottom: 68 + 4 =

Box 2 — top: 50 − 32 =; left: 4 x 4 =; right: (6 x 2) + 6 =; bottom: 75 + (50 − 75) =

Box 3 — top: (22 + 44) − 2 =; left: 10 x 5 =; right: 20 + 7 =; bottom: (15 + 15) − 10 =

Box 4 — top: 6 x 2 =; left: 24 − 38 =; right: 8 x 6 =; bottom: (9 x 3) + 6 =

Row 2

Box 1 — top: (8 x 7) + 8 =; left: 12 x 3 =; right: 8 x 3 =; bottom: 65 + 7 =

Box 2 — top: 4 x 2 =; left: 6 x 4 =; right: 24 − 9 =; bottom: 50 + 50 =

Box 3 — top: (12 + 12) − 9 =; left: 16 x 2 =; right: 6 x 2 =; bottom: (6 x 2) + 3 =

Box 4 — top: 20 − 4 =; left: 26 + 12 =; right: 25 ÷ 5 =; bottom: (7 x 4) − 8 =

Row 3

Box 1 — top: (5 x 5) − 11 =; left: (6 x 3) − 13 =; right: (13 + 13) − 2 =; bottom: 16 + 16 =

Box 2 — top: 36 − 24 =; left: 6 x 5 =; right: (9 + 9) + 9 =; bottom: 28 + 12 =

Box 3 — top: 5 x 1 =; left: (9 x 1) + 6 =; right: 9 x 3 =; bottom: 16 x 0 =

Box 4 — top: 10 x 6 =; left: 9 x 6 =; right: 8 x 1 =; bottom: 20 + 20 =

Row 4

Box 1 — top: 24 + 12 =; left: 5 x 6 =; right: (5 x 4) − 6 =; bottom: 16 + 14 =

Box 2 — top: 40 + 9 =; left: 5 x 4 =; right: 5 x 3 =; bottom: 10 x 5 =

Box 3 — top: (8 x 5) + 20 =; left: 9 x 4 =; right: (6 x 2) + 3 =; bottom: (8 + 8) + 4 =

Box 4 — top: 56 + 8 =; left: (5 x 9) − 10 =; right: (9 x 2) + 9 =; bottom: 3 x 2 =

Row 5

Box 1 — top: (8 x 3) − 12 =; left: 81 − 63 =; right: (9 x 2) − 2 =; bottom: (5 x 5) − 15 =

Box 2 — top: 24 − 4 =; left: 9 x 6 =; right: 5 x 2 =; bottom: 5 x 2 =

Box 3 — top: (7 x 3) + 28 =; left: 58 + 4 =; right: 8 x 1 =; bottom: 28 − 4 =

Box 4 — top: (8 x 8) − 4 =; left: (5 x 5) − 7 =; right: 18 + 9 =; bottom: 36 − 30 =

©The Mailbox® • TEC44034 • Dec./Jan. 2007–8 • written by Leigh Anne Newsom, Chesapeake, VA • Key p. 311

Note to the teacher: Use alone or with "All Squared Away" on page 145.

Have a Slice!

Write each fraction from below on the line next to its equivalent decimal.

A. 0.5 = _____

B. 0.2 = _____

C. 0.60 = _____

D. 0.34 = _____

E. 0.08 = _____

F. 0.44 = _____

G. 0.58 = _____

H. 0.9 = _____

I. 0.750 = _____

J. 0.31 = _____

K. 0.091 = _____

L. 0.07 = _____

M. 0.89 = _____

N. 0.05 = _____

O. 0.79 = _____

P. 0.011 = _____

Q. 0.09 = _____

R. 0.06 = _____

S. 0.80 = _____

T. 0.030 = _____

To the Top With Congruent Shapes

with ideas by Jennifer Otter, Oak Ridge, NC

TOOTHPICK CHALLENGE
Partner activity

This construction activity will have students using translations, rotations, and reflections to verify that two shapes are congruent. Begin by writing on the board the five tasks shown. Then equip each pair of students with a resealable bag containing ten wooden toothpicks. Instruct the partners to complete one task at a time using the specified number of toothpicks. Once each set of shapes is constructed, the partners decide what type of transformation (or combination of moves) can be used to prove that the figures are congruent. (See the answer key on page 312.) Have early finishers create similar problems to place at a center for more practice.

1. Use eight toothpicks to make two quadrilaterals.

2. Make two congruent trapezoids using all ten toothpicks.

3. Make two congruent triangles using six toothpicks.

4. Make three congruent triangles using nine toothpicks.

5. Make two congruent pentagons using all ten toothpicks.

CHECK THE LENGTH!
Game

Determining whether line segments are congruent is fun to do with this partner game. To prepare, give each pair of students a copy of the game cards and answer key on page 152. Instruct the duo to cut out, shuffle, and stack the cards facedown in a pile and to set the key aside. Then provide the pair with two different colors of pencils and a sheet of centimeter graph paper with axes numbered as shown to use as a gameboard.

To play, one child draws a card from the pile and then uses a colored pencil to plot and connect the points for each set of ordered pairs. When he's finished, he states whether the two resulting line segments are congruent or not. His partner uses the key to check his answer. If his answer is correct and the segments are congruent, he gets two points. If he is correct and the segments are not congruent, he gets one point. Players then switch roles and repeat the process. Play continues until all cards in the pile have been used. The player with more points wins.

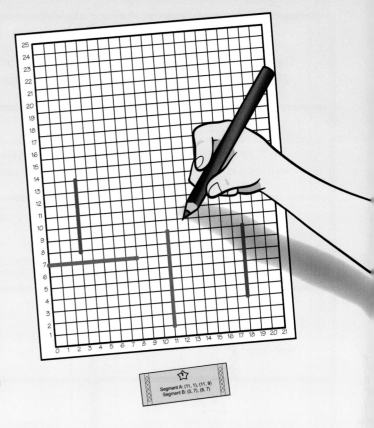

Segment A: (11, 1), (11, 9)
Segment B: (0, 7), (8, 7)

CONGRUENT OR SIMILAR?
Review activity

Prepare for this whole-class activity by giving each pair of students half of an old file folder, a marker, and four slips of paper. Have the duo label the front of its folder "Congruent" and the back "Similar." Next, have the partners briefly describe on each of two paper slips a different pair of congruent objects visible in the classroom. For example, a student may describe identical student math textbooks on one slip and same-size playground balls on the other. On each of the last two slips, have students describe different sets of objects that are similar but not congruent, such as concentric circles or pencils or straws of different lengths. Collect the completed slips and place them in a container. Then remove a slip and read its description to the class. Have each set of partners quietly discuss whether the described objects are congruent or similar and then display their answer by holding up the corresponding side of their file folder. Call on any twosome with the correct response to explain its answer.

These two objects are the only things on the tray below the whiteboard. One is red. The other is blue.

Congruent

The objects are congruent because they are the same size and same shape.

Game Cards and Answer Key

Use with "Check the Length!" on page 151.

1 Segment A: (11, 1), (11, 9) Segment B: (0, 7), (8, 7) TEC44034	**11** Segment A: (0, 17), (0, 22) Segment B: (8, 0), (8, 6) TEC44034	**Answer Key For "Check the Length!"**

2 Segment A: (9, 0), (9, 5) Segment B: (0, 15), (5, 15) TEC44034	**12** Segment A: (17, 7), (17, 16) Segment B: (9, 6), (9, 15) TEC44034
3 Segment A: (5, 2), (5, 6) Segment B: (6, 14), (6, 19) TEC44034	**13** Segment A: (0, 9), (0, 12) Segment B: (5, 13), (8, 13) TEC44034
4 Segment A: (1, 2), (4, 2) Segment B: (20, 0), (20, 4) TEC44034	**14** Segment A: (15, 2), (15, 9) Segment B: (11, 10), (11, 17) TEC44034
5 Segment A: (6, 23), (10, 23) Segment B: (2, 16), (2, 20) TEC44034	**15** Segment A: (21, 1), (21, 11) Segment B: (12, 6), (12, 16) TEC44034
6 Segment A: (3, 8), (3, 14) Segment B: (18, 3), (18, 9) TEC44034	**16** Segment A: (0, 0), (0, 3) Segment B: (13, 3), (13, 7) TEC44034
7 Segment A: (0, 4), (0, 5) Segment B: (13, 0), (13, 1) TEC44034	**17** Segment A: (12, 1), (12, 4) Segment B: (16, 9), (16, 14) TEC44034
8 Segment A: (4, 8), (4, 14) Segment B: (6, 1), (6, 6) TEC44034	**18** Segment A: (5, 0), (7, 0) Segment B: (18, 14), (20, 14) TEC44034
9 Segment A: (14, 17), (21, 17) Segment B: (3, 16), (3, 22) TEC44034	**19** Segment A: (14, 0), (19, 0) Segment B: (7, 18), (13, 18) TEC44034
10 Segment A: (6, 9), (6, 10) Segment B: (16, 2), (18, 2) TEC44034	**20** Segment A: (14, 4), (14, 12) Segment B: (10, 0), (10, 7) TEC44034

Answer Key For "Check the Length!"

1. congruent
2. congruent
3. not congruent
4. not congruent
5. congruent
6. congruent
7. congruent
8. not congruent
9. not congruent
10. not congruent
11. not congruent
12. congruent
13. congruent
14. congruent
15. congruent
16. not congruent
17. not congruent
18. congruent
19. not congruent
20. not congruent

TEC44034

Up the Wall

Match each pair of congruent shapes by writing a letter next to each number in the chart. Then cut out the shapes below. Use the cutouts to identify how the matching figure moved.

Number	Letter	Translation, Reflection, and/or Rotation
1		
2		
3		
4		
5		
6		
7		
8		
9		
10		

Why did the rock climber climb the wall?
To find out, write each letter from above on its matching numbered line below.

It was a ___ ___ ___ ___ ___
        3   8   1   2   9

place to ___ ___ ___ ___ ___!
      10   4   6   7   5

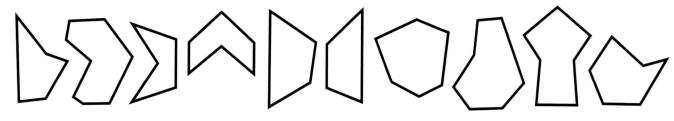

Ship Them Out!

Study the clipboard. Then use a ruler to measure the sides of each climbing hold (lettered shape). Write each shape's letter in a space on its matching box. Write the remaining letters on the storage box. If your answers are correct, the unscrambled letters on each box will spell a math word.

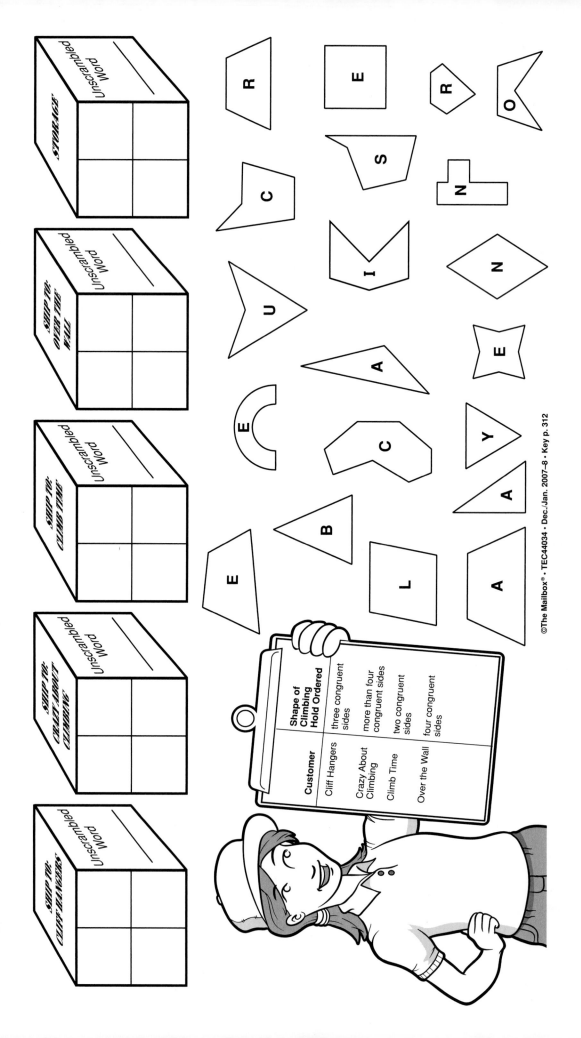

SHIP TO: CLIFF HANGERS

Unscrambled Word _____

SHIP TO: CRAZY ABOUT CLIMBING

Unscrambled Word _____

SHIP TO: CLIMB TIME

Unscrambled Word _____

SHIP TO: OVER THE WALL

Unscrambled Word _____

STORAGE

Unscrambled Word _____

Customer	Shape of Climbing Hold Ordered
Cliff Hangers	three congruent sides
Crazy About Climbing	more than four congruent sides
Climb Time	two congruent sides
Over the Wall	four congruent sides

Conquering Division

*with ideas by Michelle Bauml, Polk Elementary, Richwood, TX
and Becca DeGeorge, Neil Armstrong Elementary, Bettendorf, IA*

DUELING DIGITS
Review game

For this partner game, provide each pair of students with
two sheets of paper, a calculator, and one suit of playing
cards with the face cards and the ten removed. To begin,
Player A draws a tic-tac-toe board on a sheet of paper.
Player B draws three cards and places them faceup in a
row in the order drawn to form a dividend. He then draws
a fourth card to determine the divisor. Player A solves
the division problem on the second sheet of paper. Then
Player B checks Player A's quotient with the calculator. If
correct, Player A makes a mark on the tic-tac-toe board.
If incorrect, he marks nothing. Players alternate drawing
cards, solving problems, and making marks on the board
until one player has three marks in a row.

THE GREAT DIVIDE
Divisibility rules

To play this version of bingo, provide each child with a copy of the gameboard on page 158 and colorful paper squares to use as game markers. Instruct her to program each blank square on her gameboard with a number from the number bank. Then call out one of the following numbers: 2, 3, 4, 5, 6, 8, 9, or 10. Have each player write the announced number (divisor) on a paper square and then decide whether any number on her gameboard is divisible by that number. If so, she covers that number with the paper square. Continue calling out one number at a time in this manner until all eight divisors have been announced or one student has covered five numbers in a row.

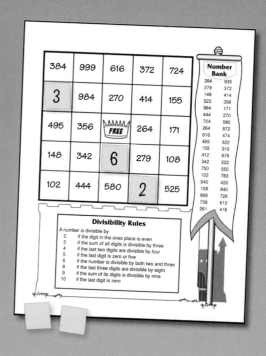

JOUSTING WITH DIVIDENDS
Mental math, division patterns

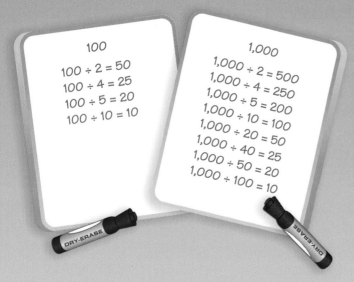

This small-group activity has students matching wits and using division facts to divide multiples of 10. Give each group a small whiteboard and a dry-erase marker. Call out a dividend, such as 100 or 1,000. Challenge each group to list on its whiteboard all the possible division sentences it can think of for that dividend and then hold up its board to be checked. Award a point to the teams listing the greatest number of correct facts and an extra point to the team that finishes first. Once the boards are cleaned, play another round. The team with the most points at the end wins.

A TRIO OF "MOAT-IVES"
Problem solving

Hone students' critical-thinking skills by having them turn sets of related numbers into word problems. Assign each child a different set of three related numbers. Have him write and illustrate on the front of an unlined sheet of paper a word problem for the numbers and then record the answer on the back. When everyone is finished, have students swap problems, solve their partner's problem on scrap paper, and then check the answer on the back of the paper. Repeat two more times. Conclude by having students discuss any challenges or surprises they encountered while creating the problems.

9, 14, 126

A royal knight and eight comrades found a box containing 126 gold coins. If each person takes the same number of coins, how many coins will each person get?

LET OUT A CHEER!
Small-group activity

Create squads of cheerleaders to help problem solvers follow the correct order of steps for long division. Divide students into squads of five. Give each squad four sheets of heavy paper. Instruct the squad to label each sheet with a different division step. Once the sheets are labeled, challenge a child from each squad to go to the board and simultaneously solve a division problem. As each child works, allow his squad members to cheer him on by holding up the card needed to complete each step in turn. Continue until every child has solved a problem on the board. For a follow-up that can generate even more team spirit, challenge each squad to create its own mnemonic for remembering the division steps. After a class vote, post the winning mnemonic on the board for easy reference.

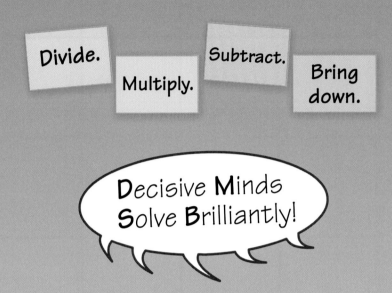

A SLIGHT SLIP-UP
Whole-class activity

To help students identify and correct common long-division errors, program unlined index cards with different problems as shown (same problem front and back). Then laminate the cards. Give each child a card and a wipe-off marker. As she solves the problem on the front of her card, instruct her to intentionally make an error in any step. For example, she could forget to record a remainder or incorrectly place the first digit of the quotient. Next, have students trade cards, flip their classmate's card over, and correctly solve the problem on the back. When she's finished, have her compare her work with the work on the front and find an error. Direct her to circle the error and then ask the classmate to confirm whether the circled part contains the mistake. Also have the partners discuss how to correct the mistakes on both cards. Then have each duo wipe both cards clean and repeat the steps for another round of practice.

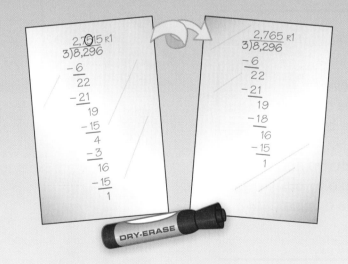

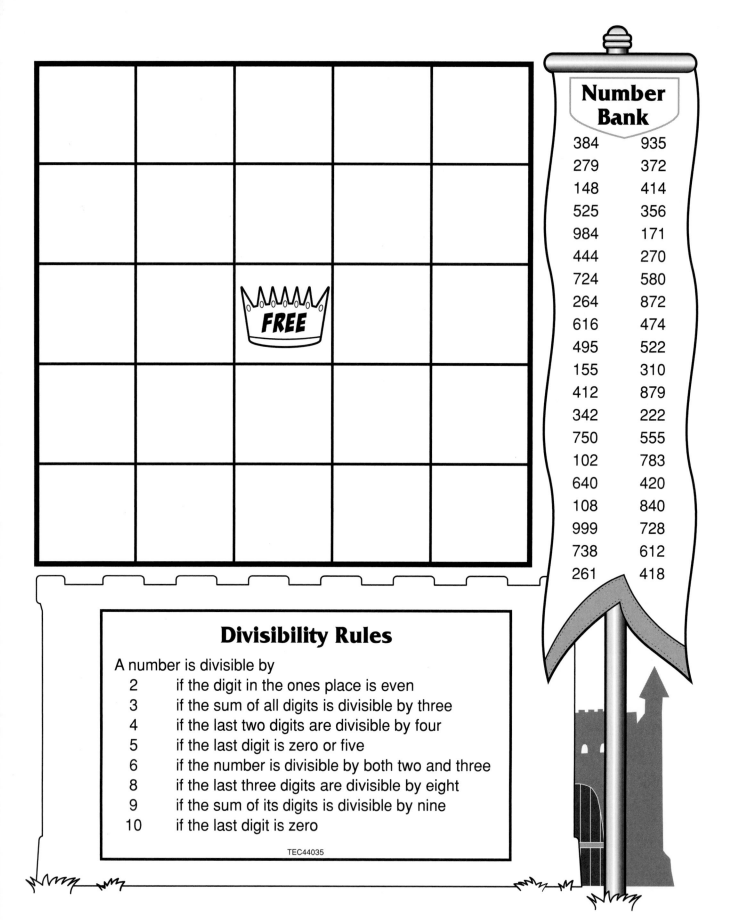

Number Bank

384	935
279	372
148	414
525	356
984	171
444	270
724	580
264	872
616	474
495	522
155	310
412	879
342	222
750	555
102	783
640	420
108	840
999	728
738	612
261	418

FREE

Divisibility Rules

A number is divisible by

2	if the digit in the ones place is even
3	if the sum of all digits is divisible by three
4	if the last two digits are divisible by four
5	if the last digit is zero or five
6	if the number is divisible by both two and three
8	if the last three digits are divisible by eight
9	if the sum of its digits is divisible by nine
10	if the last digit is zero

TEC44035

Note to the teacher: Use with "The Great Divide" on page 156. If desired, have each student cut out the chart of divisibility rules and keep it in his math folder as a handy reference.

It Costs to Conquer!

Solve the problems. Then use the information to complete the royal expense form below.

1 There are 12 knights traveling by wagon to slay the dragon. The total cost of the wagon is $1,080. How much will each knight pay? _____

2 The total cost for lodging is $7,848. How much will each knight pay? _____

3 The total cost of meals during the trip is $3,600. How much will each knight pay? _____

4 If dragon-slaying licenses for all the knights cost a total of $288, how much does one license cost? _____

5 New suits of armor for all the knights cost $2,016. How much is one suit of armor? _____

6 The king also wants the knights to claim land for his kingdom. If the land costs a total of $576, how much will each knight have to pay? _____

Thy Royal Expenses
(per knight)

Congratulations! You have been selected by the king to help slay a dragon! Here is a summary of your share of the cost.

Transportation: _____   Dragon-slaying license: _____

Lodging: _____   Suit of armor: _____

Meals: _____   Land claim: _____

All the King's Horses

Solve each problem.

1. A blacksmith is making 31 horseshoes for the king's horses. How many horses will get a complete set of new shoes?

2. A new stable is being built for 25 horses. If one stall can hold two horses, how many stalls should be built in the stable?

3. The king's army has 121 pounds of supplies to transport. Each horse will carry no more than eight pounds. How many horses will be needed to carry all the supplies?

4. The queen has bought 5,185 pounds of hay to make into bales. If it takes 25 pounds to make one bale of hay, how many hay bales can be made?

5. Each royal carriage needs six horses to pull it. There are 28 horses ready to work. How many carriages can be used?

6. A knight has six horses and a bucket of 35 carrots. How many more carrots does the knight need if he wants to give each horse six carrots?

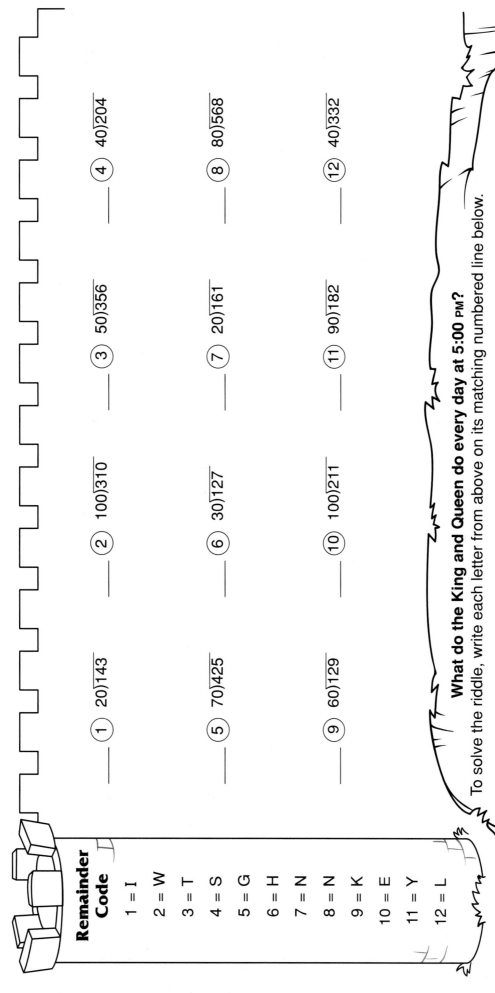

Royal Remainders

Divide. Write the matching letter for each remainder in the space provided.

Remainder Code

1 = I
2 = W
3 = T
4 = S
5 = G
6 = H
7 = N
8 = N
9 = K
10 = E
11 = Y
12 = L

____ ① 20)143

____ ② 100)310

____ ③ 50)356

____ ④ 40)204

____ ⑤ 70)425

____ ⑥ 30)127

____ ⑦ 20)161

____ ⑧ 80)568

____ ⑨ 60)129

____ ⑩ 100)211

____ ⑪ 90)182

____ ⑫ 40)332

What do the King and Queen do every day at 5:00 PM?

To solve the riddle, write each letter from above on its matching numbered line below.

They watch the " ___ ___ ___ ___ ___ ___ ___ ___ ___ ___ ___ ___ ___ ___ ___ ___ ___ ___ !"
9 8 7 5 3 1 12 10   6 12 11 4

Geometric Shapes and Figures

with ideas by Colleen Dabney, Williamsburg, VA

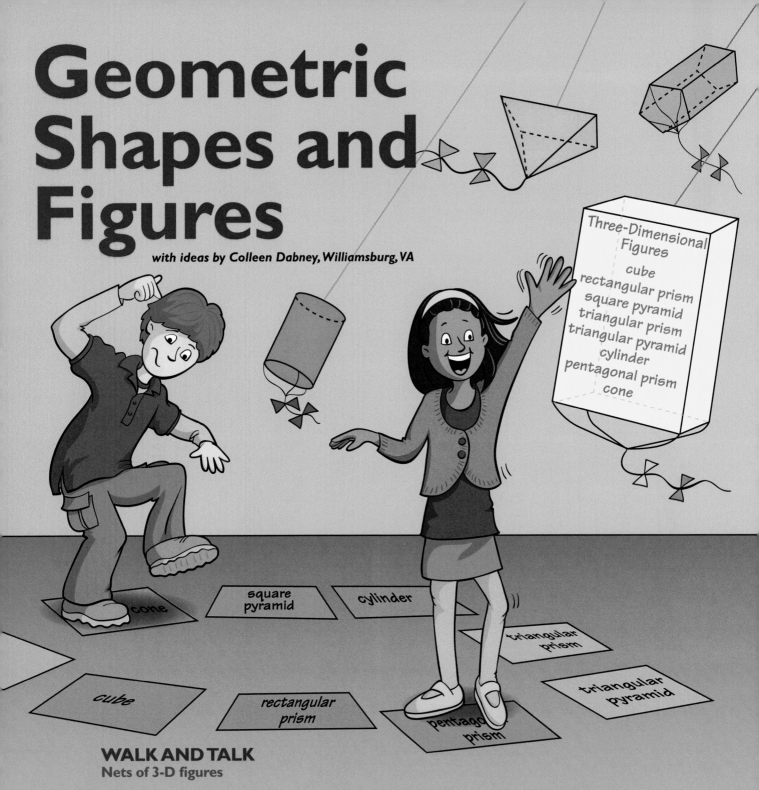

Three-Dimensional Figures
cube
rectangular prism
square pyramid
triangular prism
triangular pyramid
cylinder
pentagonal prism
cone

cube

square pyramid

cylinder

cone

rectangular prism

triangular prism

triangular pyramid

pentagonal prism

WALK AND TALK
Nets of 3-D figures

For this easy-to-play whole-class game, gather a CD of kid-pleasing music and patterns of different three-dimensional figures, such as those listed. Next, have each student label a sheet of paper with the name of one of the figures. Arrange the sheets on the floor in a circle. Then start the music and have students walk around the circle of sheets. When the music stops, direct each child to stand on a different sheet. Display one of the patterns (covering its name) and have each student who thinks she is standing on that figure's name raise her hand. If she's correct and can explain why, she stays in the game. If incorrect or if she's standing on the corresponding sheet but does not raise her hand, she returns to her desk. Continue in this manner until only one child remains. Play additional rounds as time allows. To follow up, have each student make a mobile of 3-D figures using the patterns on page 164 as directed.

QUICK DRAW
Faces, edges, and vertices

Reinforce features of 3-D figures with this clever twist on the game rock, paper, scissors. Display the chart at the right. Next, have each group of three students cut apart a copy of the eight 3-D cards on page 166 and stack them facedown. Then demonstrate how to make the three hand signals shown. To play, each trio faces away from the chart and counts to three. On "three," each player makes one of the hand signals. Next, one student turns over the pile's top card. Each player, in turn, records on paper either the number of faces, edges, or vertices (according to the hand signal he made) of the figure shown on the card. Then the threesome turns around and checks the answers with the chart. Each player with a correct answer stays in the game. A player with an incorrect answer sits out. Play continues in this manner until one group member remains. For more practice, have each child complete a copy of page 168 as directed.

Figure	Faces	Edges	Vertices
cone	1	0	1
cube	6	12	8
cylinder	2	0	0
rectangular prism	6	12	8
square pyramid	5	8	5
triangular prism	5	9	6
triangular pyramid	4	6	4

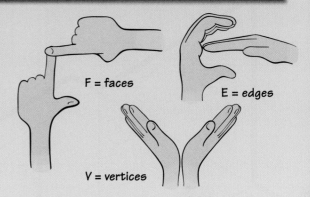

F = faces

E = edges

V = vertices

trapezoid

decagon

FLYING HIGH
Polygon attributes

Begin by assigning each child or student pair a 2-D shape. Challenge the student to use tissue paper and other materials to create and label a kite with his assigned shape. Have him write each attribute of that shape on a different bow on his kite's tail. After students share their completed projects, display the kites around the room as an eye-catching math reference. For more practice with polygons, have each child complete a copy of page 167 as directed.

THE SKY'S THE LIMIT
Relating 2-D and 3-D shapes

Use this ready-in-minutes center to help students identify the geometric-shaped faces of solid figures. Laminate the mat on page 165 and the cards and answer key on page 166. Cut the cards apart and store them with the key and sorting mat. To use the center, Student A places any 3-D figure card on the mat. Student B determines which shapes form the selected figure's faces and places the corresponding number of cards on the mat's smaller boxes. Student A then uses the answer key to check Student B's answer. Play alternates in this manner until all the 3-D figure cards have been used.

Nets of 3-D Figures

Directions:
1. Label each 2-D pattern with the name of the 3-D figure it will form. Label each remaining face with a different attribute of that figure as directed. Then lightly color each face.
2. Cut out each pattern and poke a hole at each dot.
3. Fold each figure along the lines; then tape the edges together at the tabs.
4. Use wire and string to display the figures as shown.

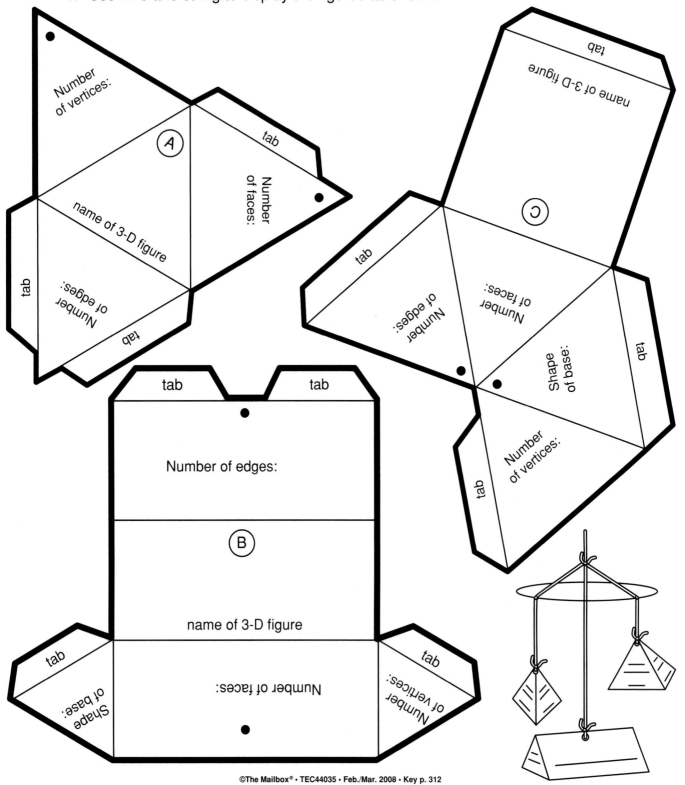

Number of vertices:

tab

A

name of 3-D figure

Number of faces:

tab

tab

Number of edges:

tab

name of 3-D figure

tab

C

Number of edges:

Number of faces:

tab

Shape of base:

tab

Number of vertices:

tab

tab

name of 3-D figure

tab

Number of edges:

B

name of 3-D figure

tab

Shape of base:

Number of faces:

tab

Number of vertices:

©The Mailbox® • TEC44035 • Feb./Mar. 2008 • Key p. 312

Note to the teacher: Use alone or with "Walk and Talk" on page 162.

THE SKY'S THE LIMIT

3-D Cards

Use with "Quick Draw" and
"The Sky's the Limit" on page 163.

2-D Cards and Answer Key

Use with "The Sky's the Limit" on page 163.

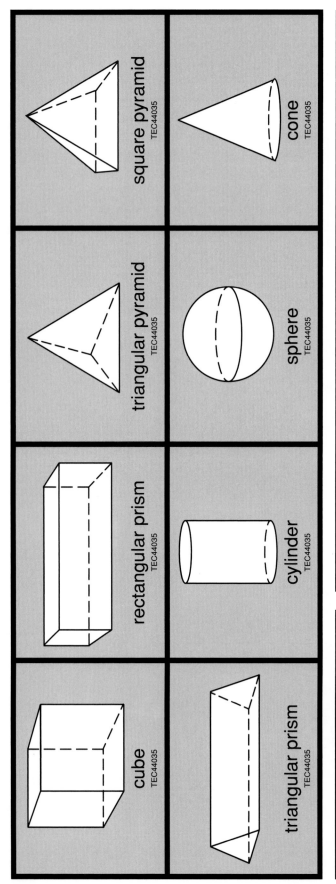

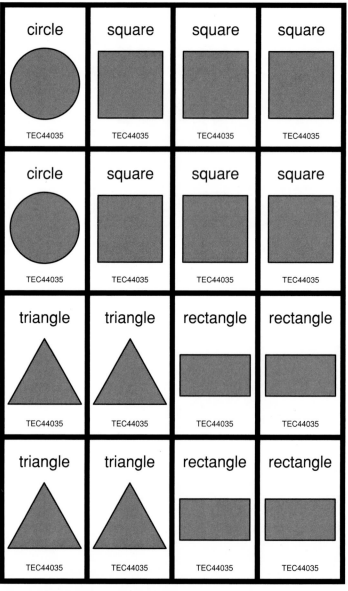

Answer Key for "The Sky's the Limit"

cube = six squares

rectangular prism = two squares, four rectangles

triangular pyramid = four triangles

square pyramid = one square, four triangles

triangular prism = two triangles, three rectangles

cylinder = two circles

sphere = none

cone = one circle

TEC44035

In a Tangle

Match each prefix to its definition by writing a letter on each kite.

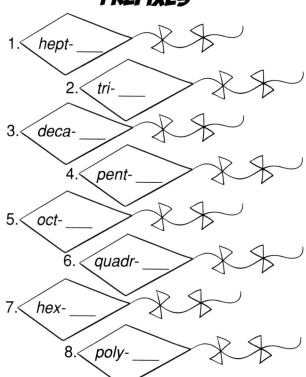

PREFIXES

1. hept-___
2. tri-___
3. deca-___
4. pent-___
5. oct-___
6. quadr-___
7. hex-___
8. poly-___

DEFINITIONS

A. many

B. three

C. four

D. five

E. six

F. seven

G. eight

H. ten

Write the name of each polygon.

9.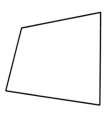

10.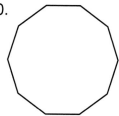

11.

_____

_____

_____

12.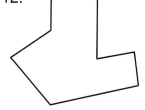

13.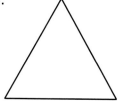

14.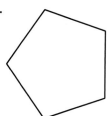

15.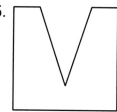

_____

_____

_____

_____

Note to the teacher: Use alone or with "Flying High" on page 163.

Take Flight

Write the letter of each kite next to its matching description. Then color each kite the correct color(s).

_____ 1. Mia's orange kite has six congruent square faces.

_____ 2. Kendra's green kite has a square base, one vertex, and five faces.

_____ 3. Brent's blue kite has congruent parallel circle bases.

_____ 4. Anne's red kite has a triangular base, four faces, four vertices, and six edges.

_____ 5. Kelli's multicolored kite has two triangular bases, five faces, and six vertices.

_____ 6. Ian's purple kite consists of two figures with a common vertex and circles for bases.

_____ 7. Tim's yellow kite has 18 edges, eight faces, and 12 vertices.

_____ 8. Sonya's pink kite has eight triangular faces and six vertices.

What do you call a kite with 12 faces?

To answer the question, write the letter of each kite on its matching numbered line below.

A __ __ __ __ __ __ __ __ __ __ __ __
   2 3 2 4 5 1 6 4 2 7 3 8

Note to the teacher: Use alone or with "Quick Draw" on page 163.

On Course With
Fractions and Decimals

with ideas by Jennifer Otter, Oak Ridge, NC

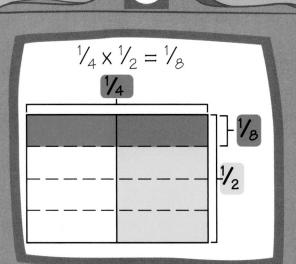

$$\frac{1}{4} \times \frac{1}{2} = \frac{1}{8}$$

$$\frac{1}{4}$$

$$\frac{1}{8}$$

$$\frac{1}{2}$$

Problems

$$\frac{1}{4} \times \frac{1}{2} = \frac{1}{8}$$

$$\frac{1}{2} \times \frac{2}{3} = \frac{1}{3}$$

$$\frac{3}{4} \times \frac{1}{2} = \frac{3}{8}$$

$$\frac{1}{3} \times \frac{1}{4} = \frac{1}{12}$$

$$\frac{1}{2} \times \frac{1}{3} = \frac{1}{6}$$

$$\frac{1}{2} \times \frac{2}{5} = \frac{1}{5}$$

GO FOR THE GREEN
Understanding the multiplication of fractions

Begin by writing on the board the six problems shown (without the answers). Have students read the problems in unison, saying "of" instead of "times" for each multiplication sign and "is" instead of "equals" for each equal sign. Next, give each child a sheet of unlined paper and blue and yellow pencils. Solve the first problem together, using the steps shown as a guide. Point out that the answer *(⅛)* is the green part of the box. Have students compare the answer to each factor. *(The answer is smaller than either factor.)* Then guide the class to understand that the product of two fractions that are each less than 1 will always be less than either factor because the process involves finding part of a part. Whether students solve the remaining problems independently or with your guidance, they'll have a better grasp of what multiplying fractions really means!

Steps:
1. Draw a box and divide it into the same number of parts as the denominator of the second fraction. With the yellow pencil, color a number of parts equal to that fraction's numerator.
2. Use dashed lines to divide the box into the same number of parts as the denominator of the first fraction. With the blue pencil, color a number of parts equal to that fraction's numerator so the colors overlap.
3. Write a fraction (in simplest form) to show what part of the box is green.

169

CAPTAIN'S CHOICE
Adding and subtracting like and unlike mixed numbers

To play this nifty game, make a copy of pages 171 and 172 for each group of four students. Instruct each foursome to cut its cards apart, fold them along the lines, and tape each one so the problem is on the front and the answer is on the back. After students arrange the cards problem-side up, each child places a game marker on a different starting circle of the gameboard. Next, one player (the captain) selects a problem that all four players solve. Then he turns the card over so players can check their answers. The student whose marker matches the solution sets the problem aside, moves his marker ahead one circle, and becomes the new captain. Play continues in this manner until one student reaches Finish. If desired, follow up by having each child complete a copy of page 173 as directed.

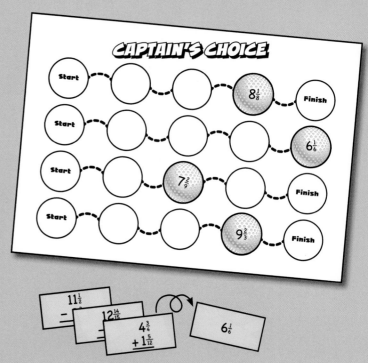

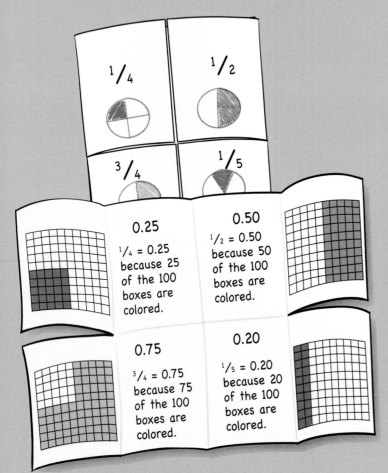

PICTURES, PLUS!
Decimal equivalents for common fractions

All students need to represent a fraction and decimal in picture form is a sheet of unlined paper, scissors, and four colored pencils. Each child folds her paper in half twice, unfolds the paper, and then folds the sides to meet at the center crease line as shown. She cuts along each side's fold line to make four flaps, labels the flaps with the fractions shown, and then draws representative pictures. Beneath each flap, she draws a 10 x 10 grid, divides it into the same number of equal parts as the matching fraction's denominator, and colors a number of boxes equal to the numerator. Then she counts the colored boxes, writes the number as a decimal, and briefly explains why that fraction and decimal represent the same value.

CAPTAIN'S CHOICE

Finish Finish Finish Finish

Start Start Start Start

Cards and Game Markers

Use with "Captain's Choice" on page 170.

$6\frac{1}{2}$ $+\ 1\frac{5}{8}$	$8\frac{1}{8}$ TEC44036	$2\frac{5}{9}$ $+\ 4\frac{2}{3}$	$7\frac{2}{9}$ TEC44036
$8\frac{5}{6}$ $-\ 2\frac{2}{3}$	$6\frac{1}{6}$ TEC44036	$7\frac{1}{4}$ $+\ 2\frac{5}{12}$	$9\frac{2}{3}$ TEC44036
$10\frac{1}{4}$ $-\ 2\frac{3}{24}$	$8\frac{1}{8}$ TEC44036	$10\frac{7}{9}$ $-\ 3\frac{5}{9}$	$7\frac{2}{9}$ TEC44036
$3\frac{2}{6}$ $+\ 2\frac{5}{6}$	$6\frac{1}{6}$ TEC44036	$12\frac{14}{15}$ $-\ 3\frac{4}{15}$	$9\frac{2}{3}$ TEC44036
$11\frac{1}{2}$ $-\ 3\frac{3}{8}$	$8\frac{1}{8}$ TEC44036	$12\frac{17}{18}$ $-\ 5\frac{13}{18}$	$7\frac{2}{9}$ TEC44036
$4\frac{3}{4}$ $+\ 1\frac{5}{12}$	$6\frac{1}{6}$ TEC44036	$11\frac{5}{6}$ $-\ 2\frac{1}{6}$	$9\frac{2}{3}$ TEC44036
$5\frac{7}{8}$ $+\ 2\frac{2}{8}$	$8\frac{1}{8}$ TEC44036	$5\frac{3}{27}$ $+\ 2\frac{1}{9}$	$7\frac{2}{9}$ TEC44036
$9\frac{5}{9}$ $-\ 3\frac{7}{18}$	$6\frac{1}{6}$ TEC44036	$4\frac{3}{5}$ $+\ 5\frac{1}{15}$	$9\frac{2}{3}$ TEC44036

"Par-fect" Fractions

Solve. Find each answer below. Write each problem number on its matching flag. One flag will not be used.

1. $\dfrac{3}{5}$
  $+ \dfrac{3}{8}$

2. $\dfrac{9}{11}$
  $- \dfrac{3}{11}$

3. $1\dfrac{7}{8}$
  $+ 3\dfrac{5}{8}$

4. $1\dfrac{4}{9}$
  $+ 3\dfrac{2}{3}$

5. $3\dfrac{2}{3}$
  $- 2\dfrac{1}{5}$

6. $4\dfrac{9}{10}$
  $+ 6\dfrac{4}{5}$

7. $\dfrac{3}{4}$
  $- \dfrac{2}{3}$

8. $\dfrac{9}{16}$
  $+ \dfrac{7}{16}$

9. $\dfrac{5}{9}$
  $- \dfrac{1}{6}$

10. $1\dfrac{5}{6}$
   $+ 5\dfrac{2}{3}$

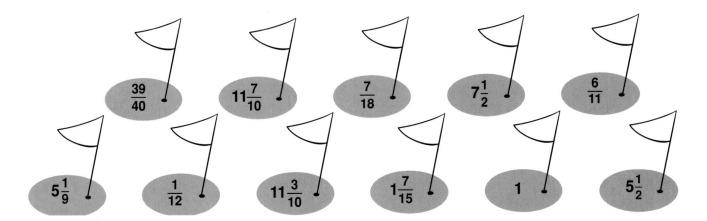

$\dfrac{39}{40}$ $11\dfrac{7}{10}$ $\dfrac{7}{18}$ $7\dfrac{1}{2}$ $\dfrac{6}{11}$

$5\dfrac{1}{9}$ $\dfrac{1}{12}$ $11\dfrac{3}{10}$ $1\dfrac{7}{15}$ 1 $5\dfrac{1}{2}$

Note to the teacher: Use alone or with "Captain's Choice" on page 170.

173

GREAT SHOT!

Estimate. Then find the actual answer.

	Problem	Estimate	Actual Answer
Round to the tens place.	1. $\quad$ 87.63 $\quad$ + 26.89		
	2. $\quad$ 19.8 $\quad$ x 36.3		
	3. $\quad$ 186.44 $\quad$ − 79.42		
	4. $\quad$ 26.24 $\quad$ x 21.7		
Use compatible numbers.	5. $\quad$ 4$\overline{)123.92}$		
	6. $\quad$ 297.70 $\quad$ − 98.65		
	7. $\quad$ 98.73 $\quad$ + 76.27		
	8. $\quad$ 6$\overline{)27.24}$		

Who made a hole in one?

To answer the question above, cut out the golf balls at the right and glue them to the top of the matching circles below to make a flap.

_____

made the hole in one.

8 Ming

7 Justin

6 Juan

5 Amber

4 Kaitlyn

3 Carmen

2 Jon

1 Clint

Estimate: 800
Actual: 718.74

Estimate: 30
Actual: 30.98

Estimate: 5
Actual: 4.54

Estimate: 600
Actual: 569.408

Estimate: 110
Actual: 107.02

Estimate: 200
Actual: 199.05

Estimate: 120
Actual: 114.52

Estimate: 175
Actual: 175.00

Playing With Probability

with ideas by Vickie Robertson, Meadow Greene Elementary, Whittier, CA

Gameboard

X~~1~~	X~~3~~	3
X~~2~~	4	5
6	X~~6~~	X~~1~~

Predictions

(²⁄₉	²⁄₉	²⁄₉)
¹⁄₉	¹⁄₉	¹⁄₉
(²⁄₉	²⁄₉	²⁄₉)

TIC-TAC-TOE
Whole-class or partner game

Begin by having each child draw two 3 x 3 grids on a sheet of paper and title them as shown. Instruct the student to randomly program his gameboard with the numbers 1 through 6, repeating a number if he wishes, but not more than twice. In each corresponding box of his predictions grid, have him write a fraction representing the number of times that number appears on his gameboard. Then have him circle on his predictions grid where he is most likely to get tic-tac-toe. Next, roll a die, call out the number rolled, and have students cross out that number in each place it is written on their gameboards. The first player to cross out three numbers in a row, column, or diagonal calls out "Tic-tac-probability!" and shares with the class whether his predictions were correct.

Types of Flowers	Favorite Flower	Probability
carnations	ll	2 out of 30
daisies	HHł HHł ll	12 out of 30
lilies	l	1 out of 30
roses	HHł	5 out of 30
tulips	HHł HHł	10 out of 30

A GARDEN VARIETY
Testing a predicted outcome

This whole-class activity makes working with probability as easy as picking flowers! Pin die-cut flowers (one per student) to a board along with a list of five different varieties of flowers. Instruct each child to label a cutout with the name of her favorite flower from the list and then make a tally mark next to the flower's name on the list. Based on the tally marks, have students predict which flower type would most likely be picked by someone, without looking, from a bouquet consisting of only those flowers. Then test the prediction by having one student at a time stand with her back to the board and close her eyes. Slowly turn her around and have her touch a flower on the display. Tally the number of times students touch each flower type. When everyone has had a turn, have students compare the actual outcome with their prediction.

> We think daisies will be picked most often!

impossible	less likely	equally likely	more likely	certain

0    $\frac{1}{4}$ $\frac{1}{2}$ $\frac{3}{4}$ 1

Events

- going to Jupiter for breakfast tomorrow *(impossible)*
- pulling a penny from a cup that contains a penny and a nickel *(equally likely)*
- spinning a number less than 6 on a spinner whose parts are numbered from 1 to 5 *(certain)*
- spinning green on a spinner that has two blue parts, two red parts, one green part, and one yellow part *(less likely)*
- pulling a red marble from a cup that has one green marble, two blue marbles, two yellow marbles, and five red marbles *(more likely)*

IMPOSSIBLE, CERTAIN, OR SOMEWHERE BETWEEN
Likelihood of an event

To understand the terms associated with probability, draw a number line on the board like the one shown. Discuss with students the relationship between each number and corresponding label on the number line. Then have students refer to the number line to help them describe the probability of events, such as those at the left.

PICK THE RIGHT DOOR!
Review activity

Which student will open a paper door that conceals a math homework pass or extra minutes of recess the whole class can enjoy? To find out, fold ten sheets of construction paper in half. Number the folded papers from 1 to 10 and, if desired, decorate each one to look like an actual door. Behind one door, tape a slip of paper labeled with a prize that benefits the entire class. Then arrange the doors in a visible location, such as a chalk tray. After having students determine the probability of choosing the correct door on the first guess ($\frac{1}{10}$), select one child to pick a door. If he chooses the correct door, award the prize to the entire class. If he is incorrect, have students determine the probability of finding the correct door on the second try ($\frac{1}{9}$); then select another student to pick a different door. Continue in this manner until the correct door is found.

> There is now a one in nine chance that someone will pick the correct door.

Name _____

Tic-Tac-Toe

In each box of the first grid below, write the probability of spinning that letter on the wheel.
In each box of the second grid below, write the probability of choosing that number from the box.
Circle the three matching answers that are in a row, in a column, or on a diagonal in each grid.

A	B	C
D	E	F
G	H	I

1	2	3
4	5	6
7	8	9

PLAY YOUR CARDS RIGHT!

A queen, a king, and a jack are face cards.

Solve. Write each answer in simplest form.

1. What is the probability of drawing a 7 from a player who has three 8s, one queen, one 7, one 5, and one 4? _____

2. What is the probability of drawing a spade from a player who has five spades, four hearts, and one club? _____

3. What is the probability of drawing a king or queen from a player who has four jacks, four queens, and four kings? _____

4. A deck of cards has 13 hearts, 13 clubs, 13 spades, 13 diamonds, and two jokers.
   What is the probability of drawing a joker? _____ A diamond? _____
   A club or a spade? _____

5. What is the probability of drawing a card greater than 4 from a player who has two 4s, three 7s, one 5, and four 3s? _____

6. What is the probability of drawing a red card from a player who has eight hearts, five spades, four diamonds, and three clubs? _____ A black card? _____

7. What is the probability of drawing a face card from a player who has three kings, two aces, one queen, and two jacks? _____

8. What is the probability of drawing a card that is not an ace from a player who has four 10s, three queens, two 6s, two aces, and one 4? _____

©The Mailbox® • TEC44036 • April/May 2008 • Key p. 312

Problem Solving?
No Problem!

with ideas by Vickie Robertson, Whittier, CA

There are three cards in the following colors: green, yellow, and red. <u>Ben</u> has a green card. <u>Kit</u> does not have a red card. <u>Joey's</u> card is not green or yellow. What color is each student's card?

	green	yellow	red
Ben	Ben	X	X
Kit	X	Kit	X
Joey	X	X	Joey

THINK IT THROUGH
Logical reasoning

To help students better understand this problem-solving strategy, here are two quick activities. For students who need a greater challenge, have them create similar problems for the class to solve!

- Label three large index cards from 1 to 3. Arrange the cards on the chalk tray blank-side out in the following order: 2, 3, 1. Then turn the middle card number-side out. Guide students to reason that the numbers are out of order (since the middle number is 3) and that the numeral 1 may not be on the first card. Help students conclude that a possible order for the numbers is 2, 3, 1; then turn the cards over to check.

- On the board, write the problem and draw the chart shown above. (Substitute three of your students' names for those in the problem.) As a student volunteer reads aloud one sentence in the problem at a time, mark the chart, as shown, using information that's directly stated and inferred.

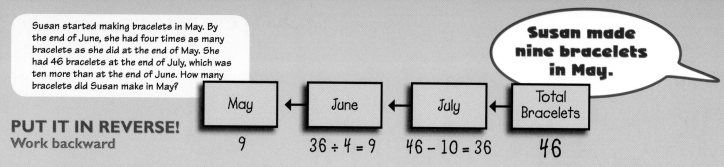

Susan started making bracelets in May. By the end of June, she had four times as many bracelets as she did at the end of May. She had 46 bracelets at the end of July, which was ten more than at the end of June. How many bracelets did Susan make in May?

Susan made nine bracelets in May.

May	June	July	Total Bracelets
9	$36 \div 4 = 9$	$46 - 10 = 36$	46

PUT IT IN REVERSE!
Work backward

Show students that sometimes going backward actually puts them ahead! Use a flow chart to solve a problem that requires this strategy (see the example). Afterward, review with students what they should do when working backward. *(Start at the end of the problem and work back to the beginning using inverse operations.)* Next, have each small group of students cut apart the cards on a copy of page 181 and turn the answer key facedown. Then instruct each child to select a problem and solve it on notebook paper using the method you just demonstrated. When she's finished, have her trade cards with another child in her group and solve the new problem. Students continue in this manner until time is up or all the problems are solved. Have students then check their answers against the key and discuss within their groups anything they did not understand.

SKETCH TO SOLVE
Draw a picture or diagram

The advantage of using this strategy is it helps students see conditions that might not be obvious when reading a problem. Have each child work with a partner to solve the problems at the left by drawing a picture (or diagram). While they work, encourage the partners to think aloud so you can check their understanding as you circulate around the room. For more practice, have each student complete a copy of page 182 as directed.

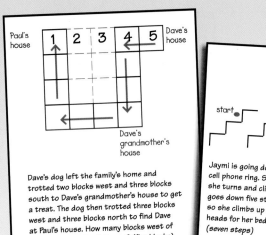

Dave's dog left the family's home and trotted two blocks west and three blocks south to Dave's grandmother's house to get a treat. The dog then trotted three blocks west and three blocks north to find Dave at Paul's house. How many blocks west of Dave's house is Paul's house? *(five blocks)*

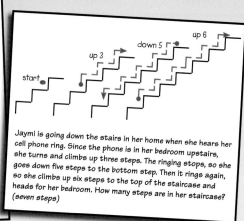

Jaymi is going down the stairs in her home when she hears her cell phone ring. Since the phone is in her bedroom upstairs, she turns and climbs up three steps. The ringing stops, so she goes down five steps to the bottom step. Then it rings again, so she climbs up six steps to the top of the staircase and heads for her bedroom. How many steps are in her staircase? *(seven steps)*

SNACK CHOICES
Make an organized list

Recording data in a systematic way makes it easier for problem solvers to review what's been listed to be sure they've left nothing out. To reinforce this strategy, give each small group of students colorful connecting cubes to represent each of the following healthy snacks: red (apple), yellow (banana), orange (orange), white (milk), and blue (grape juice). If desired, have students cut snack shapes from colorful paper instead. Instruct each group to use its manipulatives to list all the combinations of one fruit and one drink *(six combinations)*. For more practice, have each student complete a copy of page 183 as directed.

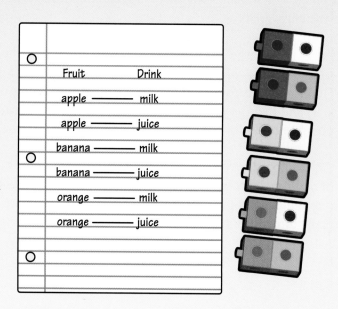

Fruit	Drink
apple	milk
apple	juice
banana	milk
banana	juice
orange	milk
orange	juice

1. Mark collects baseball cards. He gave three cards to each of four friends. Then he gave one card to his brother. If Mark has 12 cards left in his collection, how many did he originally have?

TEC44037

2. Tony bought a soccer ball for $19.95. Later, he bought a pair of sneakers that cost three times as much as the ball. After shopping, he had $7.80 left in his wallet. How much money did he have before making the purchases?

TEC44037

3. Zack's backpack weighs twice as much as Joe's. Joe's backpack weighs three times as much as Jon's. Jon's backpack weighs half as much as Chris's. Chris's backpack weighs four pounds. How much does Zack's backpack weigh?

TEC44037

4. Kiera is three years older than Katie. Katie is the same age as Melissa. Melissa is two years older than Haley. Haley is three-fourths as old as Kaitlyn. Kaitlyn is one year younger than Ashley. If Ashley is 13 years old, how old are the other girls?

TEC44037

5. Jackson shared a box of popcorn with his friends and his mom. He gave 12 pieces to his mom and then divided the remaining pieces equally among himself and his three friends. Jackson ended up with 16 pieces of popcorn for himself. How many pieces of popcorn were in the bag he shared?

TEC44037

6. Abby, Emma, and Beth are sisters. Abby is five years older than Emma. Emma is six years younger than Beth. Beth is ten years old. How old is Abby?

TEC44037

7. Erin had $5.15 left after shopping. She spent $10.58 on dog food. Then she spent $9.72 on cat food. How much money did Erin have when she started shopping?

TEC44037

8. Jeff bought a really cool T-shirt for three times as much as a pair of socks cost. His socks cost half as much as his cap. His cap cost $10.00. How much did his T-shirt cost?

TEC44037

9. At a problem-solving fair, six more kids wore shorts than jeans. Half the number of kids wearing shorts wore caps. Thirteen kids were wearing caps. How many kids wore jeans?

TEC44037

10. It is 6:00 PM, and Jordan just finished swim practice. First, he spent 45 minutes with his diving coach. Next, he swam the backstroke for 40 minutes. Then he spent one hour swimming the breaststroke. He finished practice with 35 minutes of free-style. What time did he begin practice?

TEC44037

Answer Key

1. 25 cards
2. $87.60
3. 12 pounds
4. Kaitlyn, 12; Haley, 9; Melissa, 11; Katie, 11; Kiera, 14

5. 76 pieces
6. 9 years old
7. $25.45
8. $15.00

9. 20 kids
10. 3:00 PM

TEC44037

ALL IN THE FAMILY

Solve each problem by drawing a picture or diagram in the box provided.

1. Mr. Cox drives the van when his son's scout troop collects newspapers for recycling. They begin their route at the fire station and then go five miles north, nine miles west, and eight miles south. Next, they go nine miles east. How far and in what direction do they then have to go to return to the fire station?

Answer: _____

2. Jenny is helping her mom set up square tables for a family reunion. There are seven tables. If they form a *U* shape with the tables and place them so the edges align, at how many sides will they not be able to place chairs?

Answer: _____

3. Kevin rides his bike two houses west to return a book to Miguel. Then he rides five houses east to return a soccer ball to Gabe. Gabe lives in the last house on Kevin's street. Finally, Kevin rides seven houses west to borrow a movie from Andy. Andy lives in the first house on Kevin's street. How many houses are on Kevin's street?

Answer: _____

4. Grandpa Cox likes to collect stamps. How many stamps are on the border of a 10 x 10 sheet of 100 stamps?

Answer: _____

5. Grandma Cox is decorating a row of 12 cookies. The first eight cookies have red sprinkles, and the last eight cookies have blue sprinkles. Every fourth cookie has yellow sprinkles. How many cookies have both red and blue sprinkles? How many cookies have red, blue, and yellow sprinkles?

Answer: _____

Note to the teacher: Use with "Sketch to Solve" on page 180.

Name_____

So Many Choices!

Solve each problem by making an organized list.

1. Patty can have her birthday party at a pizza parlor, a skating rink, or a pottery-making shop. She can invite three friends, five friends, or seven friends. List all the combinations of places and numbers of friends.

Place	Number of Friends

2. Will needs exact change to buy a $0.55 snack from a vending machine. List all the combinations of quarters, dimes, and/or nickels.

Quarters	Dimes	Nickels

3. Carmen can sign up for soccer, volleyball, or gymnastics. She can also take piano, violin, or drum lessons. If she has time for only one sport and one type of music lesson, list all the combinations.

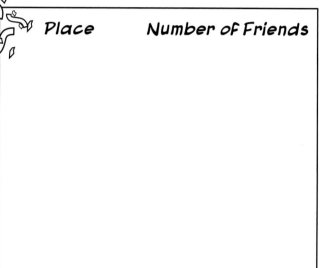

Sport	Music Lesson

4. Riley wants to take a photograph of his three best friends together. List all the ways he can have Eddie, Brandon, and Jake stand for the photo.

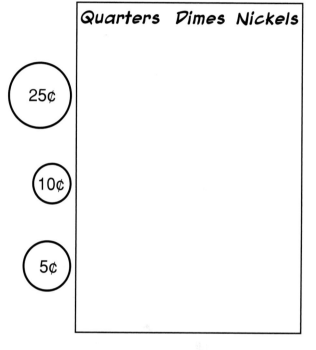

Left	Middle	Right

©The Mailbox® • TEC44037 • June/July 2008 • Key p. 313

Big Top Patterns and Functions

with ideas by Jennifer Otter, Oak Ridge, NC

JUGGLING NUMBERS
Input-output chart variation

Want a unique way for students to identify function rules? Then move this activity to the center ring! Provide each child with the materials listed below and guide her through the steps shown. When all cards are completed, have each student swap cards with a classmate, study the ten pairs of corresponding input and output numbers on that card's wheel to guess the rule used, and then lift the card's flap to check her guess. Continue trading cards as time permits.

Materials for each student: copy of page 186, scissors, glue, brad, crayons or colored pencils

Steps:
1. Color the card. Then cut out the card and the opening for its flap.
2. Fold the card along the thin solid line; then cut out the openings for the circles and for turning the wheel. Write a function rule under the flap.
3. Cut out the wheel, fold it along the line, and glue its blank sides together.
4. Label the circles on one side of the wheel with input numbers for the rule. Label each corresponding circle on the back with the matching output number.
5. Using the brad, make a hole at each dot on the wheel and card. Secure the wheel inside the card with the brad so the circles on the wheel and card are aligned, and the input numbers face the front of the card.

CRAZY QUILT
Input-output patterns

Provide each student with a copy of a
hundred chart, a half sheet of paper, and
four colored pencils of his choice. Instruct
him to label the paper with his colors, four
function rules, and four starting numbers
like the ones shown, using a different rule
and number (1 to 100) for each color.
Then have the student color his hundred
chart accordingly, mount it on a construction paper square, and tape his paper to the
back. If desired, tape the completed squares
together to form a colorful paper quilt and
display it on a wall or bulletin board.

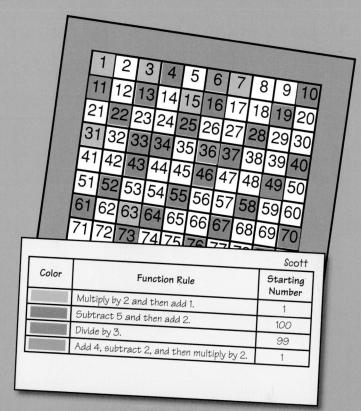

Color	Function Rule	Scott Starting Number
	Multiply by 2 and then add 1.	1
	Subtract 5 and then add 2.	100
	Divide by 3.	99
	Add 4, subtract 2, and then multiply by 2.	1

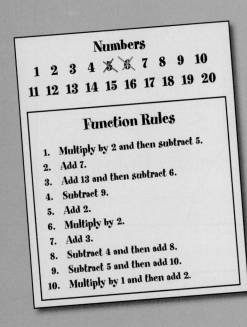

Numbers

1 2 3 4 ~~5~~ ~~6~~ 7 8 9 10
11 12 13 14 15 16 17 18 19 20

Function Rules

1. Multiply by 2 and then subtract 5.
2. Add 7.
3. Add 13 and then subtract 6.
4. Subtract 9.
5. Add 2.
6. Multiply by 2.
7. Add 3.
8. Subtract 4 and then add 8.
9. Subtract 5 and then add 10.
10. Multiply by 1 and then add 2.

PATTERN PLAY
Partner game

Give each pair of students two colored pencils, a copy of a hundred chart, and
a list of ten function rules and numbers from 1 to 20 like the one at the left.
To play, one partner selects a number and a rule. Using a colored pencil, she
shades her number on the hundred chart and crosses it out on the list. Next,
she applies the selected rule to determine the next three numbers in the pattern
and shades those numbers in the chart. Player two then takes a turn, using any
rule and any number still available but coloring only uncolored boxes. The
player with more colored squares once all the numbers are crossed out wins.
See page 187 for more practice.

PASS THE PATTERN
Small-group activity

Have each student in the group select any four numbers from 1 to 25
and write them in a sequence that follows a certain pattern. Instruct
the student to write a rule that reflects her numbers' sequence. Make
sure no one within the group repeats a number or uses the same rule.
Have the group record its work on a sheet of paper, leaving answer
blanks for the next three numbers in each sequence and an answer
line for each rule. On the back of the page, have each contributor
list the numbers that complete his set and record the corresponding
rule. Finally, have each group place its page in a clear page protector
and trade with another group. With each trade, have students in
each group study the four number sequences, agree on the missing
numbers and rule for each one, and take turns recording the answers
with a wipe-off marker before turning the page over to check. See
page 188 for more practice.

1. 1, 2, 4, 7, __, __, __
   rule:

2. 3, 6, 9, 12, __, __, __
   rule:

3. 5, 10, 15, 20, __, __, __
   rule:

4. 25, 23, 21, 19, __, __, __
   rule:

Ringmaster Card and Wheel Pattern

Use with "Juggling Numbers" on page 184.

Rule

TEC44037

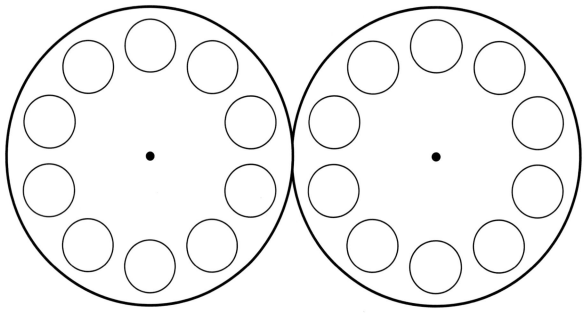

Hat Trick

Apply the corresponding rule to each input number in a set. Write the matching set of output numbers on the second hat.

INPUT Numbers	Rules	OUTPUT Numbers
A. 4, 5, 6	A. Add 3 and then multiply by 2.	A. ___, ___, ___
B. 3, 5, 7	B. Multiply by 4.	B. ___, ___, ___
C. 10, 22, 40	C. Divide by 2.	C. ___, ___, ___
D. 1, 4, 9	D. Multiply by 3 and then subtract 1.	D. ___, ___, ___
E. 7, 12, 18	E. Add 11.	E. ___, ___, ___
F. 9, 18, 21	F. Divide by 3 and then add 5.	F. ___, ___, ___
G. 2, 5, 10	G. Add 3 and then multiply by 2.	G. ___, ___, ___
H. 4, 15, 25	H. Add 10 and then subtract 5.	H. ___, ___, ___
I. 12, 16, 28	I. Add 12 and then divide by 4.	I. ___, ___, ___
J. 50, 35, 25	J. Divide by 5 and then subtract 5.	J. ___, ___, ___

Note to the teacher: Use alone or with "Pattern Play" on page 185.

Name_____

Performing for Peanuts

Complete each pattern and write the rule. Then use the code to color the shape(s) labeled with the matching answers.

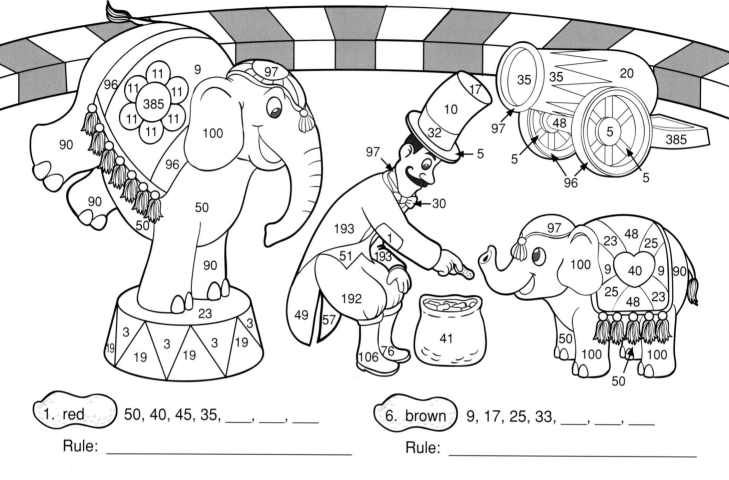

1. red 50, 40, 45, 35, ___, ___, ___

Rule: _____

2. blue 5, 7, 10, 14, ___, ___, ___

Rule: _____

3. yellow 47, 41, 35, 29, ___, ___, ___

Rule: _____

4. orange 729, 243, 81, 27, ___, ___, ___

Rule: _____

5. gray 20, 40, 30, 60, ___, ___, ___

Rule: _____

6. brown 9, 17, 25, 33, ___, ___, ___

Rule: _____

7. purple 7, 13, 25, 49, ___, ___, ___

Rule: _____

8. pink 320, 160, 80, 40, ___, ___, ___

Rule: _____

9. green 3, 6, 12, 24, ___, ___, ___

Rule: _____

10. black 1, 6, 16, 31, ___, ___, ___

Rule: _____

Note to the teacher: Use alone or with "Pass the Pattern" on page 185.

LANGUAGE ARTS SPOTLIGHT

Language Arts Spotlight

Reading Placemats

After you read a selection, write its title on the line.
Show the selection to a parent or your teacher and
have him or her initial the plate.
Then draw an item on your placemat according to
the code.

Please complete this
assignment by
Sept. 28
date

Type of selection: _Poem_
Title: _"One Inch Tall"_

Type of selection: _Newspaper_
Title: _Sunday funnies from September 16_

Type of selection: _Magazine_
Title: _Nickelodeon_

Type of selection: _Directions_
Title: _"Assembling a Model Airplane"_

Type of selection: _Science Article_
Title: _"Learn About a Bee"_

Type of selection: _Folktale_
Title: _Paul Bunyan_

Tia's Reading Placemat

Create-Your-Placemat Code
Add items to your placemat in this order as
shown:
1. napkin   4. knife
2. fork   5. spoon
3. plate   6. the title "[Your Name]'s
                    Reading Placemat"

Tony's Reading Placemat

Reading Placemats
Fictional and informational text

Motivate students to read a variety of texts with an activity that's perfect for the first month of school. Program a copy of page 192 with a due date and six different types of reading selections, such as a folktale, magazine article, newspaper section, poem, set of directions, and myth. Also place at a center the supplies listed. Give each child a copy of page 192 and a 9" x 12" piece of tagboard to use as a placemat. After he reads a selection, have him complete the form as directed and trace one item onto his placemat using the materials at the center. When he has read all six selections, the result is a complete place setting. Reward students who complete their place settings with a special treat to enjoy on their reading placemats!

Donna G. Pawloski, Primos Elementary, Primos, PA

Supplies:
tracers: plastic fork, spoon, and knife;
  dinner napkin; 6" tagboard circle
pencil
crayons, markers, or colored pencils

Quick Spell
Spelling review

Draw on a sheet of paper a grid such as the one shown. Write a letter in each grid box, including at least five of each vowel and three of each consonant. Make a class supply of the grid on colorful paper and laminate the copies. Then have each student cut apart one grid and place the letters in a sandwich bag. To play, have each child spread his letters out on his desk and place his hands in his lap. Call out a word and say, "Go!" The first person to spell the word using his letters raises his hand. If he is correct, the student earns a point. If he's incorrect, check the spelling of the second child to raise her hand. Reward the first student to score a predetermined number of points with a small prize or class privilege.

Sue Burriss, Taylor County Middle School, Campbellsville, KY

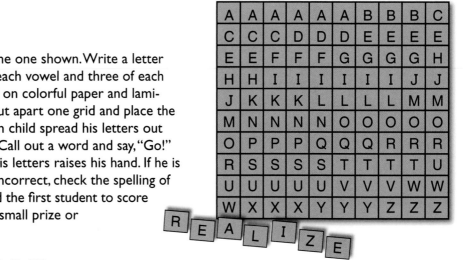

A	A	A	A	A	B	B	B	C
C	C	C	D	D	D	E	E	E
E	E	F	F	F	G	G	G	H
H	H	I	I	I	I	I	I	J
J	K	K	K	L	L	L	L	M
M	N	N	N	O	O	O	O	O
O	P	P	P	Q	Q	R	R	R
R	S	S	S	S	T	T	T	U
U	U	U	U	U	V	V	V	W
W	X	X	X	Y	Y	Y	Z	Z

REALIZE

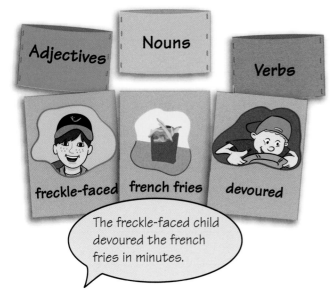

Adjectives   Nouns   Verbs

freckle-faced   french fries   devoured

The freckle-faced child devoured the french fries in minutes.

Picture-Perfect
Identifying parts of speech, writing sentences

For this nifty hands-on lesson, have each child fold three sheets of paper in half, staple the sides, and label the resulting pockets as shown. Next, direct her to cut out magazine pictures that represent different nouns, verbs, and adjectives. Then have her mount each picture on construction paper, add the word, and place the picture in the appropriate pocket. Have students meet in groups and combine their pictures. Then have each group choose one noun, one verb, and one adjective to use in a creative sentence. After groups share their sentences, repeat the activity. At the end of the lesson, challenge each child to collect her pictures and refile them in the correct pockets.

Kim Bostick, Old Town Elementary, Winston-Salem, NC

Wanted: Super Speakers
Making effective presentations

Write on the board the names shown below, explaining that they are unwanted characters in regard to class presentations. (Change any names that match those of students in your class.) After discussing the characters' poor speaking traits plus the qualities of effective speakers, divide students into groups. Have each group select a character listed or create a new one. Then challenge each group to create an "Unwanted" poster that includes an illustration of the character and a description of his or her speaking weaknesses. Have each group share its poster and give examples of how to improve the character's presentation skills. Display the posters throughout the year to remind students of presentation pitfalls to avoid.

Terry Healy, Marlatt Elementary, Manhattan, KS

Freddy Footshuffler	Mona Monotone	Lulu Lookdown
Ida I. Canthearyou	Tony Toofast	

UNWANTED!
Mona Monotone

Ms. Monotone never changes her voice when she speaks. She doesn't use her voice to emphasize key points. Her tone and volume always stay the same. She doesn't speak with any feeling or emotion. Mona has been known to put her listeners to sleep!

Reading Placemats

After you read a selection, write its title on the line.
Show the selection to a parent or your teacher and
    have him or her initial the plate.
Then draw an item on your placemat according to
    the code.

Please complete this
assignment by
_____
date

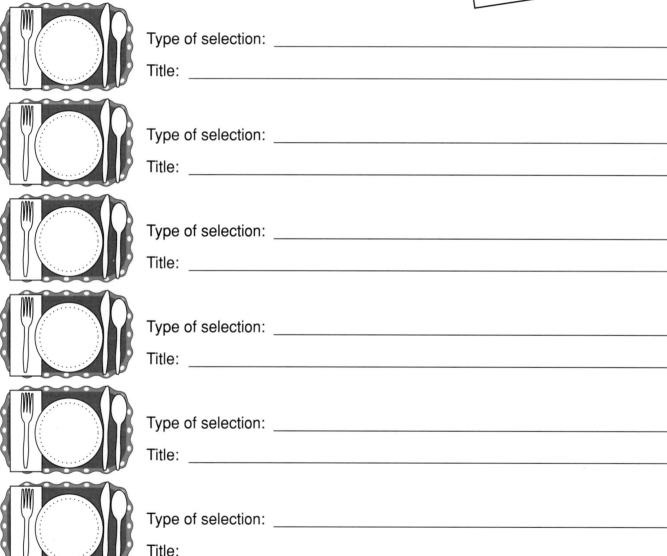

Type of selection: _____

Title: _____

Type of selection: _____

Title: _____

Type of selection: _____

Title: _____

Type of selection: _____

Title: _____

Type of selection: _____

Title: _____

Type of selection: _____

Title: _____

Tia's Reading Placemat

Create-Your-Placemat Code
Add items to your placemat in this order as
shown:
1. napkin   4. knife
2. fork   5. spoon
3. plate   6. the title "[Your Name]'s
            Reading Placemat"

©The Mailbox® • TEC44032 • Aug./Sept. 2007

Language Arts Spotlight

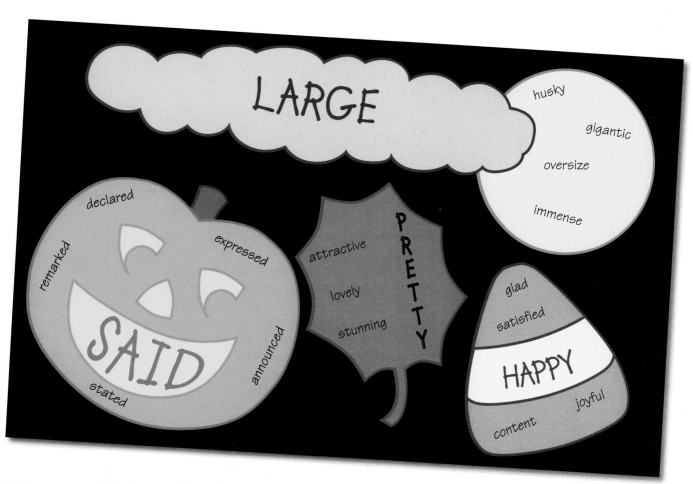

LARGE

husky
gigantic
oversize
immense

declared
remarked
expressed
announced
stated
SAID

attractive
PRETTY
lovely
stunning

glad
satisfied
HAPPY
content
joyful

Vetoed Vocabulary

Synonyms

Help your students create a display that doubles as a visual thesaurus! Post a list of overused words, such as *said, do, happy, mean, sad, like, good, large, pretty, walk, nice,* and *bad.* Have each student find synonyms for three or more of the words using a thesaurus. Then have him incorporate the words into a collage based on a favorite theme, such as a sport, hobby, or holiday. The student lists each tired word and its synonyms on one of the collage's cutouts as shown. After a sharing session, display the collages on a bulletin board or wall for students to use as references for future writing assignments.

Michelle Palmer, Schaumburg, IL

Web of Words
Vocabulary

Build your students' word wisdom with a scavenger hunt activity you can use throughout the year. Give each child a copy of page 195 to complete as directed. If desired, award a bonus or extra-credit point for each web section that includes three different word sources.

Kim Minafo, Dillard Drive Elementary, Raleigh, NC

Name Ben

Web of Words

Write a vocabulary word beside each small spider. When you see a word used, fill in a space below the word. Use the guidelines to help you.

Can you fill in three spaces for each word?

arrival
oxygen
altitude
uphill
incredible
crest
peak
heroic
ascending
breathtaking

GUIDELINES

Where should I look? Everywhere! Try books, Web sites, songs, signs, magazines, newspapers, menus, cards, dictionaries, game rules, directions, products around your house, and other places.

What do I write in the space? List where you found the word and, if applicable, a page number.

May I Quote You?
Using quotation marks

To prepare for this punctuation activity, have each student write her name on a paper slip and drop it into a container. Post a question, such as one of those shown, on the board. Then have each student draw a classmate's name. Provide several minutes for each child to find the classmate whose name she drew and record his response to the question. When the student returns to her desk, have her rewrite the response as a direct or divided quotation, using correct punctuation. Have students swap papers to check each other's work. Then, if desired, post another question and repeat the activity.

Lindsay Smith, St. Elizabeth Seton School, Pickering, Ontario, Canada

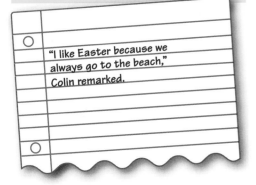

What is your favorite holiday? Why?

What famous person would you most like to share lunch with? Why?

What is your favorite color? Why?

What do you like the most about your home? Why?

Should the school year be shorter? Why or why not?

"I like Easter because we always go to the beach," Colin remarked.

Hidden Adjective Pictures
Using adjectives

For a fun parts of speech activity, have each student list a noun from a story he is currently writing and three adjectives to describe it. Next, have the student draw a picture of his noun, adding features that represent the adjectives. For example, in the picture shown, the noun *farmer* is illustrated to suggest the adjectives *hardworking* (the hoe), *curious* (the question mark), and *mean* (the slanted eyebrows). Have students share their pictures in small groups, challenging each other to guess the hidden adjectives in each one.

Veronica B. Krapf, The Davis Academy, Atlanta, GA

Adjective: curious

Adjective: mean

Noun: farmer

Adjective: hardworking

Web of Words

Write a vocabulary word beside each small spider.
When you see a word used, fill in a space below the word. Use the guidelines to help you.

Can you fill in three spaces for each word?

GUIDELINES

Where should I look? Everywhere! Try books, Web sites, songs, signs, magazines, newspapers, menus, cards, dictionaries, game rules, directions, products around your house, and other places.

What do I write in the space? List where you found the word and, if applicable, a page number.

©The Mailbox® • TEC44033 • Oct./Nov. 2007

Note to the teacher: Use with "Web of Words" on page 194.

195

Language Arts Spotlight

the very fast runner
a dripping-wet runner

Revised Descriptors

the extremely speedy sprinter
a totally drenched jogger

the pretty beach house
a sunny day
a boat moving slowly

Revised Descriptors

the lovely seaside cottage
a cloudless and radiant day
a sailboat drifting lazily

The Modifier Gallery

Descriptive adjectives and adverbs

Try this idea to encourage your young writers to use modifiers that help readers visualize the images being described. To do this, display each of several interesting magazine pictures above separate sheets of paper. Have students walk around the makeshift gallery and label each chart with descriptive phrases that include adjectives and adverbs. After every child has labeled at least one chart, draw a line under the last phrase on each chart. Instruct pairs of students to each choose one phrase and revise it using more interesting adjectives and adverbs (see the examples). Then have the partners write their improved phrases below the charts' black lines.

Cheryl Rule, Mt. Airy Middle School, Mt. Airy, MD

Connection Chains
Comprehension

Help students make connections to what they read by posting three labels, as shown, on a bulletin board. After students read a selection, have each child label a colorful paper strip with a connection he made. Then have him share his connection with the class. When the class decides which type of connection his example represents, the student staples his strip in a loop onto the paper chain that has been started under the matching label. When the chains reach a predetermined length, remove them and start over!

Andrea Hetzke, Oakdale Christian Academy, Chicago, IL

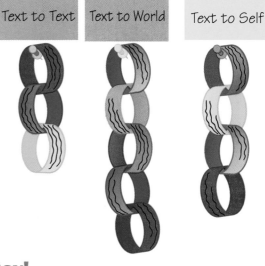

What a Day!
Synonyms and antonyms, using a thesaurus

For a fun way to build vocabulary and thesaurus skills, write "It was a _____ day" on the board. Ask students to name adjectives that could be used in the blank. List the words on a chart. Next, read aloud the classic picture book *Alexander and the Terrible, Horrible, No Good, Very Bad Day* by Judith Viorst. Invite students to name synonyms for the adjectives in the title. Add these to the list. Then have each child follow these steps:

1. Choose a word from the chart. Use a thesaurus to find four synonyms and four antonyms for the word. Write the words on scrap paper.
2. Divide a sheet of unlined paper into four blocks and title it using your synonyms. Then draw and color four different comic strip–style pictures that illustrate the title.
3. Repeat Step 2 on another sheet of paper using your antonyms.

After students share their work, post the picture pairs on a display titled "What a Day!"

Kim Minafo, Raleigh, NC

Weighty Words
Vocabulary brainteaser

Looking for a great vocabulary builder or fun free-time activity? Just turn to the reproducible activity on page 198. Give each child a copy of the page and allow several days for completion. Or place copies at a center for early finishers to tackle. Then have students pair up and use calculators to check each other's answers.

Kim Minafo

Weighty Words

The chart below assigns a weight to each letter in the alphabet.
Using the chart, find and list a word for each challenge 1–10.
Show your work on another sheet of paper.

Find...

1. Two words with a sum less than 20 pounds   1. _____

2. A word weighing less than your teacher's last name   2. _____

3. Two words with the same weight   3. _____

4. Two words with a difference of four pounds   4. _____

5. A word that weighs less than your last name   5. _____

6. Two synonyms that weigh within three pounds of each other   6. _____

7. A ten-pound verb   7. _____

8. An adjective that weighs at least 30 pounds   8. _____

9. Two words with a product under 30 pounds   9. _____

10. Two words with a sum greater than the number of   10. _____
    students in your class

Letter Weight

Letter	Weight		Letter	Weight		Letter	Weight
A	3 lb.		J	6 lb.		S	3 lb.
B	5 lb.		K	7 lb.		T	5 lb.
C	4 lb.		L	4 lb.		U	3 lb.
D	3 lb.		M	2 lb.		V	8 lb.
E	1 lb.		N	3 lb.		W	7 lb.
F	6 lb.		O	2 lb.		X	9 lb.
G	5 lb.		P	4 lb.		Y	8 lb.
H	5 lb.		Q	8 lb.		Z	9 lb.
I	2 lb.		R	5 lb.			

Antonyms

happy : depressed as seal : open	comfort : annoy as soothe : vex
loud : faint as quiet : noisy	guilty : innocent as broad : narrow

Synonyms

thin : narrow as yell : shout	steal : plunder as launch : start
trouble : bother as scalding : hot	early : premature as rough : coarse

Object—Action

broom : sweep as kitten : purr	phone : ring as bird : chirp
tornado : destroy as oven : bake	earthworm : dig as horse : gallop

Part—Whole

keyboard : computer as player : team	student : class as musician : band
country : continent as fin : fish	letter : alphabet as tree : forest

Build a Better Vocabulary

Analogies

To nail down stronger vocabulary skills, try this fun-to-do activity. After a review of the four types of analogies shown, each child colors and cuts out the brick and roof patterns from a copy of page 201. He glues the roof patterns on a large sheet of construction paper as shown. Then he groups the labeled bricks under the matching roofs. (There are four bricks for each roof. For the answer key, see page 313.) Finally, the student adds two blank bricks to each house and labels each one with a related analogy of his own. Provide time for students to share their original analogies before displaying the projects in your classroom.

Kim Minafo, Apex, NC

Double-Crossed!
Synonyms

Introduce this vocabulary builder by writing "BIG," "CHILLY," and "STORY" on the board. Add the two synonyms shown to *BIG*. Then ask students to identify two synonyms to add to *CHILLY* and *STORY* (see the examples). Next, have students use thesauruses to create their own synonym crosswords, starting with words of their choice or words in the list. When students are finished, have a volunteer write his starting word on the board and challenge classmates to guess the two synonyms that go with it. Adapt this idea to use with other categories, such as antonyms or curriculum topics. (For example, start with PRESIDENTS and add presidents' last names to it.)

Isobel L. Livingstone, Rahway, NJ

```
J       H
U       U
M       U
B I G
O       E


                I
                C
CHILLY              STORY
O                   A   A
L                   L   R
D                   E   N
```

Starter Synonyms

splendid	admire
speak	happy
brave	small
excellent	pale
lovely	soft
quiet	house
rapid	strange

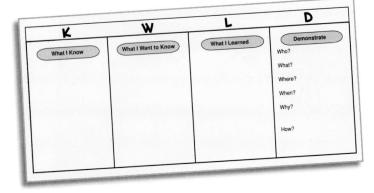

K	W	L	D
What I Know	What I Want to Know	What I Learned	Demonstrate
			Who?
			What?
			Where?
			When?
			Why?
			How?

KWLD Charts
Summarizing

A small addition to the KWL comprehension strategy can mean big improvements in summarizing skills. Before students read a nonfiction text, give each child a copy of a chart like the one shown. Brainstorm with students what they already know about the text's topic. Then have each student fill in his *K* column. In the *W* column, have students list questions they have about the topic. Then have students read the selection. After reading, discuss the text and have each student complete the *L* column. Finally, have each student answer as many questions about the selection as possible in the *D* column and use that information to summarize the text.

Sandra K. H. Wright, Dallas Public Schools, Dallas, TX

How? When? Where?
Adverbs

Have each student write three sentences with the same subject and action verb. Then have her add an underlined adverb to each sentence using the following code:
- Sentence 1: Add an adverb that answers "How?" about the verb.
- Sentence 2: Add an adverb that answers "When?" about the verb.
- Sentence 3: Add an adverb that answers "Where?" about the verb.

Have the student copy and illustrate each sentence on paper that's been divided into sections as shown. Then have her write in the final section two other adverbs for each question. Bind the cartoons in a class book titled "Adverb Adventures."

adapted from an idea by Mary Stinchfield, Northbridge Middle School Whitinsville, MA

1. The tiny boy sang <u>loudly</u>.

2. The tiny boy sang <u>early</u>.

3. The tiny boy sang <u>inside</u> the car.

How?
terribly, quietly
When?
yesterday, late
Where?
here, nearby

Erica

Brick and Roof Patterns

Use with "Build a Better Vocabulary" on page 199.

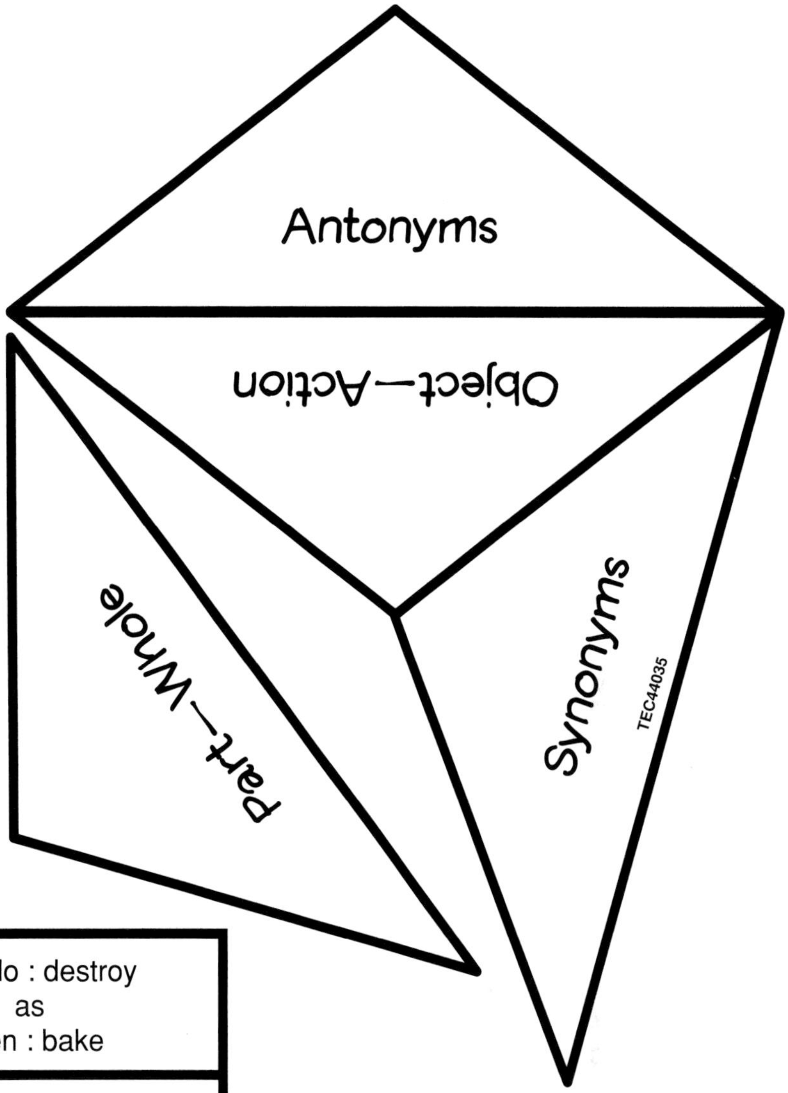
Antonyms
Object—Action
Part—Whole
Synonyms
TEC44035

student : class
as
musician : band

happy : depressed
as
seal : open

phone : ring
as
bird : chirp

country : continent
as
fin : fish

loud : faint
as
quiet : noisy

thin : narrow
as
yell : shout

guilty : innocent
as
broad : narrow

keyboard : computer
as
player : team

steal : plunder
as
launch : start

trouble : bother
as
scalding : hot

broom : sweep
as
kitten : purr

comfort : annoy
as
soothe : vex

letter : alphabet
as
tree : forest

earthworm : dig
as
horse : gallop

tornado : destroy
as
oven : bake

early : premature
as
rough : coarse

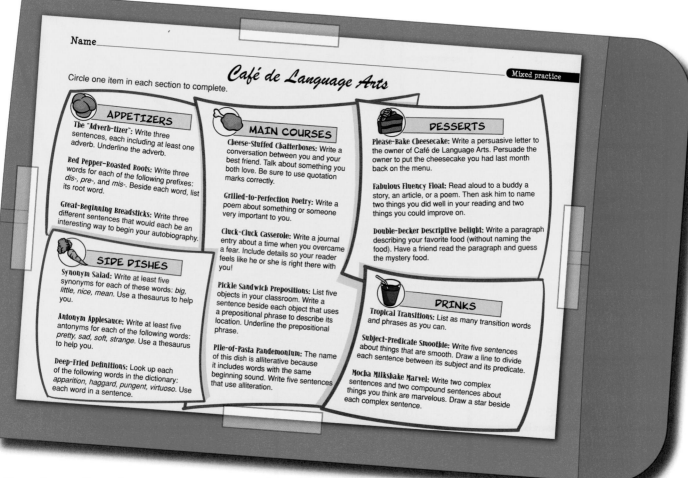

Café de Language Arts

Skills review

Place an order for independent practice of key language arts skills by giving each student a copy of page 204. Direct each child to circle a task of his choice from each menu section. If desired, have the student tape his menu to a large envelope, as shown, and store his work inside. After removing and assessing students' work, keep the envelopes. Then redistribute them later in the year and have each student use a different highlighter to select five additional tasks to complete. Bon appétit!

Joseph Lemmo, Chapman Intermediate School, Woodstock, GA

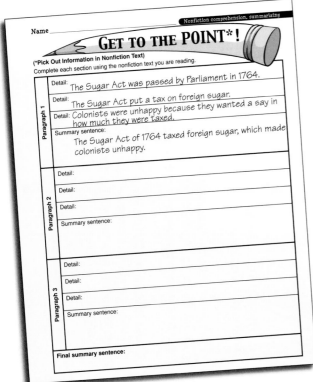

Name _____

GET TO THE POINT*!

(*Pick Out Information in Nonfiction Text)
Complete each section using the nonfiction text you are reading.

Paragraph 1

Detail: The Sugar Act was passed by Parliament in 1764.

Detail: The Sugar Act put a tax on foreign sugar.

Detail: Colonists were unhappy because they wanted a say in how much they were taxed.

Summary sentence: The Sugar Act of 1764 taxed foreign sugar, which made colonists unhappy.

Paragraph 2

Detail:

Detail:

Detail:

Summary sentence:

Paragraph 3

Detail:

Detail:

Detail:

Summary sentence:

Final summary sentence:

Get to the POINT!
Nonfiction comprehension, summarizing

Finding important details in a factual passage can be difficult for students. To strengthen this skill, give each child one or more copies of page 205 (depending on the passage's length). As students read a nonfiction passage, have them "pick out information in nonfiction text" (POINT) to fill in the organizer. Then have each student follow the steps below to summarize the passage.

Diane Marshall, Salem, AL

Steps:
1. As you read the first paragraph, pick three important details and list them on the organizer where indicated.
2. Use the details to write a one-sentence summary.
3. Repeat Steps 1 and 2 for the other paragraphs in the passage.
4. When you've finished reading, use the three summary sentences to write a final sentence that summarizes the entire text.

Extra! Extra!
Verbs

For this great grammar activity, collect old newspapers. Have each child fold a sheet of construction paper in half twice, unfold her paper, and label the four quadrants as shown. Explain that tired verbs are overused verbs, like *said* and *run,* and new verbs are interesting or unfamiliar verbs students don't normally use in their writing. Then have the student cut out words from the newspaper and glue each example in the appropriate section. Use the projects to assess students' knowledge of verb use. If desired, display the papers to create a giant verb bank students can refer to when writing.

Carol Lawrence, Madera, CA

Action Verbs: drove, vote, BUY, tackle

Tired Verbs: Run, look, laugh

Helping Verbs: can, may, will

New Verbs: excavate, plunge, REBUKE, deploy

GET LOST in your vacation planning with the Blunder Road Atlas! It's sure to take you farther than you've ever dreamed!

Blunder Road Atlas First Edition

What Went Wrong?
Wordplay, creative writing

To extend a lesson on advertising techniques, write on the board the ad text shown. Explain that a friend posted the ad on his Web site, but no one is buying the *Blunder Road Atlas.* Guide students to identify what went wrong with the ad:
- The word *blunder* doesn't build confidence that the maps will help a traveler.
- The word *lost* may make you think the maps won't help you find your destination.
- The phrase "…take you farther than you ever dreamed!" could mean you'll get hopelessly off course if you use the atlas's maps.

After discussing the ad's humorous wordplay, challenge students to work alone, with a partner, or in a small group to create a "What went wrong?" ad for a product or service. Then provide time for students to share their ads.

Paula Epker, Hannibal, MO

Name _____

Café de Language Arts

Circle one item in each section to complete.

APPETIZERS

The "Adverb–tizer": Write three sentences, each including at least one adverb. Underline the adverb.

Red Pepper–Roasted Roots: Write three words for each of the following prefixes: *dis-*, *pre-*, and *mis-*. Beside each word, list its root word.

Great–Beginning Breadsticks: Write three different sentences that would each be an interesting way to begin your autobiography.

SIDE DISHES

Synonym Salad: Write at least five synonyms for each of these words: *big, little, nice, mean*. Use a thesaurus to help you.

Antonym Applesauce: Write at least five antonyms for each of the following words: *pretty, sad, soft, strange*. Use a thesaurus to help you.

Deep–Fried Definitions: Look up each of the following words in the dictionary: *apparition, haggard, pungent, virtuoso*. Use each word in a sentence.

MAIN COURSES

Cheese–Stuffed Chatterboxes: Write a conversation between you and your best friend. Talk about something you both love. Be sure to use quotation marks correctly.

Grilled–to–Perfection Poetry: Write a poem about something or someone very important to you.

Cluck–Cluck Casserole: Write a journal entry about a time when you overcame a fear. Include details so your reader feels like he or she is right there with you!

Pickle Sandwich Prepositions: List five objects in your classroom. Write a sentence beside each object that uses a prepositional phrase to describe its location. Underline the prepositional phrase.

Pile–of–Pasta Pandemonium: The name of this dish is alliterative because it includes words with the same beginning sound. Write five sentences that use alliteration.

DESSERTS

Please–Bake Cheesecake: Write a persuasive letter to the owner of Café de Language Arts. Persuade the owner to put the cheesecake you had last month back on the menu.

Fabulous Fluency Float: Read aloud to a buddy a story, an article, or a poem. Then ask him to name two things you did well in your reading and two things you could improve on.

Double–Decker Descriptive Delight: Write a paragraph describing your favorite food (without naming the food). Have a friend read the paragraph and guess the mystery food.

DRINKS

Tropical Transitions: List as many transition words and phrases as you can.

Subject–Predicate Smoothie: Write five sentences about things that are smooth. Draw a line to divide each sentence between its subject and its predicate.

Mocha Milkshake Marvel: Write two complex sentences and two compound sentences about things you think are marvelous. Draw a star beside each complex sentence.

©The Mailbox® • TEC44036 • April/May 2008

Note to the teacher: Use with "Café de Language Arts" on page 202.

GET TO THE POINT*!

(*Pick Out Information in Nonfiction Text)

Complete each section using the nonfiction text you are reading.

Paragraph 1	Detail:
	Detail:
	Detail:
	Summary sentence:
Paragraph 2	Detail:
	Detail:
	Detail:
	Summary sentence:
Paragraph 3	Detail:
	Detail:
	Detail:
	Summary sentence:
	Final summary sentence:

Degrees of Synonyms
Word choice

Too often students look up a word in a thesaurus without considering which synonym listed best supports the meaning they want to convey. To encourage better word choice, give each child a copy of a thermometer pattern from page 209. Point out that the hottest temperatures, or strongest synonyms, are at the top of the thermometer, while the coolest temperatures, or weakest related words, are at the bottom. Next, have students write *hot* in the thermometer's bulb. On the board, list the following words: *warm, scorching, toasty, fiery,* and *sizzling.* Have students look up the words in a dictionary, compare their definitions, and then record the words on the pattern from weakest to strongest. Discuss students' rankings and reach a class consensus. Then write the synonyms on a copy of the pattern in the order students agreed upon and post it on your word wall. Periodically, repeat the activity with other starter words, such as those shown below.

Elizabeth Davis, Balsz Elementary, Phoenix, AZ

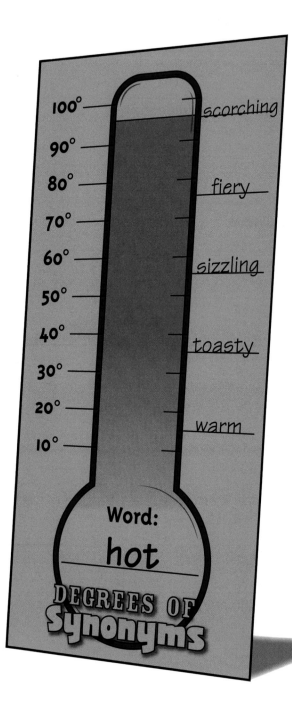

Additional starter words
love, hate, good, mad, rich, sick, happy, sad

Animal Quotes
Direct quotations

For a fun way to practice punctuating a speaker's exact words, post an interesting picture of one or more animals. (Used calendars and magazines and the Internet are great sources.) Have each student write on scrap paper a comment the animal might make if it could talk. Next, instruct her to rewrite the comment as a quotation on a paper strip and then ask a partner to edit the sentence's punctuation. After the writer makes any corrections, have her turn in the strip for checking. Post correctly punctuated sentences with the picture. To keep the practice going strong, change the picture frequently.

"But Mom, I don't want to go into hibernation yet!" Little Bear cried.

Butterflies

Up through the wispy clouds
Above the bright green treetops,
Down to the blooming flowers
To a place among the petals.

Jared

Preposition Poetry
Using prepositional phrases

To follow up a lesson on prepositions, have each student choose a topic, such as butterflies or basketball, for a poem. Instruct him to begin each line of the poem with a different prepositional phrase that relates to his topic. After he writes a predetermined number of lines, have him ask a partner to edit his work. If desired, have the student copy his poem's final version on a paper cutout representing his topic and then post the cutout on a display titled "Preposition Poetry."

Linda Ellis, Locke Hill Elementary, San Antonio, TX

Question Makers, Inc.
Nonfiction reading comprehension

Use this ongoing activity to build important reading skills. Each week or two, set out a variety of nonfiction books, magazines, and other texts (one per student). After reading one of the selections, a student writes on an index card her name, the selection's title, and three questions about the selection. Then she writes the answers on the card's back, paper-clips the card to the selection, and returns the selection to the designated area. Once all the selections have at least one card attached to them, redistribute the selections. Have each student read her new selection and answer one set of questions. Then have her flip over the card to check her work. If time allows, have students trade selections and then read and answer questions about a different topic.

Leigh Newsom, Cedar Road Elementary, Chesapeake, VA

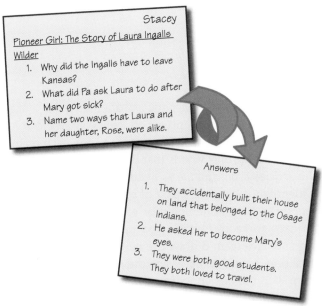

Stacey

Pioneer Girl: The Story of Laura Ingalls Wilder

1. Why did the Ingalls have to leave Kansas?
2. What did Pa ask Laura to do after Mary got sick?
3. Name two ways that Laura and her daughter, Rose, were alike.

Answers

1. They accidentally built their house on land that belonged to the Osage Indians.
2. He asked her to become Mary's eyes.
3. They were both good students. They both loved to travel.

Reading Graphs
Skill review

Use the reproducible on page 210 to reinforce the skills your students need to practice most! Preview a reading selection to identify four skills embedded in it, such as contractions, words with prefixes or suffixes, alliteration, similes, or compound words. List the selection's title where indicated and each skill in a box as shown. Then make student copies. After a student reads the selection, have him list in the boxes examples from the selection and draw a bar to indicate the number of different examples he found for each category. To use the reproducible again, simply label a blank graph with another selection's title and skills before making copies.

Deborah S. Alexander, Titche Elementary, Dallas, TX

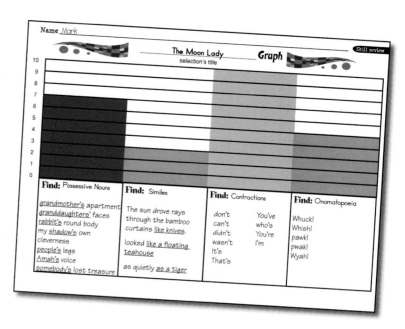

Name _Mark_

The Moon Lady — Graph
selection's title — Skill review

Find: Possessive Nouns	Find: Similes	Find: Contractions	Find: Onomatopoeia
grandmother's apartment granddaughters' faces rabbit's round body my shadow's own cleverness people's legs Amah's voice somebody's lost treasure	The sun drove rays through the bamboo curtains like knives. looked like a floating teahouse as quietly as a tiger	don't You've can't who's didn't You're wasn't I'm It's That's	Whuck! Whish! pawk! pwak! Wyah!

On a Roll!
Reviewing compound and complex sentences

Begin by having students brainstorm a list of six topics. Number the topics, and give each group of students a die. One student in each group rolls the die to determine the topic. Then he rolls the die again. If he rolls an odd number, each student writes a compound sentence about the topic. If he rolls an even number, each child writes a complex sentence. When all students have written their sentences, they pass their papers to the right for peer editing. Afterward, everyone returns the papers to their owners and repeats the steps until time is up. This quick activity also is a fun way to practice writing facts and opinions or causes and effects.

Topics
1. music videos
2. cell phones
3. fun ways to relax
4. Mt. Everest
5. sharks
6. the drought in our area

Scare the shark away from me, or I'll scream at the top of my lungs.

Letter Lineup
Parts-of-speech review

Place a set of plastic magnetic alphabet letters in a bag and divide the class into two teams. A player on Team A draws four letters and places them on the whiteboard in any order. Then each team writes a sentence using, in order, only words that begin with the letters on the board and the articles *a, an,* and *the* as needed. After a team writes its sentence, it identifies each word's part of speech as shown. As teams share their sentences, award one point for each complete sentence and one point for each correctly identified part of speech. Then return the letters to the bag and have Team B draw the next four letters. Continue in this manner until time runs out, increasing the number of letters drawn if desired. The team with the higher score wins.

	noun	action verb	adjective	noun
○	Gary	munched	a vanilla	éclair.

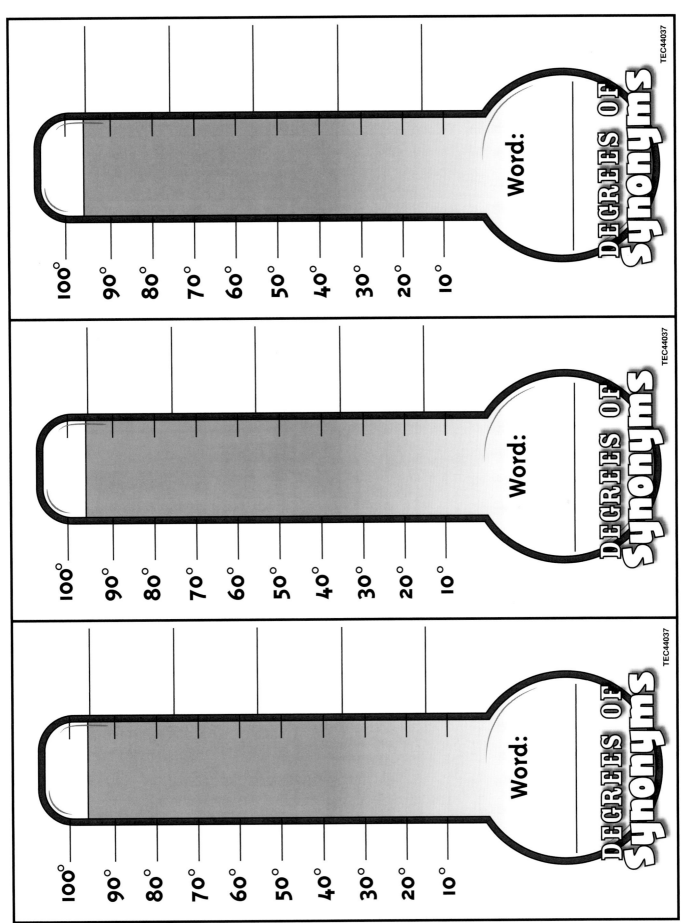

TEC44037

TEC44037

TEC44037

DEGREES OF Synonyms

DEGREES OF Synonyms

DEGREES OF Synonyms

Word:

Word:

Word:

100° 90° 80° 70° 60° 50° 40° 30° 20° 10°

100° 90° 80° 70° 60° 50° 40° 30° 20° 10°

100° 90° 80° 70° 60° 50° 40° 30° 20° 10°

Skill review

Graph

_____
selection's title

10										
9										
8										
7										
6										
5										
4										
3										
2										
1										
0										

Find:

Find:

Find:

Find:

©The Mailbox® · TEC44036 · June/July 2008

Note to the teacher: Use with "Reading Graphs" on page 208.

MATH MAILBAG

MATH MAILBAG

gameboard

6, 5 4 4, 3 3 3

throwaway area

2 1 1

Put It in Its Place!
Place value

This easy game is great as a time filler. Have each child use a nonerasable pen to draw a gameboard of seven answer blanks (with commas where shown) plus three more to use for throwaway numbers. Then roll a die and announce the number rolled. Have each child decide where to write the announced number to try to eventually create the largest number possible. After ten rolls, have students share their answers. Declare the child with the largest number the winner. In the event of a tie, declare multiple winners. Play more rounds as time allows. To vary the game, have students create the smallest number possible or draw a gameboard that includes a decimal. Or replace three sides of the die with the digits 7, 8, and 9!

Julie Asti, St. Leo School, Ridgway, PA

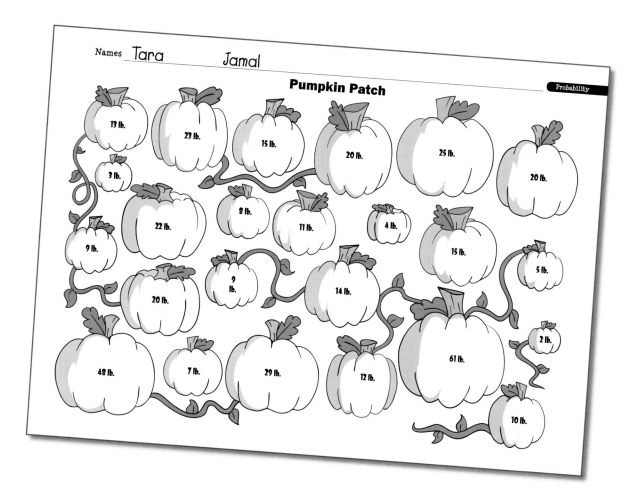

Pumpkin Patch

Probability

Pumpkin-Patch Probability

Problem solving

This partner activity is sure to please! Give each pair of students a copy of the pumpkin patch on page 215. Instruct the pair to write on each of five paper strips a probability question that can be answered using the pumpkin patch. (See the examples.) Collect the strips and read aloud one problem at a time. Each twosome that solves the problem correctly gets to color one pumpkin on its page. The first duo to color all 24 pumpkins wins.

Jennifer Otter, Oak Ridge, NC

Sample questions:
1. What is the probability of choosing a pumpkin that weighs exactly 20 pounds? ($^3/_{24}$, or $^1/_8$)
2. What are the odds of picking a pumpkin that weighs less than seven pounds? ($^4/_{24}$, or $^1/_6$)
3. What is the probability of picking a pumpkin that does not weigh exactly 14 pounds? ($^{23}/_{24}$)
4. What is the probability of choosing a pumpkin whose weight is a prime number? ($^9/_{24}$, or $^3/_8$)
5. What are the odds of choosing a pumpkin whose weight is an even number? ($^{11}/_{24}$)

Same As, Less Than, or Greater Than
Fractions

Reviewing equivalent fractions and comparing fractions is a fun thing to do no matter what the season with this easy-to-adapt activity. Instruct each child to cut out a seasonal shape, label it with fraction problems that match the skill being reviewed, and then color the cutout, adding appropriate details. To solve the problems, have students trade cutouts and write their answers on paper. Or laminate the cutouts and place a few of them at a time at a center to give individual students or small groups more practice.

Cindy Pyscher, Clarkston Elementary, Clarkston, MI

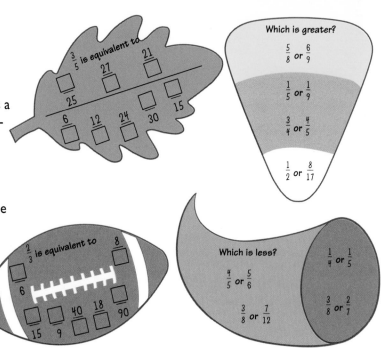

Fine-Feathered Friend
Place value

To create this gobbling-good math aid, have each child cut out a circle, six tail feathers, and a turkey head from colorful paper as shown. Instruct her to label each feather with a different place value from ones to hundred thousands. Then have her assemble the turkey with glue so its head and neck are between each trio of feathers and represent the comma separating the two three-digit periods. To complete the project, she adds a beak, eyes, wattle, wings, and feet. Allow her to keep the turkey in her math folder and refer to it when she is completing classwork, reading large numbers, or recording dictated numbers.

Kristi Root, Burris Elementary, Mitchell, IN

Disappearing Numbers
Multiples

This whole-class or small-group activity makes multiplication facts fun to practice! Begin by having students count in unison by twos, by fives, and then by tens to establish a pattern. Next, invite ten volunteers to the front of the room and have them try to count by sevens. Write each consecutive multiple on the board as it is said. Then have students read the multiples in unison. After the third reading, erase one of the numbers and have students read them again and supply the missing multiple. When students are finished, erase a second number and have students read the listed numbers again and supply both missing multiples. Continue in this manner, erasing one additional number each time, until all ten numbers have been erased and students have supplied all the missing multiples. Repeat the activity with other multiples whenever you need a terrific time filler!

Adam Eisenson, Easley Elementary, Durham, NC

Names _____

Pumpkin Patch

20 lb.

5 lb.

2 lb.

10 lb.

25 lb.

15 lb.

61 lb.

4 lb.

20 lb.

14 lb.

12 lb.

11 lb.

15 lb.

8 lb.

9 lb.

29 lb.

23 lb.

22 lb.

20 lb.

7 lb.

13 lb.

3 lb.

9 lb.

48 lb.

©The Mailbox® · TEC44033 · Oct./Nov. 2007

Note to the teacher: Use with "Pumpkin-Patch Probability" on page 213.

215

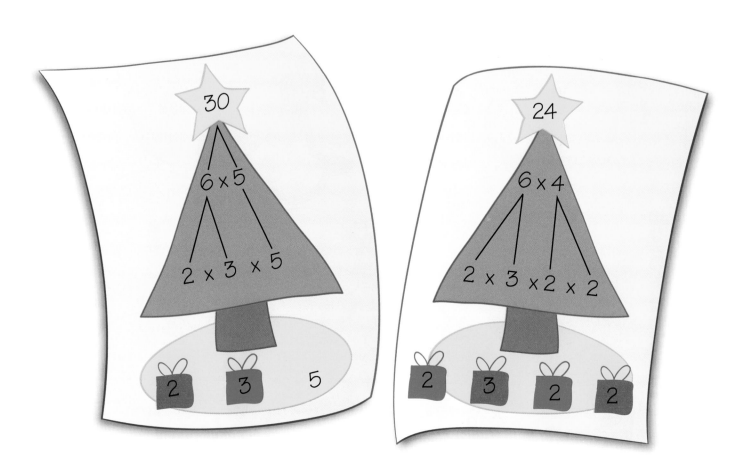

Trim the Trees!
Prime factorization, common factors

Deck your halls this December with pairs of factor trees! Have each child write a different composite number at the top of each of two sheets of paper and draw a star around each number. Next, he extends two lines (branches) from each number and writes two of its factors. He continues factoring it in this way until only prime numbers are left. Then he draws a triangle around each set of factored numbers to create a tree shape and adds a tree trunk and tree skirt. Since no Christmas tree is complete without packages underneath, have him copy the prime factors onto the trees' skirts, box the common factors, and then do the coloring!

Barbara Majoy, Meadowlawn School, Sandusky, OH

Not Your Ordinary Bingo
Mean, median, mode, and range

In honor of Bingo's Birthday Month, review statistics skills by giving this familiar game a different twist. Have each child draw a 5 x 5 grid on his paper and randomly program it with the digits 1–6. To play, roll a die five times and announce which statistic—mean (rounded to the nearest whole number), median, mode, or range—students should find with the numbers rolled. Then have each student use a colored pencil to shade the calculated answer on his gameboard. Explain that only one space can be shaded for each calculation, even if an answer appears more than once on the gameboard. If a set of numbers has more than one mode, either mode can be used as an answer. If no space matches an answer or a set of numbers has no mode, the student does not color a space. Play continues until one player colors five spaces horizontally, vertically, or diagonally.

Jennifer Otter, Oak Ridge, NC

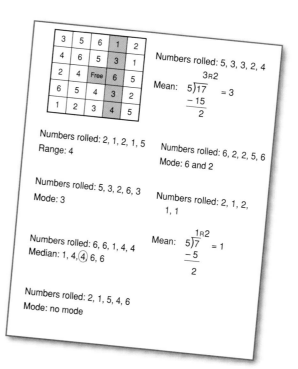

Numbers rolled: 5, 3, 3, 2, 4

Mean:
$$5\overline{)17} = 3 \quad \begin{array}{r} 3\text{R}2 \\ -15 \\ \hline 2 \end{array}$$

Numbers rolled: 2, 1, 2, 1, 5
Range: 4

Numbers rolled: 6, 2, 2, 5, 6
Mode: 6 and 2

Numbers rolled: 5, 3, 2, 6, 3
Mode: 3

Numbers rolled: 2, 1, 2, 1, 1

Mean:
$$5\overline{)7} = 1 \quad \begin{array}{r} 1\text{R}2 \\ -5 \\ \hline 2 \end{array}$$

Numbers rolled: 6, 6, 1, 4, 4
Median: 1, 4, ④ 6, 6

Numbers rolled: 2, 1, 5, 4, 6
Mode: no mode

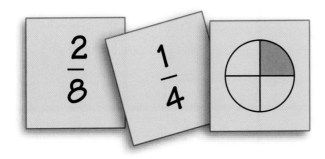

All Sides Covered
Surface area

This partner activity is perfect for getting students wrapped up in area! Collect various-size boxes so that each pair of students has a different box. Have partners pretend they are gift wrappers at a department store during the holidays and that the boxes are gifts that need to be wrapped. Instruct each duo to use a ruler to measure the sides of its box, calculate the area of each side, and add the six products together to determine the amount of paper needed to cover its box. When everyone is finished, display the boxes in random order. Challenge students to guess which box has the greatest surface area and which has the smallest surface area. Then, as the partners share their calculations, arrange the boxes in order from greatest surface area to smallest. If desired, display a roll of gift wrap and reveal its total number of square feet. Have students determine how many of the boxes could be wrapped using the paper.

Shawna Miller, Denton, TX

Match Three!
Fractions

Pairs of students make connections between pictorial and equivalent forms of common fractions with this fun version of the game Concentration. Give each twosome a copy of the cards on page 218 to cut apart, shuffle, and arrange facedown in an array. Each player takes a turn turning over three cards at a time instead of two. The player who makes the most three-way matches wins. To extend the learning, have students cut index cards into sixths and make additional game cards using different fractions.

Renee Silliman, Spring Shadows Elementary, Houston, TX

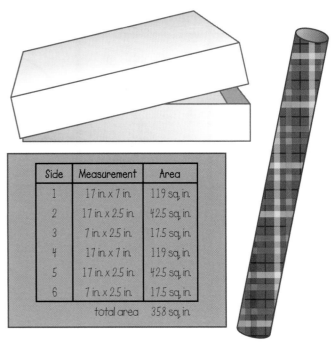

Side	Measurement	Area
1	17 in. x 7 in.	119 sq. in.
2	17 in. x 2.5 in.	42.5 sq. in.
3	7 in. x 2.5 in.	17.5 sq. in.
4	17 in. x 7 in.	119 sq. in.
5	17 in. x 2.5 in.	42.5 sq. in.
6	7 in. x 2.5 in.	17.5 sq. in.
	total area	358 sq. in.

Fraction Cards

Use with "Match Three!" on page 217.

$\dfrac{1}{5}$ TEC44034	 TEC44034	$\dfrac{2}{10}$ TEC44034	$\dfrac{5}{8}$ TEC44034	 TEC44034
$\dfrac{10}{16}$ TEC44034	$\dfrac{2}{3}$ TEC44034	 TEC44034	$\dfrac{4}{6}$ TEC44034	$\dfrac{1}{1}$ TEC44034
  TEC44034	$\dfrac{2}{2}$ TEC44034	$\dfrac{4}{5}$ TEC44034	 TEC44034	$\dfrac{8}{10}$ TEC44034
$\dfrac{3}{5}$ TEC44034	 TEC44034	$\dfrac{6}{10}$ TEC44034	$\dfrac{2}{5}$ TEC44034	 TEC44034
$\dfrac{4}{10}$ TEC44034	$\dfrac{1}{4}$ TEC44034	 TEC44034	$\dfrac{2}{8}$ TEC44034	$\dfrac{1}{3}$ TEC44034
  TEC44034	$\dfrac{2}{6}$ TEC44034	$\dfrac{1}{2}$ TEC44034	 TEC44034	$\dfrac{2}{4}$ TEC44034

MATH MAILBAG

Message	Probability
Cool Cat	$^2/_{25}$
Puppy Love	$^2/_{25}$
Hug Me	$^1/_{25}$
Sweet Talk	$^2/_{25}$
Be Mine	$^5/_{25}$, or $^1/_5$
Top Dog	$^1/_{25}$
Love Bird	$^1/_{25}$
Class Act	$^2/_{25}$
#1 Fan	$^2/_{25}$
Be My Hero	$^2/_{25}$
Charm Me	$^2/_{25}$
I Love You	$^3/_{25}$

Likely Conversations
Probability

For this sweet activity, provide each student with a small box of conversation hearts. Instruct him to sort his candies into different groups by message, not color. Next, have him make a chart showing the probability of a person choosing (without looking) a candy labeled with each different message. When the charts are finished, ask each child to report his findings. Tally the data on the board. Then allow students to enjoy their sweet treats while they discuss which messages are most and least likely to be found in similar boxes of candies and why.

Melissa Barbay, Devers School, Devers, TX

Shopping Scenarios
Positive and negative integers

This real-world activity focuses on bank balances. Have each student pretend she has her own account at a bank. Challenge her to create a word problem about a shopping experience at her favorite store and write it on a sticky note. Next, label two columns on the board as shown, and have students take turns sharing their shopping scenarios with the class. Have the class decide whether each completed transaction will result in a positive or negative bank balance. Then have the sharer post her sticky note under the appropriate heading.

Jennifer Otter, Oak Ridge, NC

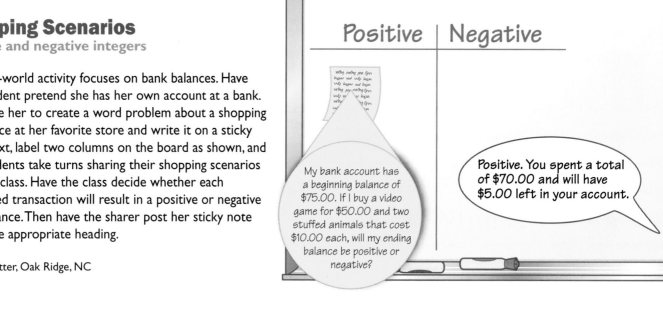

Positive | Negative

My bank account has a beginning balance of $75.00. If I buy a video game for $50.00 and two stuffed animals that cost $10.00 each, will my ending balance be positive or negative?

Positive. You spent a total of $70.00 and will have $5.00 left in your account.

Terrific Tops

$\frac{3}{8}$ of the shirts have stripes

$\frac{6}{8}$, or $\frac{3}{4}$, of the shirts have stars

$\frac{2}{8}$, or $\frac{1}{4}$, of the shirts have green stripes

$\frac{7}{8}$ of the shirts have three different colors

An Eye for Detail
Fractions

Prepare for this partner activity by having students bring in a variety of sales catalogs or store circulars. Then have each pair cut out six to eight colorful examples from a category of its choice and glue the cutouts to a section of bulletin board paper. Also have each duo label its paper with fractional descriptors that represent characteristics of their examples and share the descriptors with the class. For practice with converting fractions to decimals, have each child complete a copy of page 221 as directed.

adapted from an idea by Leigh Anne Newsom, Cedar Road Elementary Chesapeake, VA

Shamrocks and Pots of Gold
Ordered pairs on a grid

If your students sometimes have trouble remembering to first move right and then up when finding or plotting numbers on a grid, use this partner game as a review! Give each child a copy of centimeter grid paper and have him number its axes. Then instruct him to color 32 green dots (representing shamrocks) and eight yellow dots (representing pots of gold) at intersecting lines anywhere on his grid. To play, he calls out a pair of numbers, such as (10, 6), and records the number pair on another sheet of paper to track his guesses. His opponent reveals whether he has found a four-leaf clover (worth one point), a pot of gold (worth five points), or neither. He records his points on his tracking sheet. Play then alternates until time is called. The player with more points wins.

adapted from an idea by Rob Siebert, Mt. Pulaski Grade School Mt. Pulaski, IL

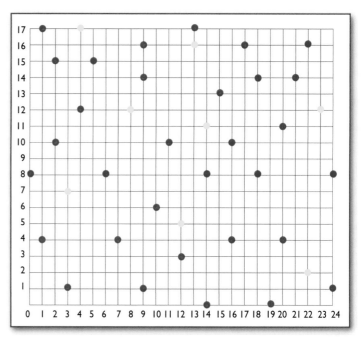

Name _____

Fix the Menu!

Write each fraction as a decimal so customers will know how much each item costs.
Then choose one item from each section and find the total cost of a meal.

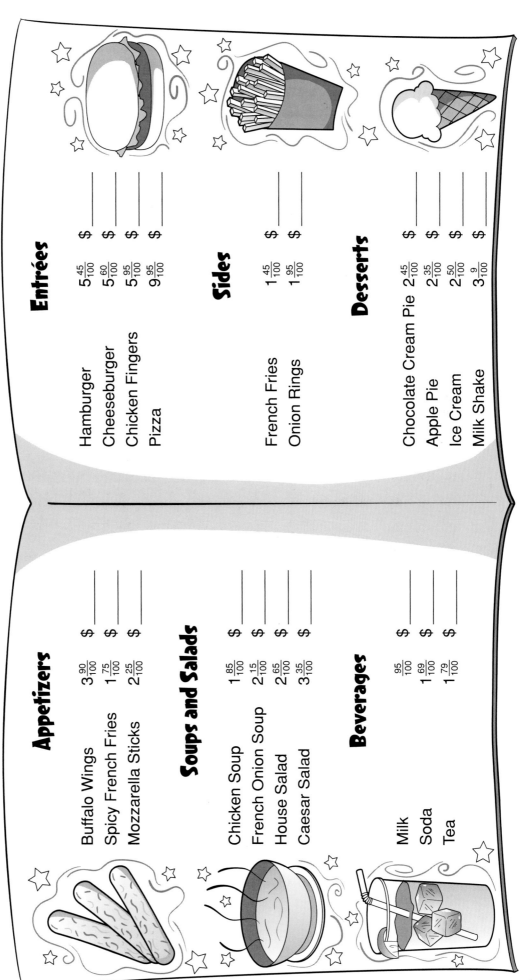

Appetizers

Buffalo Wings	$3\frac{90}{100}$	$ ____
Spicy French Fries	$1\frac{75}{100}$	$ ____
Mozzarella Sticks	$2\frac{25}{100}$	$ ____

Soups and Salads

Chicken Soup	$1\frac{85}{100}$	$ ____
French Onion Soup	$2\frac{15}{100}$	$ ____
House Salad	$2\frac{65}{100}$	$ ____
Caesar Salad	$3\frac{35}{100}$	$ ____

Beverages

Milk	$\frac{95}{100}$	$ ____
Soda	$1\frac{69}{100}$	$ ____
Tea	$1\frac{79}{100}$	$ ____

Entrées

Hamburger	$5\frac{45}{100}$	$ ____
Cheeseburger	$5\frac{60}{100}$	$ ____
Chicken Fingers	$5\frac{95}{100}$	$ ____
Pizza	$9\frac{95}{100}$	$ ____

Sides

French Fries	$1\frac{45}{100}$	$ ____
Onion Rings	$1\frac{95}{100}$	$ ____

Desserts

Chocolate Cream Pie	$2\frac{45}{100}$	$ ____
Apple Pie	$2\frac{35}{100}$	$ ____
Ice Cream	$2\frac{50}{100}$	$ ____
Milk Shake	$3\frac{9}{100}$	$ ____

©The Mailbox® • TEC44035 • Feb./Mar. 2008 • Key p. 313 • written by Jeannine Cintorino, Valley Stream, NY

Carrot Patch
Perimeter and Area

True

Good Carrots

False

Bad Carrots

Directions:
1. Draw a card.
2. Read the statement and decide whether it is true or false.
3. Place the card on the matching carrot top.
4. After sorting all the cards, turn them over to check your work.

If each side of a hexagon is ten feet long, the hexagon's perimeter is 70 feet.

The perimeter of a pentagon whose sides measure eight feet, eight feet, five feet, five feet, and six feet is 32 feet.

If one side of an equilateral triangle measures three centimeters, its perimeter is nine centimeters.

Carrot-Patch Problems

Perimeter and area

This self-checking activity is one a student can take to his seat to complete. Laminate the sorting mat on page 224 and the cards on page 225. Cut the cards apart, fold each card along the broken line so its text is to the outside, and tape the edges. Store the mat and cards in a manila envelope. To complete the activity, a student just follows the directions on the mat.

Teresa Vilfer-Snyder, Fredericktown, OH

If one side of a regular octagon is five centimeters long, the octagon's perimeter is 40 centimeters.

A trapezoid whose sides measure three feet, six feet, three feet, and 12 feet has a perimeter of 24 feet.

Chime In First!
Rounding and estimating

Use this math version of Around the World to review estimation strategies. Begin by asking the first two students to stand. Then present a problem either orally, on the overhead, or on the board. The first student to answer correctly moves to stand beside the next classmate while you prepare the next problem. The student who did not answer first sits down. If students answer simultaneously, use a tie-breaker problem. Play continues in this manner. The last student standing wins.

Jennifer Otter, Oak Ridge, NC

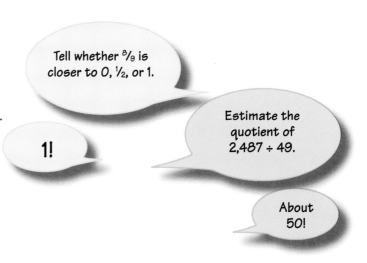

Tell whether $^8/_9$ is closer to 0, $\frac{1}{2}$, or 1.

1!

Estimate the quotient of 2,487 ÷ 49.

About 50!

25% OFF

TOP 25 HIT SONGS

Regular price $16.00
Sale price ?

To find a sale price:
1. Change the discount percent to a decimal or use the discount fraction.
   25% = 0.25   (25% = ¼)
2. regular price x decimal (or fraction) = savings
   $16.00 x 0.25 = $4.00
   ($16.00 x ¼ = $4.00)
3. regular price – savings = sale price
   $16.00 – $4.00 = $12.00

Falling Prices
Finding percentages

To help students become savvy shoppers, have them calculate the cost of sale merchandise they might find in their favorite stores. Post and discuss an example like the one shown. Next, list on the board two popular items along with a regular price and the percentage (or fraction) off for each item. (A Sunday newspaper is a good source.) Have students work alone or with a partner to find each item's reduced price. When students are finished, check the answers together. If desired, have students calculate each sale price with 7 percent tax added. Continue in this manner as time permits.

Spring Fever Reliever
Measurement, graphing, and data analysis

If warmer temperatures are making your students antsy, get them out of their seats with this physical math activity. Have groups of students make standing long jumps, measuring to the nearest quarter inch and recording three jumps per person. Instruct each group to make a bar graph showing each jumper's best distance and then calculate the data's range, median, mode, and mean. For a greater challenge, compile the data to compare the average distance jumped by the boys in each group to the girls in each group and have each child display the results in a double-bar graph.

Devin Ann Colby, Fountain Green Elementary, Bel Air, MD

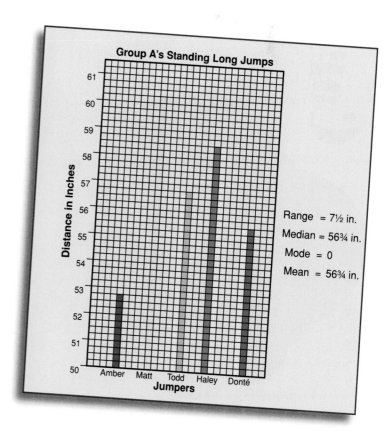

Group A's Standing Long Jumps

Distance in Inches / Jumpers: Amber, Matt, Todd, Haley, Donté

Range = 7½ in.
Median = 56¾ in.
Mode = 0
Mean = 56¾ in.

223

Carrot Patch

Perimeter and Area

False

True

Directions:
1. Draw a card.
2. Read the statement and decide whether it is true or false.
3. Place the card on the matching carrot top.
4. After sorting all the cards, turn them over to check your work.

Bad Carrots

Good Carrots

The perimeter of a square whose sides are each four centimeters in length is 16 centimeters. TEC44036 **True**	If one side of a square is seven inches long, the square's area is 28 square inches. TEC44036 **False**	A quadrilateral whose sides measure six feet, nine feet, 11 feet, and two feet has a perimeter of 24 feet. TEC44036 **False**
If one side of a square is three inches long, the square's area is 12 square inches. TEC44036 **False**	A parallelogram whose base measures 20 yards and whose height measures 15 yards has an area of 300 square yards. TEC44036 **True**	The perimeter of a pentagon whose sides measure eight feet, eight feet, five feet, five feet, and six feet is 32 feet. TEC44036 **True**
The area of a rectangle that measures 12 inches by 8 inches is 20 square inches. TEC44036 **False**	If one side of an equilateral triangle measures three centimeters, its perimeter is nine centimeters. TEC44036 **True**	A swimming pool that is ten yards long and five yards wide has an area of 15 square yards. TEC44036 **False**
If each side of a hexagon is ten feet long, the hexagon's perimeter is 70 feet. TEC44036 **False**	One side of a rhombus measures five inches. The perimeter of the rhombus is 25 inches. TEC44036 **False**	If one side of a regular octagon is five centimeters long, the octagon's perimeter is 40 centimeters. TEC44036 **True**
The area of a right triangle whose base is 12 inches and whose height is eight inches is 48 square inches. TEC44036 **True**	A trapezoid whose sides measure three feet, six feet, three feet, and 12 feet has a perimeter of 24 feet. TEC44036 **True**	If a rectangle measures 40 inches by 30 inches, its area is 700 square inches. TEC44036 **False**

A Slew of Clues

Name the solid figure being described. Use the words on the shoeprints for help. Then draw a picture of the figure.

cube

1 I have one more circular face than a cone. I am a

_____

_____.

2 I have two fewer vertices than a rectangular prism. I am a _____

_____.

pentagonal prism

triangular pyramid

3 I have the same number of edges as a cube. I am a

_____

_____.

4 I have four fewer edges than a rectangular prism. I am a

_____

_____.

sphere

5 I have five more square faces and four more edges than a square pyramid. I am a

_____

_____.

6 I have one less face, one less vertex, and two fewer edges than a square pyramid. I am a

_____

_____.

cylinder

triangular prism

rectangular prism

7 I have no faces, no vertices, and no edges. I am a

_____

_____.

8 I have two faces that are pentagons and five faces that are rectangles. I am a

_____

_____.

square pyramid

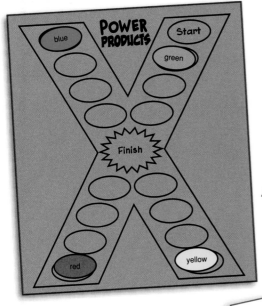

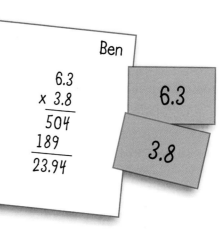

Ben

$$\begin{array}{r} 6.3 \\ \times\ 3.8 \\ \hline 504 \\ 189 \\ \hline 23.94 \end{array}$$

6.3

3.8

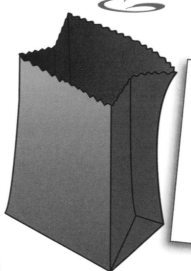

Ava

$$\begin{array}{r} 0.74 \\ \times\ 3.5 \\ \hline 370 \\ 222 \\ \hline 2.590 \end{array}$$

0.74

3.5

Power Products

Multiplication

This four-player game is an "x-cellent" way to review multiplication of whole numbers, fractions, or decimals. Give each group a copy of page 229 and a bag of index cards, each card labeled with a number you want students to multiply. Instruct one member of each group to cut out and distribute the game markers at the bottom of the page. Then have each child color his marker accordingly and place it on a space marked "Start." To play, each student takes two cards from the bag and uses a sheet of scratch paper to find the product of the cards' numbers. After players use calculators to verify their answers, the player with the highest product moves his marker to the next space. Players then return their cards to the bag and continue playing in the same manner until one player reaches "Finish."

Jennifer Otter, Oak Ridge, NC

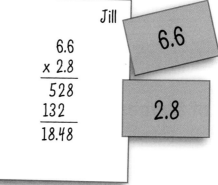

Jill

$$\begin{array}{r} 6.6 \\ \times\ 2.8 \\ \hline 528 \\ 132 \\ \hline 18.48 \end{array}$$

6.6

2.8

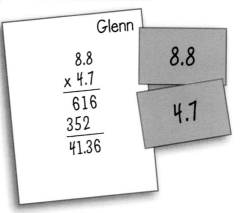

Glenn

$$\begin{array}{r} 8.8 \\ \times\ 4.7 \\ \hline 616 \\ 352 \\ \hline 41.36 \end{array}$$

8.8

4.7

Trade It!
Reviewing basic operations

For this class activity, have each child personalize a copy of a trading card from page 230. Next, announce the basic operation you want students to review. Have each child write on the back of his card a problem of that type. When he's finished, instruct him to divide both sides of a sheet of paper into four equal sections. Then have him swap his trading card with a classmate and copy and solve that child's problem in one section of his paper. Have students continue trading cards until each child has solved a problem in each of his paper's eight sections. Finally, invite each student to the board to solve his own problem. Have students check their work, giving themselves three points for attempting a problem and two more if the answer is correct!

Sarah Volinski, John T. Pirie Fine Arts & Academic Center, Chicago, IL

What's the Weight?
Metric units of mass

Students gain a better understanding of grams and kilograms with this activity. Display a paper clip, a medium-size apple, and a small textbook. Ask students to predict which object weighs about a gram, about 200 grams, and about a kilogram. Once the class agrees on each item's approximate weight, have volunteers test the predictions by weighing each item on a metric scale. Next, have each child choose an object from the classroom, weigh it on the scale, and then write on an index card a riddle about her object's weight. When students have finished their riddles, have each child trade cards with a partner and solve her partner's riddle.

adapted from an idea by Stephanie Willet-Smith, Huntersville, NC

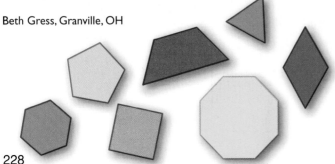

Lots of Shapes
Polygons

To help students understand the differences and similarities of various types of polygons, have each child complete a copy of page 231 as directed. If desired, provide construction paper cutouts of the polygons listed on the page for students to use as manipulatives.

Beth Gress, Granville, OH

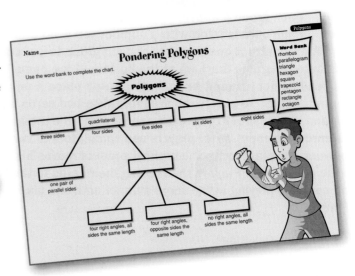

228

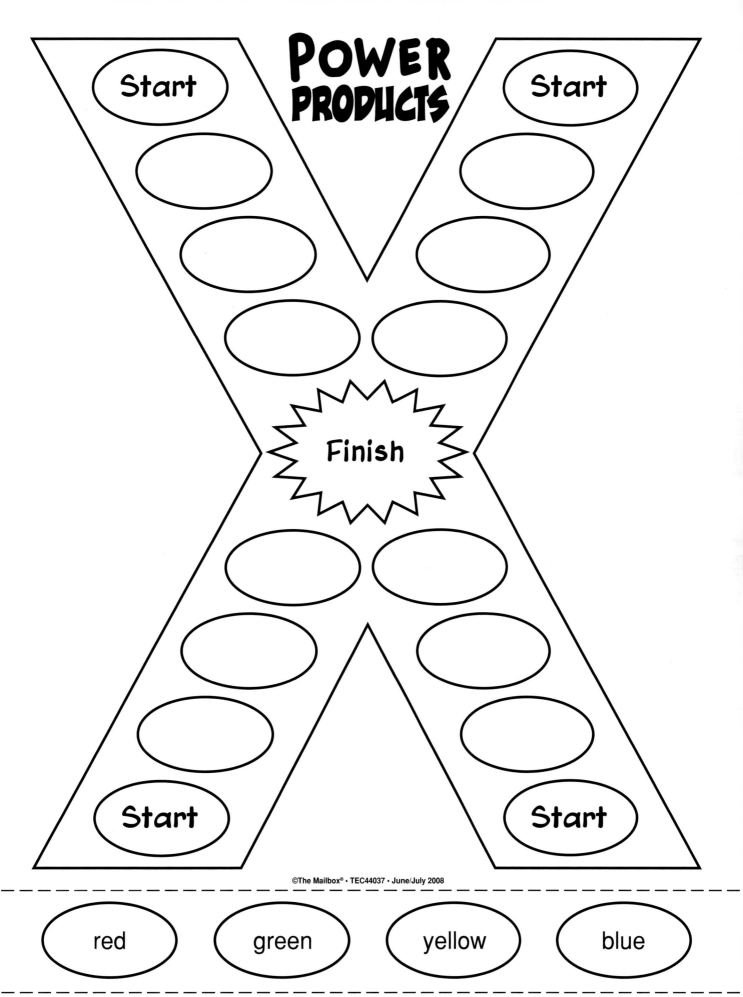

POWER PRODUCTS

Start

Start

Finish

Start

Start

red   green   yellow   blue

Note to the teacher: Use with "Power Products" on page 227.

Trading Card Patterns
Use with "Trade It!" on page 228.

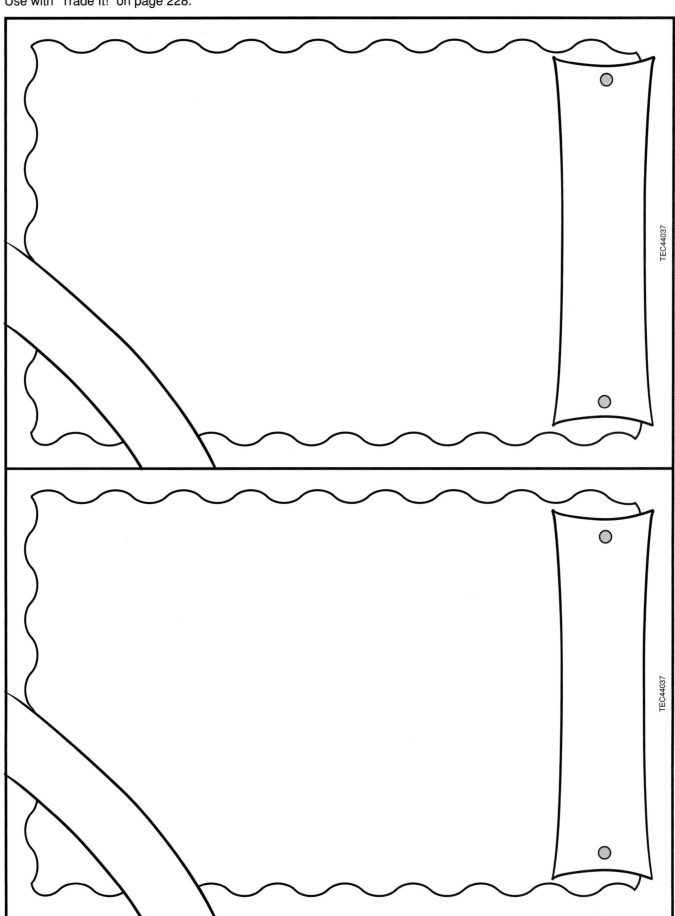

TEC44037

TEC44037

Name

Pondering Polygons

Use the word bank to complete the chart.

Word Bank
rhombus
parallelogram
triangle
hexagon
square
trapezoid
pentagon
rectangle
octagon

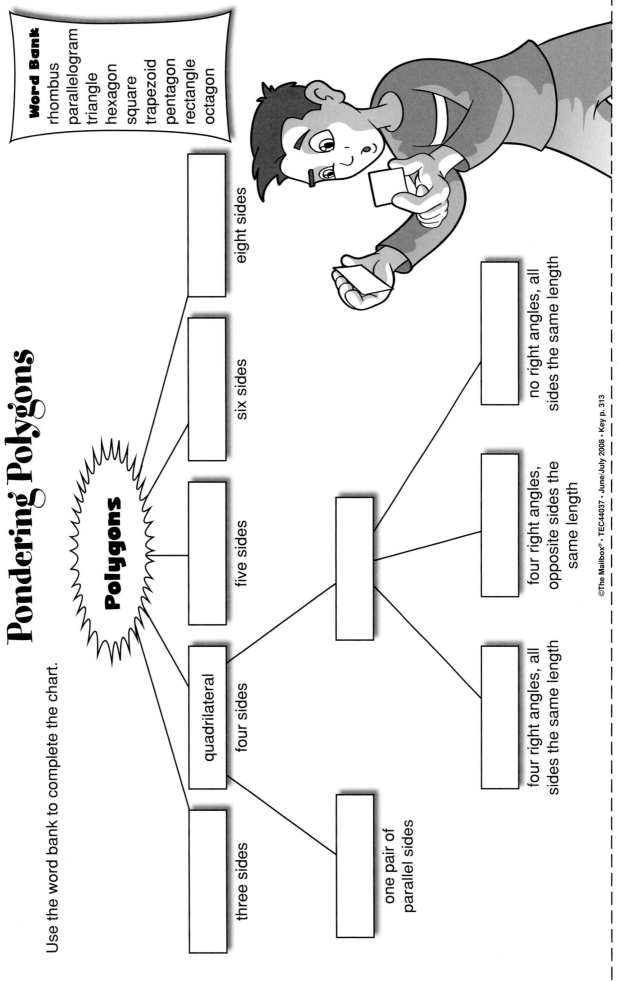

Polygons

three sides

quadrilateral — four sides

five sides

six sides

eight sides

one pair of parallel sides

four right angles, all sides the same length

four right angles, opposite sides the same length

no right angles, all sides the same length

©The Mailbox® • TEC44037 • June/July 2008 • Key p. 313

Note to the teacher: Use with "Lots of Shapes" on page 228.

Name _____

TRIPLE SCOOPS

Cut apart the ice cream scoop cards below.
Then glue each card above its matching cone.

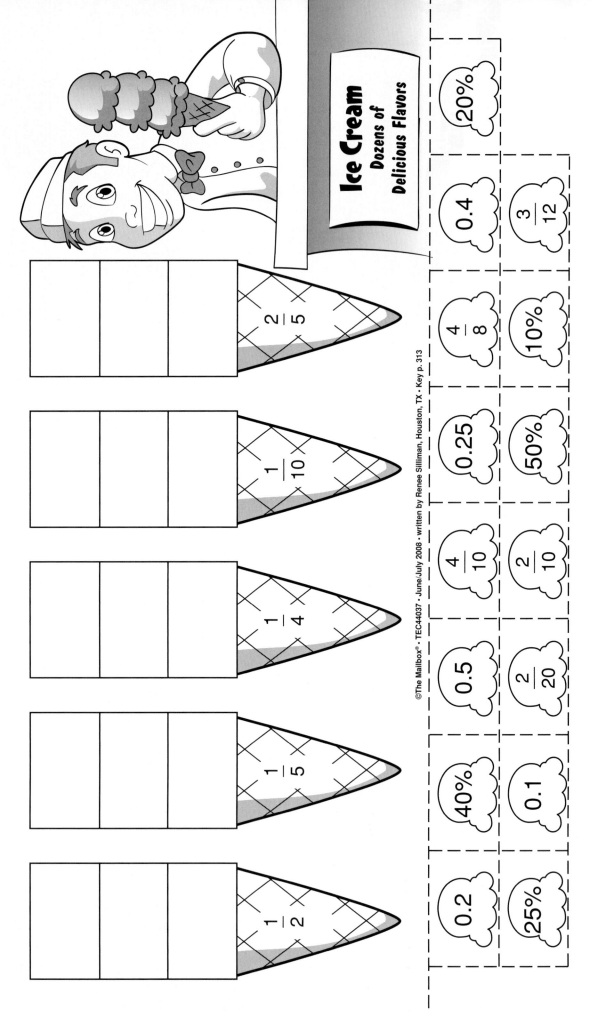

Ice Cream
Dozens of Delicious Flavors

$\frac{2}{5}$ $\frac{1}{10}$ $\frac{1}{4}$ $\frac{1}{5}$ $\frac{1}{2}$

©The Mailbox® · TEC44037 · June/July 2008 · written by Renee Silliman, Houston, TX · Key p. 313

20% 0.4 $\frac{4}{8}$ 0.25 $\frac{4}{10}$ 0.5 40% 0.2

$\frac{3}{12}$ 10% 50% $\frac{2}{10}$ $\frac{2}{20}$ 0.1 25%

232

WRITE ON!

Got Elements?
Narrative writing

Help budding authors fully develop their story-writing skills with an effective tool they can use all year long. Make copies of a form such as the one shown. After a student has completed a rough draft of his story, have him complete a copy of the form, using as much detail as possible to answer the questions. Then have the student use the form to revise his draft. Completing the form will surface elements he has forgotten to include or a lack of sufficient details. Adapt the form so students can also use it to analyze a fictional selection they've just read.

Christina Bryant, Huffman Middle School, Humble, TX

Name _____

? ? ? Got Elements? ? ? ?
1. What is the **plot** of your story?
   _____
2. What is the **setting** of your story?
   _____
3. Name the **protagonist(s)**.
   _____
4. Name the **antagonist(s)**.
   _____
5. What is the **conflict** in your story?
   _____
6. What is the **resolution** in your story?
   _____

August 29

Dear Grandma,
    For a week now, I've been dreaming of your mouthwatering apple pie! There are so many reasons why I love it and why you should bake one for me before another week goes by. First, ~~~~~~~~~ ~~~~~~~~~~ ~~~~~

Love,
Claire

A Pinch of Persuasion
Persuasive writing

Spice up letter-writing practice with a fun activity that will prove how convincing your students can be. After reviewing the format of a friendly letter, ask each child to list several of her favorite dishes. Then have her write a letter to persuade the person who normally fixes one of the dishes to do just that! Once the letter has been edited and revised, have the student copy it onto a white paper plate, adding decorations with crayons or colored pencils. After posting the plates on a bulletin board, have the writers take the letters home and deliver them to their recipients. In the days that follow, set aside time for students to share whether their persuasive pleas worked!

Joseph Lemmo, Chapman Intermediate School, Woodstock, GA

Pick a Prompt!
Journal writing

In a hurry to find an engaging writing prompt? Try one of these!
- If someone were to write a picture book about your life, what would the book's title be? Explain.
- Summer's almost over. Pretend that you can change one thing about this summer. What would you change and why?
- Write a paragraph that describes at least three ways you are different from the kid you were a year ago.
- What's the best thing about your bedroom? The worst?

Alex's
BIG
ADVENTURE

Mammals
Are warm-blooded
Are covered with hair or fur
Give birth to live young
(except for two)

Both
Are vertebrates
Have lungs
Are members of the animal kingdom

Reptiles
Are cold-blooded
Are covered with scales
Lay eggs

Batty Venn Diagram
Comparing and contrasting, paragraph writing

Sharpen writing skills this October using a unique Venn diagram. Make a class supply on gray paper of a simple bat. Have each student label the wings with the names and characteristics of two items (see the box of suggestions). Then have him write on the bat's body traits the items share. After a student completes his diagram, have him use it to write a compare-and-contrast paragraph. Create a supersimple display by having each child post his batty diagram alongside an edited copy of his paragraph.

Brooke Beverly, Dudley Elementary, Dudley, MA

Compare and contrast two

- characters in the same story or book
- events in the historical period you are studying
- literary genres you like to read
- geometric shapes you can see in the classroom
- nonfiction picture books on the same topic
- animal groups (for example, mammals and reptiles)

Timesaving Writing Labels
Managing the writing process

Eliminate the confusion of "Is this your rough draft or final draft?" with the help of your computer's label-making program. Make labels with messages such as the ones shown, using different colors or fonts to distinguish student labels from ones you use. Place the student labels at a center. Instruct students to label their assignments to indicate which draft they have completed. Use the teacher labels to save time when you're evaluating work.

adapted from an idea by Virginia Zeletzki, Banyan Creek Elementary
Delray Beach, FL

Go to the next step.

Final Draft

Student Labels
Rough Draft
First Draft
Final Draft

Teacher Labels
Read but not corrected
Correct and return.
Please see me.
Incomplete
Go to the next step.
Please self-edit.
Creative work!

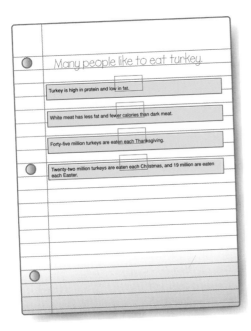

Many people like to eat turkey.

Turkey is high in protein and low in fat.

White meat has less fat and fewer calories than dark meat.

Forty-five million turkeys are eaten each Thanksgiving.

Twenty-two million turkeys are eaten each Christmas, and 19 million are eaten each Easter.

Let's Talk Turkey!
Topic sentences, paragraph writing

For this partner activity, each pair of students cuts apart the turkey fact strips on page 237 and sorts them by topic into four groups. For each group, students write a topic sentence on a separate sheet of paper and arrange the facts under it to form a good paragraph. After taping the facts in place, the pair chooses one paragraph to rewrite on another sheet of paper. Encourage students to combine or revise facts to make the best paragraph possible and to include a title. Post the paragraphs with cutout feathers on a display titled "Let's Talk Turkey!"

Cynthia Holcomb, San Angelo, TX

Pick a Prompt!
Journal Writing

No time to scare up a writing activity? Use one of these prompts!

- Leaves change color in the fall. What's one thing about yourself you hope will *never* change? Explain your answer.

- Pretend you write for a kids' magazine. Write a brief article that explains to your readers how to go trick-or-treating safely.

- Persuade a family that has always served turkey on Thanksgiving Day to eat pizza on the big day instead.

- Think about a person you are thankful to know. Tell a story about an experience you had with him or her.

I hope I never stop being a good soccer player!

Use with "Let's Talk Turkey!" on page 236.

Turkey is high in protein and low in fat.

TEC44033

A wild turkey can run as fast as 20 miles per hour.

A turkey can see movement from almost 100 yards away.

The leading turkey-producing states in 2003 were Arkansas, Minnesota, Missouri, North Carolina, and Virginia.

White meat has less fat and fewer calories than dark meat.

Domesticated turkeys, which are raised on farms, cannot fly.

TEC44033

Forty-five million turkeys are eaten each Thanksgiving.

When turkeys are excited, their heads change colors.

Twenty-two million turkeys are eaten each Christmas, and 19 million are eaten each Easter.

Wild turkeys stay in trees at night.

All male turkeys and some female turkeys have beards. These beards are black hairlike feathers on their breasts.

TEC44033

The heaviest domesticated turkey ever raised weighed 86 pounds.

Wild turkeys can fly as fast as 55 miles per hour for short distances.

TEC44033

In 2003, turkey growers in the United States raised 270 million turkeys.

Though they don't have ears like humans, turkeys have good hearing.

Today wild turkeys can be found in every state except Alaska.

WRITE ON!

Kentucky Santa

State Santa Subs
Narrative writing, research skills

To introduce this jolly writing activity, announce that Santa is taking a year off from his exhausting holiday duty and that each state must now find its own St. Nick substitute. Next, assign each student a state to research. Then have her complete a copy of the narrative-writing activity on page 240. Have her also draw a picture of her one-of-a-kind Santa sub to display with her story!

Cynthia Nash, Harrison Elementary, Warsaw, IN

Name _____

My State's Santa

Narrative writing

Fill in the organizer using information about your assigned state,
Kentucky

Gone Fishing

What will your Santa wear?

What or who might he meet along the way?

What kind of transportation will Santa use?

What route will Santa take around your state?

What other special characteristics does your state's Santa have?

On your own paper, write a story about the Christmas Eve when your state's Santa delivered gifts.

Thanks for the Fruitcake?
Audience and purpose

To prepare for this thank-you note activity, discuss with students the importance of thanking gift givers even if they aren't thrilled with the present they receive. Then share the thank-you note framework shown. Next, fill a bag with paper slips labeled with gifts (some good, some not so good) and fill another bag with silly gift-giver names. Then have each child draw a slip from each bag and write a thank-you note. To share the notes, have each child redraw a gift-giver slip and pretend to be that person. Instruct the classmate who wrote to that gift giver to deliver his note to him or her; then have the gift giver read it aloud to the class.

Courtney English, Southeast Middle School, Salisbury, NC

Thank-You Note Framework
- Beginning: Thank the giver and mention the gift.
- Middle: Explain how you plan to enjoy or use the gift.
- Ending: End with a positive comment or wish.

banana-cherry-and-avocado fruitcake

Grandma Chompers

Dear Grandma Chompers,
Thank you so much for the large banana-cherry-and-avocado fruitcake you gave me for Christmas. Though I've never had fruitcake, I sure have heard a lot about it! I plan on serving it next week when you come over for dinner. I am really looking forward to seeing you and Grandpa Chompers!
Love,
Amelia

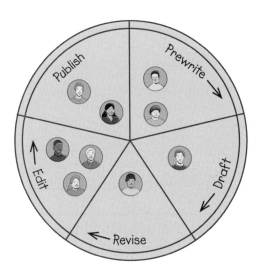

Pizza Pan Organizer
Writing process

Keep track of where each student is in the writing process with the help of a large metal pizza pan. Use a permanent marker to divide the pan into one section for each writing process step. Next, glue a photo of each student on a cardboard circle. If desired, laminate the circles. Then attach a piece of magnetic tape to the back of each circle. As a child moves through the writing process, he places his photo in the appropriate section of the pan. A quick glance tells you where each student is in his work.

Linda Biondi, Pond Road Middle School, Robbinsville, NJ

Pick a Prompt!
Journal writing

If your holiday wish list includes sensational writing prompts, try these!

- You have just awakened to find Frosty the Snowman at the foot of your bed. Write the conversation you have with him.
- Persuade Santa to come to your house and fill your stocking a week before Christmas Eve.
- Tell about your most vivid holiday memory. What happened and how did it make you feel?
- Describe the sights, sounds, and smells of a crowded mall during the last shopping day of the holiday season.

DUDE, YOU OVERSLEPT!

My State's Santa

Fill in the organizer using information about your assigned state,

_____.

What will your Santa wear?

What kind of transportation will Santa use?

What route will Santa take around your state?

What or who might he meet along the way?

What other special characteristics does your state's Santa have?

On your own paper, write a story about the Christmas Eve when your state's Santa delivered gifts.

Looking around, the pickle sees a peaceful, interesting room. The room has round tables with chairs. In one corner, there are large fluffy pillows and an orange rug. The rug is fuzzy and very soft. There is a shelf at the front of the room that is full of colorful magazines. Stacked as they are, the magazines remind the pickle of a patchwork quilt. On the desk is a silver vase of beautiful yellow flowers. They smell like expensive perfume. The

Pickle In a Pickle
Descriptive writing, sensory details

How do you help a pickle that's in a pickle? Find out with a silly writing prompt that provides serious practice with key writing skills. Share with students the prompt at the top of page 243. Then have each student complete a copy of the page. Read each resulting description aloud, omitting any mention of the pickle's actual location. Then challenge the class to identify the pickle's hiding place. For fun, have each student use construction paper and other art materials to create his pickle character. Post each pickle character with its description on a display titled "In a Pickle!"

Jo Ann Brandenburg, Ashland, KY

Drawing Directions
Expository writing

For a high-interest activity on writing directions, ask your librarian to gather one or more of Ed Emberley's cartooning books, such as *Ed Emberley's Drawing Book of Animals* or *Ed Emberley's Picture Pie*. In these books, Emberley gives step-by-step diagrams (with little or no text) showing how to draw simple animals and objects. Place the books at a center. A student chooses a diagram and writes a list of directions that could be recorded beneath each of the diagram's illustrations. Then he gives his list to a partner to see if she can recreate the picture. For a whole-class activity, display several students' directions using an overhead projector and challenge the class to recreate the pictures. Have the class suggest ways to revise directions that need improvement.

Kathryn Sandler, Shekou International School, Shekou-Shenzhen, China

How to Draw a Bird
1. Draw a circle. Divide the circle into fourths.
2. Erase the fourth that is on the top right. Then erase the other dividing lines. Color the shape red. This makes a bird's body.
3. Draw two black parallel lines sticking out from the bottom of the body to make the bird's legs.
4. Draw a triangle poking into the back of the bird's body to make the bird's tail. Color it red.
5. Draw a small triangle at the front of the body to make a beak. Color it yellow.
6. Draw a black eye on the bird.

Hey, I got a letter from Jack!

Possible Stories

Snow White and the Seven Dwarfs
Cinderella
Jack and the Beanstalk
Rumpelstiltskin
The Elves and the Shoemaker
Hansel and Gretel
The Three Billy Goats Gruff

P.S. Please Write Back!
Narrative writing, letter writing

Practice key writing skills with an activity that's close to being letter-perfect! Discuss with students how a story could be told through a series of delightful letters exchanged between fairy-tale characters, such as Peter Rabbit, Goldilocks, and the three pigs. Next, brainstorm with students a list of other familiar traditional stories or fairy tales (see the list shown). Then have each student or student pair write two or three short letters between characters from different stories. If desired, have the student illustrate each letter. Then have her bind her work between decorated covers to make her own letter-based picture book.

Laura Corwon, Parma Park Elementary, Parma Heights, OH

School is now dismissed.

Pick a Prompt!
Journal writing

- In a letter to your school board, persuade board members to vote to allow an early dismissal on Valentine's Day.

- Presidents' Day is in February. If you could spend a day hanging out with the president, what would you like to do? Explain.

- St. Patrick's Day is associated with good luck. If you could give good luck to any person in the world (besides yourself), to whom would you give it? Why?

- March weather can be very unpredictable. Would your friends describe you as being predictable most of the time or unpredictable? Explain.

Pickle In a Pickle

Read.

Last night an uneaten pickle escaped from the lunchbox you forgot to take home. It became lost in your school. Fortunately, the pickle found a phone and called you to describe its location.

EEK! I'm **lost**!

Complete.

Fill in the organizer with the details the pickle gave you about this place in your school.

What does the
pickle see?

What does the
pickle smell?

What does the
pickle hear?

What does the
pickle taste?

Where is your
pickle located?

What things has the
pickle touched?

Write.

On another sheet of paper, write a description of this location. Use the details from above.

Note to the teacher: Use with "Pickle In a Pickle" on page 241.

243

Isn't the Future Fabulous?
Narrative writing, writing a five-paragraph essay

Fast-forward to the future with a writing activity that includes a helpful graphic organizer. To begin, give each student a copy of page 246 and list on the board the text shown. Then tell students they have won a one-day trip to the distant future in a time machine. Explain that they are each allowed to visit one of the places listed. After each child writes a destination in the title blank, have him complete the planning sheet as directed and then use it to help him write a five-paragraph essay about his journey. If desired, have students who finish their essays early create a time machine to display with the completed stories.

adapted from an idea by Jennifer Hileman, Harvest Christian School, Kittanning, PA

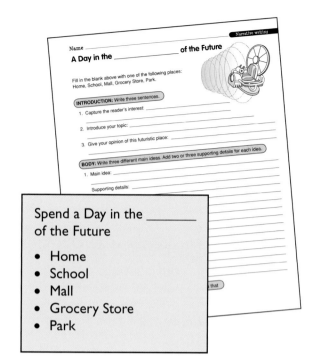

Spend a Day in the _____ of the Future

- Home
- School
- Mall
- Grocery Store
- Park

Persuasive Paragraph Framework

1. Topic sentence stating your position
2. Reason 1 (with a transition word)
3. Supporting ideas
4. Reason 2 (with a transition word)
5. Supporting ideas
6. Reason 3 (with a transition word)
7. Supporting ideas
8. Concluding sentence(s)

When you're so hungry you could eat a bear, grab a big bowl of beets instead!

Food for Thought
Persuasive writing

Strengthen writing and critical-thinking skills with this activity, which focuses on not-so-favorite foods. Ask each student to draw (or cut from an old magazine) a picture of a food she totally dislikes. Next, have each child write a paragraph to persuade others that her selected food is not the worst but is the *best* on the planet! To help students plan and organize their paragraphs, display the framework shown. Remind students to use transition words—such as *another, in addition,* or *finally*—to signal the reader that a new reason is being given. To extend the activity, have each student create a magazine advertisement or a television commercial promoting her food.

Barrilyn Kaa, Fountain Valley, CA

Pick a Prompt!
Journal writing

- April Fools' Day is April 1. Tell about a time you did something that made you feel very foolish.

- Describe the sights, sounds, and smells of your classroom on a rainy April day.

- Write a letter to persuade your school superintendent that spring break should be two weeks long.

- Mother's Day is the second Sunday in May. Write a list of directions titled "Ten Ways to Make Your Mom REALLY Happy."

Never stick a small bucket on a big head!

A Noun With Personality

Hey, Friendship, it's for you!

Step 1

Circle an abstract noun in the list.

Step 2

Answer these questions about your abstract noun.

What is your noun often seen doing? _____
_____

What are some of your noun's favorites, such as favorite color,
food, or music? _____
_____

What does your noun like to do for fun? _____
_____

What makes your noun very happy? _____
_____

What really gets on your noun's nerves? _____
_____

What things is your noun good at doing? _____
_____

What things is your noun not so good at doing? _____
_____

What major goal does your noun have? _____
_____

Abstract Nouns
Affection
Anger
Boredom
Confidence
Embarrassment
Enthusiasm
Fear
Freedom
Friendship
Hope
Injustice
Jealousy
Joy
Loneliness
Love
Peace
Sadness
Shame

Step 3

Use your answers above in a descriptive paragraph about your noun.
Write your paragraph on a separate sheet of paper.

A Day in the _____ of the Future

Fill in the blank above with one of the following places:
Home, School, Mall, Grocery Store, Park.

INTRODUCTION: Write three sentences.

1. Capture the reader's interest: _____

_____

2. Introduce your topic: _____

_____

3. Give your opinion of this futuristic place: _____

_____

BODY: Write three different main ideas. Add two or three supporting details for each idea.

1. Main idea: _____

_____

Supporting details: _____

_____

_____

2. Main idea: _____

_____

Supporting details: _____

_____

_____

3. Main idea: _____

_____

Supporting details: _____

_____

_____

CONCLUSION: On the back of this page, write sentences that

- Summarize your main ideas
- Restate your opinion using different words

Note to the teacher: Use with "Isn't the Future Fabulous?" on page 244.

WRITE ON!

Enjoying a sunset horseback ride in Jamaica

pink, blue, and purple sky

waves lapping the shore

salty taste on my lips

small colorful fish in the water

splashes of water as the horses walk

creak of the saddles

light breeze blowing my face

crystal clear blue water

Can't You Just Picture It?

Narrative or descriptive writing, sensory details

Here's how to turn pictures from used magazines and a stack of file folders into reusable tools that help students add vivid details to their stories and descriptions. Glue on the left side of each opened file folder a magazine picture with an interesting setting. Add a caption that gives information about where the picture was (or might have been) taken; then laminate the folders. Invite each student to choose a folder and an overhead pen. As you ask the questions shown, have him list sensory details about the pictured setting on the folder's right side. Then have him use the details to write a brief story about or description of the picture. At the end of the activity, he wipes the folder clean so it's ready to use again!

Tracy Swain, H. Ashton Marsh School, Absecon, NJ

Questions
- What do you see in your picture?
- What colors do you see?
- What sounds do you hear?
- What do you taste?
- What do you feel with your sense of touch?
- What scents do you smell?

Tie It All Together!
Prewriting for an informational report

Help students learn to write organized reports using the handy graphic organizer on page 249. After each student writes his report's title or topic on the tie rack, have him list each subtopic on a tie's knot. Then he's ready to jot related details on the ties. When it's time to write the rough draft, he'll have no trouble tying his information together into a well-organized report.

Kim Minafo, Apex, NC

To boost reading comprehension, have students use the organizer to organize their thoughts about a nonfiction text they've read!

Name _____

Tie It All Together! [Prewriting]

Title/topic: _____

Subtopic   Subtopic   Subtopic   Subtopic

Details   Details   Details   Details

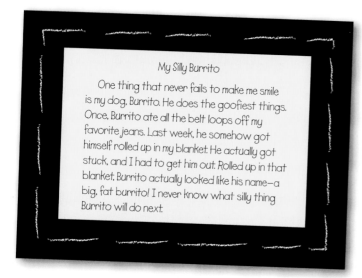

My Silly Burrito

One thing that never fails to make me smile is my dog, Burrito. He does the goofiest things. Once, Burrito ate all the belt loops off my favorite jeans. Last week, he somehow got himself rolled up in my blanket. He actually got stuck, and I had to get him out. Rolled up in that blanket, Burrito actually looked like his name—a big, fat burrito! I never know what silly thing Burrito will do next.

Miles of Smiles
Personal narrative

For this smile-inducing activity, each student brainstorms a list of things that make her smile. After five minutes, the student chooses from her list one item and talks about it with a partner. When everyone has shared, each child writes nonstop for five minutes (without worrying about spelling or punctuation) about her chosen topic. At the end of the time limit, students edit and then recopy their work on large index cards. If desired, have each student tape her card on black paper and draw white chalk lines around the border to simulate a highway. Post the projects on a display titled "Miles of Smiles."

Christina Bryant, Huffman Middle School, Humble, TX

Pick a Prompt!
Journal writing

- Pretend you're an adult who never gets the summer off like most schoolchildren do. Write a journal entry telling how you feel as you leave for work on the first day of your kids' summer vacation.

- Lots of new movies come out in the summer months. If you were to make a movie based on this school year, what would you title it and what would be the movie's main events? Explain.

- In Australia, winter lasts from June to August. Would you like having cold weather during your summer vacation? Why or why not?

- Imagine that it is 20 years from now. You open the newspaper, and a headline is about you. What is the headline, and why are you in the news?

What I wouldn't give to take the whole summer off!

See page 250 for a great end-of-the-year writing activity!

Tie It All Together!

Name

Title/topic: _____

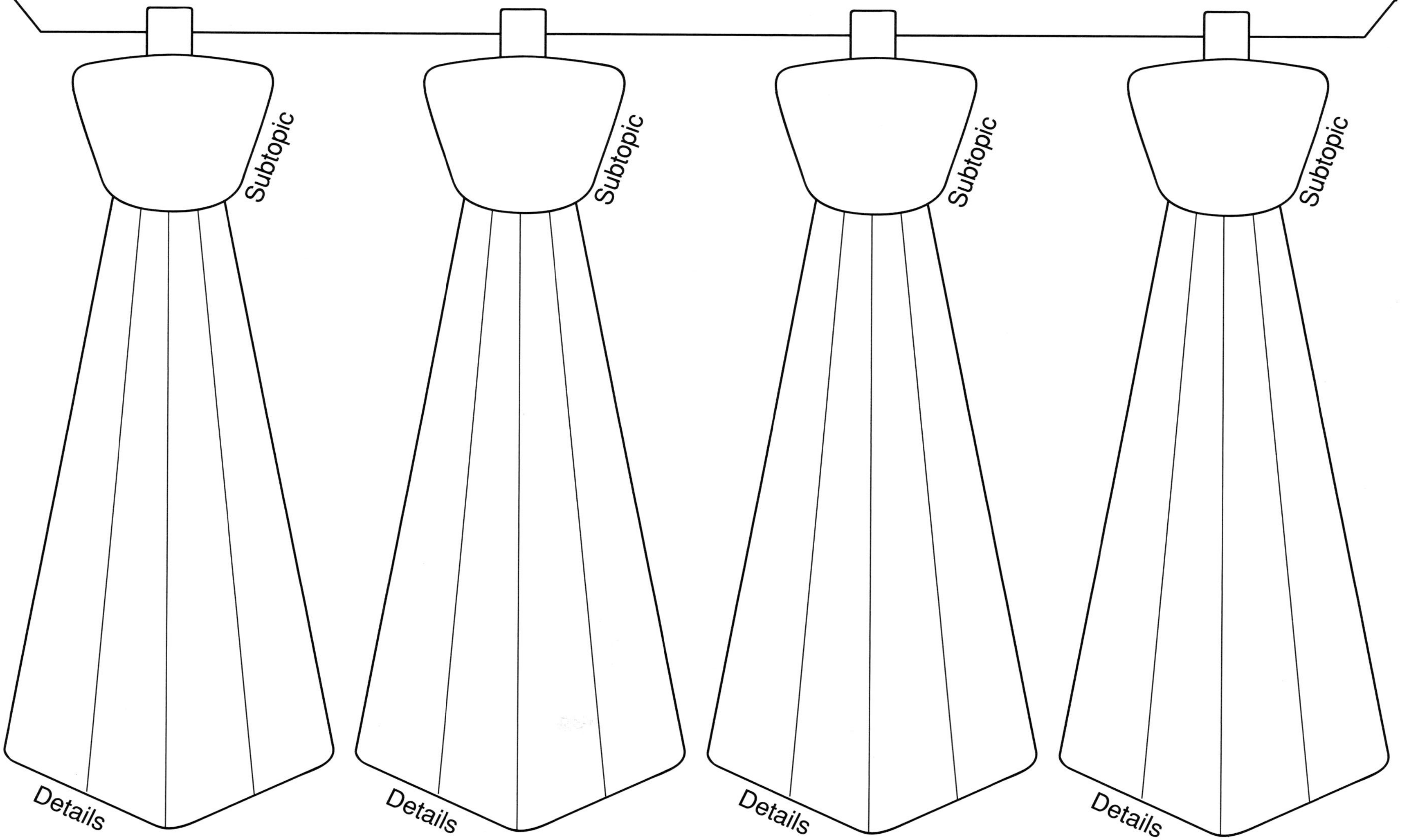

Subtopic

Subtopic

Subtopic

Subtopic

Details

Details

Details

Details

Note to the teacher: Use with "Tie It All Together!" on page 248.

Moving Up

A group of students who will be in your grade next year have asked for your help. They are nervous about next year and want to know what to expect. Your job is to convince them that they will have a great year.

I'm a little nervous...

Step 1: State why you think these younger kids should look forward to next year.

Step 2: What questions will these kids ask you when you tell them not to worry about next year?

-
-
-

Step 3: How will you answer those questions?

-
-
-

Step 4: On another sheet of paper, write an essay to convince the students in the grade below yours that they can look forward to next year. Keep the questions they might ask in mind to help you write a stronger essay.

SIMPLY SCIENCE

"Sediment-al" Journey

Earth science

Reinforce an understanding of erosion and deposition with this moving activity. Scatter one-inch color tiles on the classroom floor. Next, review with students how the forces of erosion—water, wind, and glaciers—move sediment. Then divide students into four teams: water, wind, glaciers, and deposition. Give the erosion teams about 20 seconds to move from one side of the room to the other, picking up tiles as they go. When they're finished, discuss what happened to the tiles *(they were moved)* and what forces caused the movement *(wind, water, and glaciers)*. Instruct the erosion teams to give their tiles to members of the deposition team. Have those students put the tiles back on the floor. Again, discuss what happened to the tiles *(they were moved)*. Also discuss whether all tiles were returned to their original positions *(no)*. Finally, have students tell what landforms could be built by the process they modeled *(sand dunes, deltas, etc.)*.

Amy Heuer, West Lane Elementary, Jackson, MO

It's "Element-ary," Watson!
Physical science

"What does chemistry have to do with my life anyway?" Have students answer that question for themselves by completing this unique project. After teaching about elements and the periodic table, give each child a copy of the chart on page 254 to use as a reference. Have him create a poster that features a title and a grid or chart that includes 20 elements arranged by atomic number with each element's name and symbol. Have him also include a picture or an object for each element that represents how it is a part of his life. For example, copper can be represented by a penny and sodium by a fast-food packet of salt. Then provide time for students to share their posters with the class or in a small group.

Melody J. Hagans, West Lane Elementary, Jackson, MO

Where Does It Belong?
Life science

Bring order to classifying living things with this bulletin board activity. After studying the classifications of living things, gather nature books and magazines that contain colorful pictures. Also divide a board into five equal sections, labeling one section for each kingdom. Next, divide students into five groups: plants, animals, fungi, protists, and monerans. Give each group one or two sentence strips, several large index cards, and access to the books and magazines. Instruct the group to label its sentence strip with characteristics of its assigned kingdom and glue magazine cutouts or make original drawings of examples of living things from that kingdom on the cards. When the groups are finished, have them share their work with the class. Then display each group's work in the appropriate section of the board.

adapted from an idea by Shawna Miller, Denton, TX

Monerans
one-celled, no cell nuclei, some make their own food, some feed on other living things

bacteria

Edible Moon Phases
Earth science

Culminate a study of the moon with an out-of-this-world activity that includes a yummy treat! Give each child a MoonPie cookie, a plastic knife, a paper plate, and a copy of the moon phase illustrations on page 255. Then divide students into eight groups, one for each moon phase. Instruct each child to remove her cookie's wrapper, place the cookie in the center of her plate, and trace around the cookie to make a circle. Then have her refer to her copy of the illustrations and carefully cut her cookie to represent her group's assigned moon phase. After you check her work, she can eat her treat!

Laurel Aikin, Bayside Academy, Daphne, AL

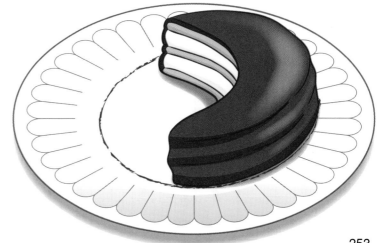

Periodic Chart of Elements

Element	Symbol	Atomic Number	Element	Symbol	Atomic Number	Element	Symbol	Atomic Number	Element	Symbol	Atomic Number
Hydrogen	H	1	Titanium	Ti	22	Technetium	Tc	43	Gadolinium	Gd	64
Helium	He	2	Vanadium	V	23	Ruthenium	Ru	44	Terbium	Tb	65
Lithium	Li	3	Chromium	Cr	24	Rhodium	Rh	45	Dysprosium	Dy	66
Beryllium	Be	4	Manganese	Mn	25	Palladium	Pd	46	Holmium	Ho	67
Boron	B	5	Iron	Fe	26	Silver	Ag	47	Erbium	Er	68
Carbon	C	6	Cobalt	Co	27	Cadmium	Cd	48	Thulium	Tm	69
Nitrogen	N	7	Nickel	Ni	28	Indium	In	49	Ytterbium	Yb	70
Oxygen	O	8	Copper	Cu	29	Tin	Sn	50	Lutetium	Lu	71
Fluorine	F	9	Zinc	Zn	30	Antimony	Sb	51	Hafnium	Hf	72
Neon	Ne	10	Gallium	Ga	31	Tellurium	Te	52	Tantalum	Ta	73
Sodium	Na	11	Germanium	Ge	32	Iodine	I	53	Tungsten	W	74
Magnesium	Mg	12	Arsenic	As	33	Xenon	Xe	54	Rhenium	Re	75
Aluminum	Al	13	Selenium	Se	34	Cesium	Cs	55	Osmium	Os	76
Silicon	Si	14	Bromine	Br	35	Barium	Ba	56	Iridium	Ir	77
Phosphorus	P	15	Krypton	Kr	36	Lanthanum	La	57	Platinum	Pt	78
Sulfur	S	16	Rubidium	Rb	37	Cerium	Ce	58	Gold	Au	79
Chlorine	Cl	17	Strontium	Sr	38	Praseodymium	Pr	59	Mercury	Hg	80
Argon	Ar	18	Yttrium	Y	39	Neodymium	Nd	60	Thallium	Tl	81
Potassium	K	19	Zirconium	Zr	40	Promethium	Pm	61	Lead	Pb	82
Calcium	Ca	20	Niobium	Nb	41	Samarium	Sm	62	Bismuth	Bi	83
Scandium	Sc	21	Molybdenum	Mo	42	Europium	Eu	63	Polonium	Po	84

Element	Symbol	Atomic Number
Astatine	At	85
Radon	Rn	86
Francium	Fr	87
Radium	Ra	88
Actinium	Ac	89
Thorium	Th	90
Protactinium	Pa	91
Uranium	U	92
Neptunium	Np	93
Plutonium	Pu	94
Americium	Am	95
Curium	Cm	96
Berkelium	Bk	97
Californium	Cf	98
Einsteinium	Es	99
Fermium	Fm	100
Mendelevium	Md	101
Nobelium	No	102
Lawrencium	Lr	103
Rutherfordium	Rf	104
Dubnium	Db	105
Seaborgium	Sg	106
Bohrium	Bh	107
Hassium	Hs	108
Meitnerium	Mt	109
Darmstadtium	Ds	110
Roentgenium	Rg	111

©The Mailbox® • TEC44032 • Aug./Sept. 2007

Note to the teacher: Use with "It's 'Element-ary,' Watson!" on page 253.

Moon Phases

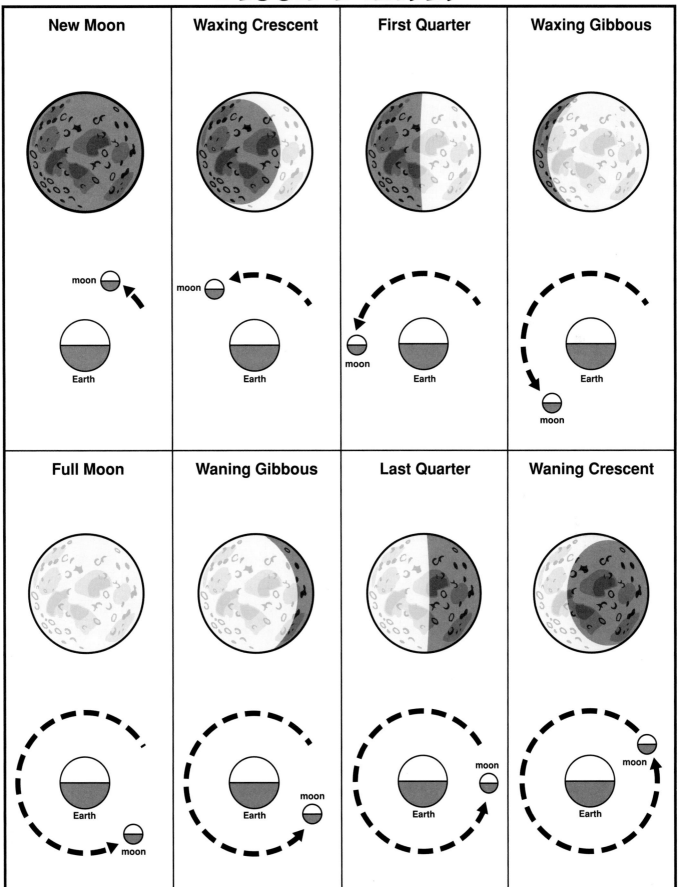

New Moon	Waxing Crescent	First Quarter	Waxing Gibbous
moon / Earth	moon / Earth	moon / Earth	Earth / moon

Full Moon	Waning Gibbous	Last Quarter	Waning Crescent
Earth / moon	Earth / moon	Earth / moon	Earth / moon

Drip Tips

Life science

Try this easy experiment to demonstrate a rain forest plant adaptation known as a *drip tip*. A drip tip is a pointed shape that helps extra water drain off a leaf. Without it, a leaf would be vulnerable to mold and insects. After students complete the activity, have them discuss these questions:

- How did water flow over each shape? *(Water will flow more quickly off the leaf cutout; it will puddle more in the center of the square and circle shapes.)*
- Which shape caused water to run off more quickly and efficiently? *(The leaf cutout was the most efficient shape.)*
- What might happen to leaves if they did not have drip tips? *(The leaves could become vulnerable to mold and insects.)*

Elizabeth M. Loeser, Jacksonville, FL

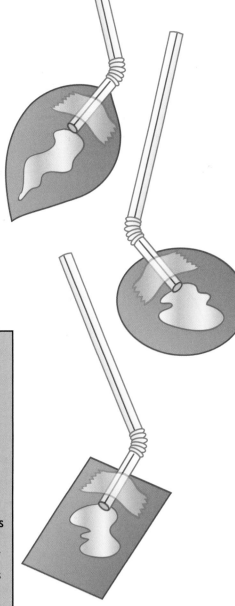

Materials for each student or small group:
copy of page 258
poster board
scissors
3 plastic flexible straws
tape
measuring cup or beaker of water colored with food coloring
dishpan, large bowl, or sink

Steps:
1. Trace the patterns on page 258 onto the poster board. Cut the tracings out.
2. Bend each straw into an L shape. Tape the first inch of the short end of the straw to a cutout where indicated so that the straw opening points to the center of the shape.
3. Hold the shape over the dishpan so that the long part of the straw is vertical and the shape is horizontal. Slowly pour water into the straw. Observe how the water flows over each shape.

Cloud Couplets
Earth science

To help students remember the different kinds of clouds, integrate a little poetry into your weather unit. Divide the class into groups and assign each group a cloud type. Challenge each group to create a couplet that describes its assigned cloud. After checking the poems for accuracy, have each group use construction paper, cotton balls, and other art materials to make a model featuring its cloud couplet.

Holly S. McCully, West Elementary, East Rochester, OH

Cumulonimbus clouds mean a storm is near.

Look out! Thunder and wind could soon be here!

Can You Hear Me Now?
Life science

tick tick

For this perfect-for-Halloween science activity, explain to students that bats use echoes of their own high-pitched squeaks to help them navigate as they fly at night. The sound bounces off objects, and the bat's large ears catch the sound. To simulate this adaptation, tape a large sheet (such as 22" x 28") of thin poster board to create a cone with a one- or two-inch opening in the small end. Have a student sit two feet from a ticking alarm clock and listen for its sound. Then have her place the small end of the cone near her ear with the large end toward the clock and listen again. The student should be able to hear the clock more clearly with the cone. Explain that the cone acts like a bat's ears, catching more sound waves than the smaller human ear. Place the cone and clock at a center so the rest of the class can try the batty experiment during free time.

Jennifer Otter, Oak Ridge, NC

Under Pressure
Physical science

Demonstrate depth and water pressure with this simple experiment. Poke two holes in the side of a two-liter soda bottle—one at the top and one at the bottom. Cover each hole with duct tape. Then fill the bottle with water and secure the cap. Have a student hold the bottle over an empty dishpan. Simultaneously remove both pieces of tape, asking students to observe from which hole water sprays farther away from the bottle *(the bottom hole)*. Ask students whether they can explain the results *(the water pressure near the bottom hole is higher because of the weight of the water)*. Explain that water pressure in the ocean increases greatly with depth. This means that divers must use special equipment to protect themselves from the extremely high water pressure.

Bonnie Pettifor, Urbana, IL

Shape Patterns
Use with "Drip Tips" on page 256.

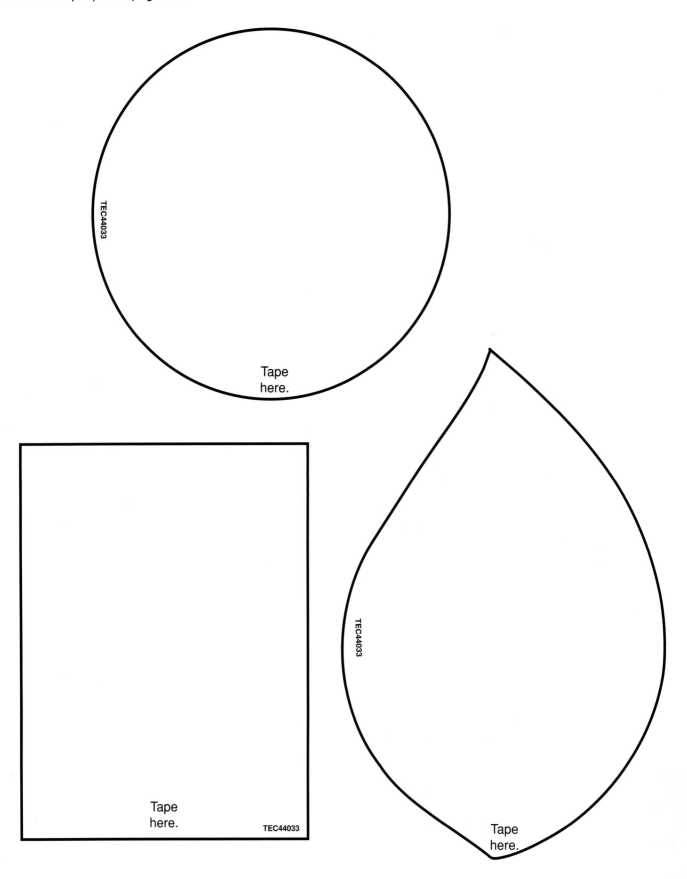

TEC44033

Tape
here.

Tape
here.

TEC44033

TEC44033

Tape
here.

SIMPLY SCIENCE

Treasures From the Sea

Directions:
1. Shuffle the cards and stack them on the mat.
2. Draw a card.
3. Decide whether the resource on the card is renewable or nonrenewable.
4. Place the card on the matching treasure chest.
5. When all the cards have been placed, check your answers with the key.

Renewable Resources

Nonrenewable Resources

clams

iron

sea salt

natural gas

tuna

©The Mailbox® • TEC44034 • Dec./Jan. 2007–8

Deep-Sea Treasures

Earth science

Transform students into explorers who discover the ocean's renewable and nonrenewable resources with the help of this cool sorting center. Mount pages 261 and 262 on separate sheets of construction paper. Cut out the cards and answer key on page 262 and place them in a large plastic bag along with the sorting mat on page 261. Send an individual child or a small group of students to the center to sort the cards according to the directions on the mat. After students check their answers with the key, be sure they shuffle the cards for the next player or players.

Diane Coffman, Lawrence, KS

Paper Bag Lungs
Life science

When teaching about the respiratory system, have students make these nifty models. Give each child two lunch-size paper bags, two plastic straws, markers, and tape. Instruct him to draw bronchioles and alveoli on the front of each bag (lung) and add labels as shown. Next, have him twist each bag around one end of a straw, secure it with tape, and then tape the straws together at the top to represent a trachea (windpipe). After students practice breathing in and out through their models to observe how the lungs inflate and deflate, have the class discuss the function of each illustrated part.

Christmas Circuitry
Physical science

December is a perfect time for teaching about series and parallel circuits. Why? Because of all the holiday lights being displayed! Plug in a set of lights with large bulbs that stay lit when a bulb is removed. Ask students to guess which type of circuit the set represents (series or parallel) and to explain their decisions. Then, using an oven mitt, remove one of the bulbs and have students observe what happens. *(The rest of the bulbs stay lit.)* Repeat the procedure using a set of lights with small twinkling bulbs that do not stay lit when a bulb is removed. After discussing the difference between the sets of lights, label each set correctly.

Mary Flowers, St. Simon School, Los Altos, CA

Pencil-Box Ecosystem
Life science

If your students have trouble understanding the difference between a population and a community of living organisms, just ask them to take out their pencil boxes! Instruct each child to pick up any item in her box. Explain that it represents a living organism, such as an oak tree, a field mouse, or a spider monkey. Next, have her group together in her box all like items. Explain that each group of items represents a population of like organisms living in a larger community with other living organisms, such as birds, flowers, or insects. Then explain that everything in her box plus the box itself and other nonliving things in it (air, dust, and dirt) represent an ecosystem.

Molly Jones, St. Bernadette School, Omaha, NE

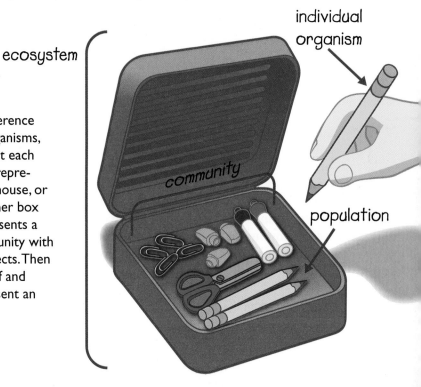

Treasures From the Sea

Directions:
1. Shuffle the cards and stack them on the mat.
2. Draw a card.
3. Decide whether the resource on the card is renewable or nonrenewable.
4. Place the card on the matching treasure chest.
5. When all the cards have been placed, check your answers with the key.

Place shuffled cards here.

Nonrenewable Resources

Renewable Resources

Resource Cards and Answer Key

Use with "Deep-Sea Treasures" on page 259 and the sorting mat on page 261.

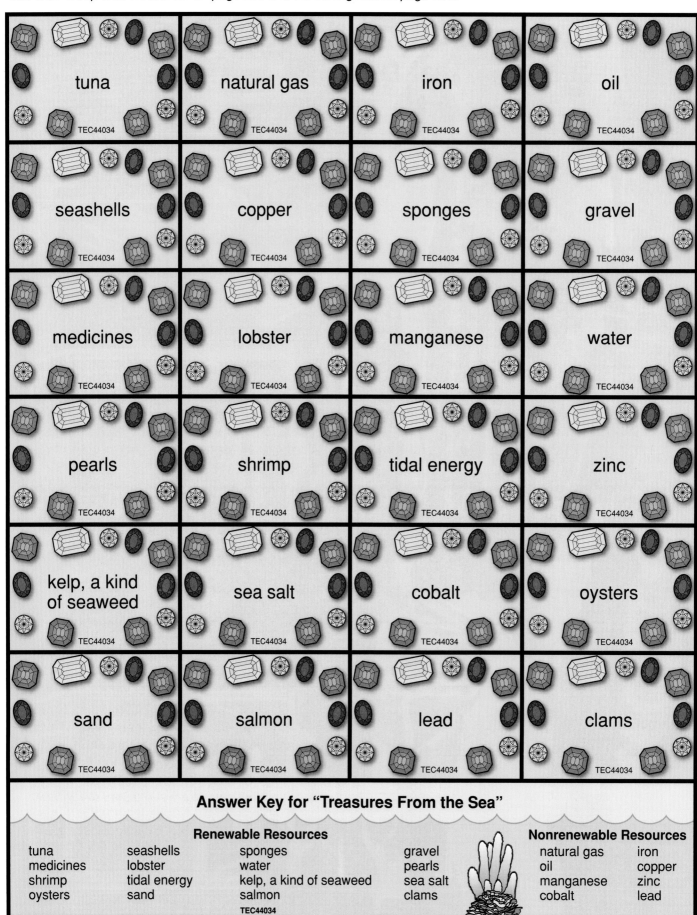

tuna	natural gas	iron	oil
TEC44034	TEC44034	TEC44034	TEC44034

seashells	copper	sponges	gravel
TEC44034	TEC44034	TEC44034	TEC44034

medicines	lobster	manganese	water
TEC44034	TEC44034	TEC44034	TEC44034

pearls	shrimp	tidal energy	zinc
TEC44034	TEC44034	TEC44034	TEC44034

kelp, a kind of seaweed	sea salt	cobalt	oysters
TEC44034	TEC44034	TEC44034	TEC44034

sand	salmon	lead	clams
TEC44034	TEC44034	TEC44034	TEC44034

Answer Key for "Treasures From the Sea"

Renewable Resources

tuna	seashells	sponges	gravel
medicines	lobster	water	pearls
shrimp	tidal energy	kelp, a kind of seaweed	sea salt
oysters	sand	salmon	clams

TEC44034

Nonrenewable Resources

natural gas	iron
oil	copper
manganese	zinc
cobalt	lead

Target Practice

Physical science

Use this discovery idea to help students understand how force affects motion. It involves some friendly competition as well!

Materials for each group of four students: bottle of water, 12" length of string, chair, small box, 30" length of foil, masking tape, yardstick

Directions:
1. Tie one end of the string around the bottle's neck. Tie the other end to the chair's back so the bottle dangles between the chair legs about an inch above the floor.
2. Place the box at one end of the foil. Arrange the foil so the box sits in front of the bottle. Tape the ends of the foil to the floor.
3. Pull the bottle back a short distance and then release it. Measure and record the distance the box travels.
4. Repeat Step 3 several more times, pulling the bottle farther back each time.
5. Using the tape, form a target (eight-inch square within a 24-inch square) a few inches from the end of the foil.
6. Take turns pulling the bottle back far enough to make the box stop within the target. Record each player's score (landing in the large square = 1 point, landing in the small square = 5 points).
7. Declare the group with the most points the winner.

Liz Harrell, Cornwall on Hudson, NY

May I Take Your Order?
Life science

Serve up a hearty helping of decision making with this fun activity. Discuss healthy foods with students and how they are prepared. Then have students work alone or in pairs to design a menu for a new healthful-foods restaurant called The Heart Rock Café. After brainstorming clever names for menu items, have students design their own menus, including descriptions of several items from each food group. Have students develop a symbol for each food group that will show customers the group to which a particular menu item belongs. For example, a red apple symbol can indicate a fruit-group item. Explain that a menu item may include foods from more than one group and should be labeled accordingly. For example, frozen yogurt may be marked with symbols for the fruit group and the milk group. Conclude by having students exchange completed menus, order balanced meals from each other, and assess each other's menu choices for nutritional value.

Bonnie Pettifor, Urbana, IL

I'll have the Guitar Guy's Grilled Chicken Salad with a Crowd-Pleasing Fruit Smoothie, please.

Seasons Model
Earth science

A new season begins in March. To help students understand the connection between the changing of the seasons and our planet's rotation and revolution, have them build models of Earth in four different positions around the Sun.

Materials for each group of students: 5 Ping-Pong balls (one yellow, four white), darning needle, 5 round toothpicks, 3 markers (blue, green, and black), foam plate

Steps:
1. Use the needle to poke holes through the top and out the bottom of each white ball. Insert a toothpick through the holes in each ball to represent Earth's axis. Repeat with the yellow ball (sun), but make only one hole so the toothpick protrudes from one end only.
2. Use the markers to make each white ball look like Earth.
3. Turn the plate upside down and insert the balls, tilting the ball at summer *toward* the sun and those at each of the other seasons *away from* the sun as shown.
4. Draw arrows to show the direction of Earth's revolution around the sun.
5. Slowly turn each miniature globe on its axis to show how Earth rotates in each position to create day and night as it revolves around the sun.

Ruth Menzer, Southwest Elementary
Pratt, KS

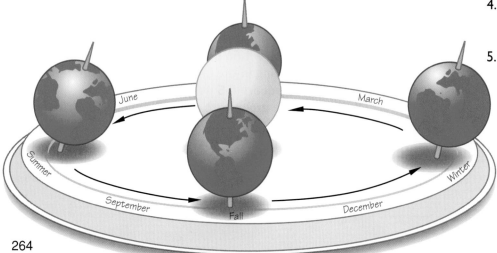

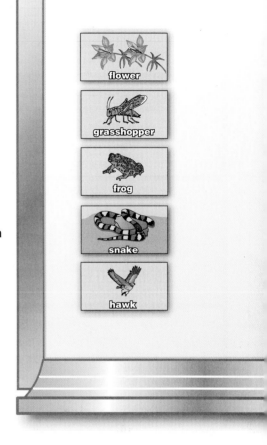

Continue the Chain
Life science

Providing the next link in a food chain is fun when it's part of a game. Cut apart the game cards on page 266 and affix a strip of magnetic tape to the back of each one. To play, randomly arrange several game cards on a whiteboard and divide students into teams. Select one game card to begin a vertical food chain. Then invite a player from Team 1 to earn a point for his team by choosing a game card that shows a plant or animal that could be the next link in that food chain. Alternate play until none of the remaining choices work. Declare the team with more points the winner.

Louella Nygaard, Thorne Bay School, Thorne Bay, AK

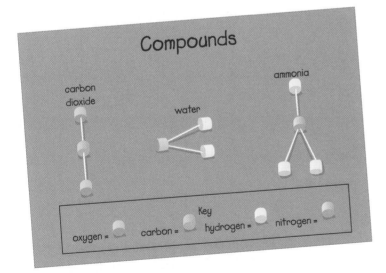

Marshmallow Models
Physical science

Here's a sweet way to learn about basic compounds. Place a supply of multicolored mini-marshmallows, toothpicks, markers, glue, and unlined paper at a center. Also display a chart of the three structures shown. To complete the activity, a student first uses the marshmallows' colors to create a color code for the following elements: oxygen, carbon, hydrogen, and nitrogen. Next, using the chart as a guide, she constructs a model of carbon dioxide, water, and ammonia. Then she glues her three models to the unlined paper and labels each one as shown.

Dr. Barbara B. Leonard, Winston-Salem, NC

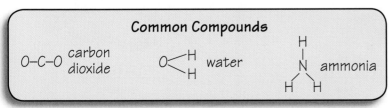

Game Cards

Use with "Continue the Chain" on page 265.

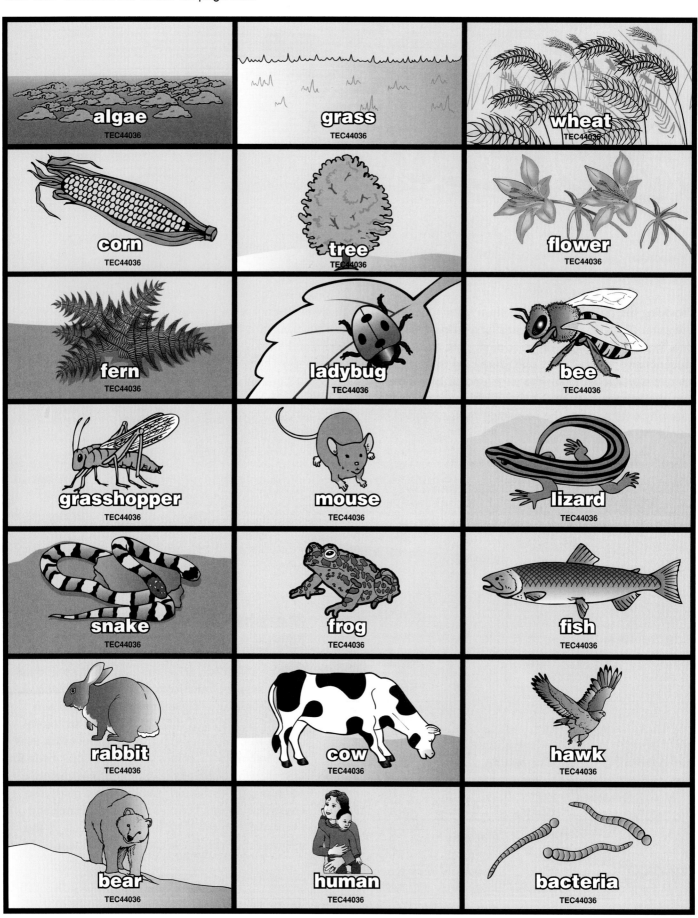

algae
TEC44036

grass
TEC44036

wheat
TEC44036

corn
TEC44036

tree
TEC44036

flower
TEC44036

fern
TEC44036

ladybug
TEC44036

bee
TEC44036

grasshopper
TEC44036

mouse
TEC44036

lizard
TEC44036

snake
TEC44036

frog
TEC44036

fish
TEC44036

rabbit
TEC44036

cow
TEC44036

hawk
TEC44036

bear
TEC44036

human
TEC44036

bacteria
TEC44036

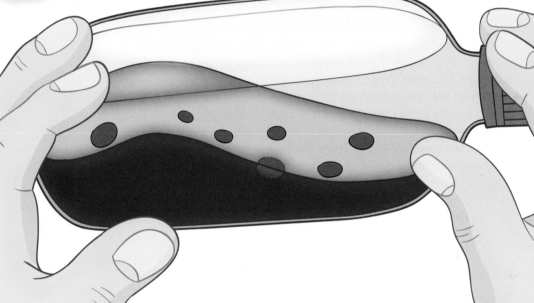

Making Waves

Earth science

To demonstrate the movement of ocean waves, pour one cup of water into a small plastic bottle and gently mix in a few drops of blue food coloring. Add one cup of mineral oil; then tightly replace the bottle cap. If desired, add a small amount of sand to the bottle to observe how waves move sand along the ocean floor. To create waves, have each student take a turn holding the bottle horizontally and then alternately raising and lowering each end like a slow-moving seesaw. Follow up with a discussion about how the water in a wave moves *(in circles, almost returning to where it starts),* what causes most waves *(the wind),* and the energy and power of ocean waves.

Dr. Barbara B. Leonard, Winston-Salem, NC

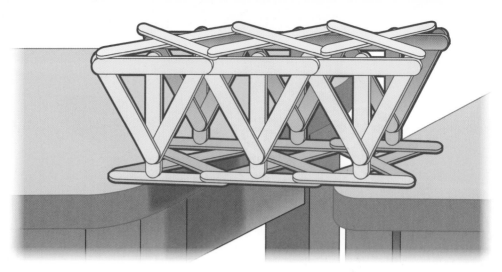

Building Bridges
Physical science

This activity encourages students to consider the forces that act on a bridge. To begin, divide the class into groups and provide each group with 50 craft sticks and a bottle of white glue. Challenge each group to use the provided materials to design and build a bridge that spans at least 12 inches. When the bridges are completed, have students predict which bridge design they think will hold the most weight. Discuss what will happen if a bridge is not able to handle a given weight load (*the extra tension will cause the bridge to snap*). Then test each bridge by positioning it to span the open space between two equal-height student desks that are about 10 inches apart. Place weights on the bridge one at a time until the bridge snaps or a predetermined weight limit has been reached. Record the amount of weight each bridge is able to hold. Then discuss with students why the design of certain bridges—such as a truss bridge with a triangular frame—makes them better able to handle tension, and therefore hold more weight, than other bridges.

Pamela Crabb, Lake Whitney Elementary, Winter Garden, FL

Possible items to use as weights (make sure all students use the same items) include Unifix cubes, playing cards, gram weights, wooden blocks, textbooks, and dictionaries.

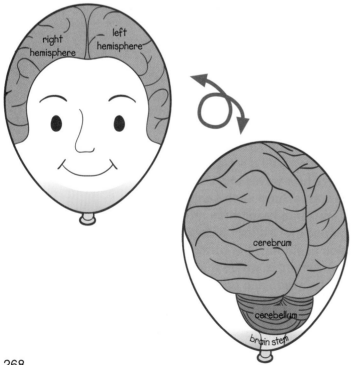

Balloon Brain
Life science

These realistic models help students learn the areas of the human brain. Give each child a 12-inch white balloon and three different-colored permanent markers. Instruct her to blow up her balloon until it is full-size and then tie it off. Next, have her draw a face on one side of her balloon and label the forehead as shown. Then, to divide the balloon (brain) into two halves (hemispheres), instruct her to draw a line that starts between the forehead's labeled parts and extends over the top of the balloon and ends above its knot. Finally, have the student use different markers to draw and label on the back of the balloon the cerebrum, the cerebellum, and the brain stem as shown. If desired, have her also label each area of the brain with the function(s) for which it is responsible.

Dr. Barbara B. Leonard, Winston-Salem, NC

EXPLORING SOCIAL STUDIES

EXPLORING Social Studies

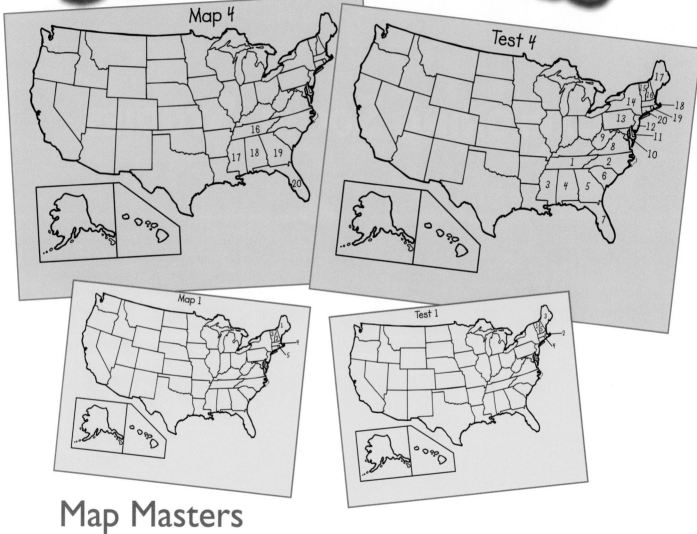

Map 4

Test 4

Map 1

Test 1

Map Masters
Geography

If your students have trouble identifying the 50 U.S. states, this ongoing activity can help. Begin by giving each child a copy of the map on page 272 with five northeastern states numbered 1–5. Give him one week to learn the location of those five states. On test day, give him a copy of the same map but with the numbers rearranged. If he correctly identifies those states, give him another copy of the map with a new chunk of states numbered. If he does not identify the first five states correctly, have him study the same map for another week. Continue in this manner, testing five new states at a time (plus the previously learned states) on the same day each week until all 50 have been mastered. Then present each map master with a special certificate that recognizes his achievement.

Sharon Vance, Nash Elementary, Kaufman, TX

Expandable Study Guide
Culture

Remembering characteristics of different cultural groups, such as Native Americans, can be easier if students use this easy-to-adapt tool. For each tribe studied, have each child complete and decorate two different booklet pages from a copy of page 273 and cut them out. Have her fold a half-inch tab on the right edge of each of two 4" x 6" pieces of construction paper. To join the pieces, instruct her to glue the unfolded edge of one piece into the valley of another. Then have her decorate the first page as the cover and glue her completed booklet pages to the next two pages as shown. After she adds pages for additional tribes she studies, have her cut off the unused tab.

Debbie Berris, Poinciana Day School, West Palm Beach, FL

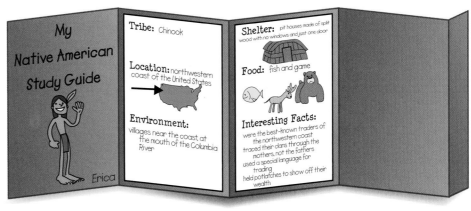

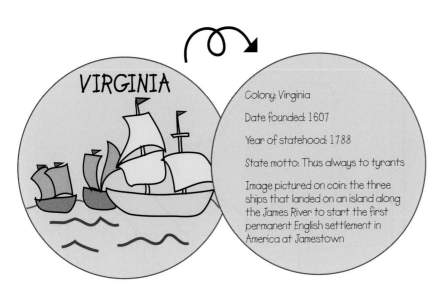

Mottoes and More
History

Capitalize on the U.S. Mint's state quarter program to help students learn more about America's 13 original colonies. Have each child research one of the colonies to learn the date it was founded, the year it became a state, and its motto. Next, have him draw a picture of that state's quarter on the front of a large paper circle and label the back with the facts he learned. When he's finished, have him write a paragraph explaining why he thinks the image pictured on the quarter was chosen to represent that state and then share his thoughts with the class.

Kellie Ouzts, County Line Elementary, Winder, GA

State Flag Makeover
History

After students study your state's flag and understand what its colors and symbols represent, announce that the governor wants a new flag. On a copy of the flag pattern on page 274, have each child design a flag on which everything included represents something important about your state. In addition, have her write a paragraph explaining why she included each item. Once students share the designs and paragraphs with the class, mount them on a display titled "Which New Design Do You Prefer, Governor?"

Teresa Vilfer-Snyder, Fredericktown Intermediate, Fredericktown, OH

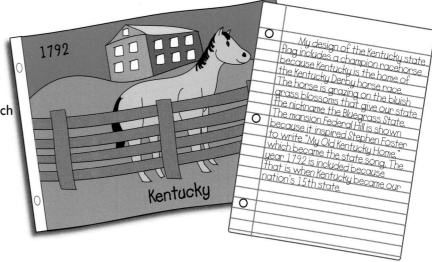

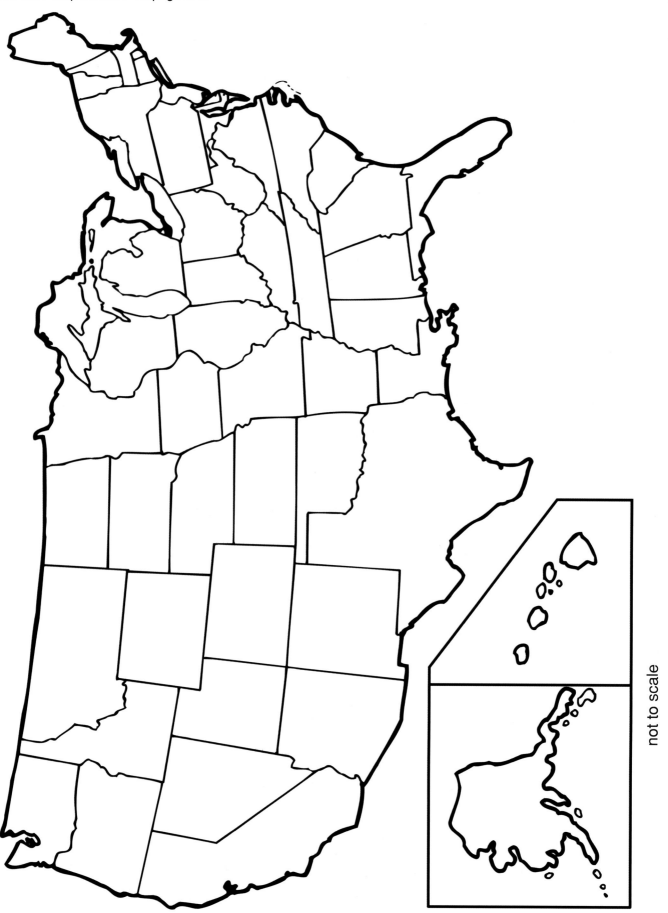

not to scale

Use with "Expandable Study Guide" on page 271.

Page 1

Tribe: Location: Environment: TEC44032	Tribe: Location: Environment: TEC44032	Tribe: Location: Environment: TEC44032

Page 2

Shelter: Food: Interesting Facts: TEC44032	Shelter: Food: Interesting Facts: TEC44032	Shelter: Food: Interesting Facts: TEC44032

Flag Pattern

Use with "State Flag Makeover" on page 271.

TEC44032

EXPLORING
Social Studies

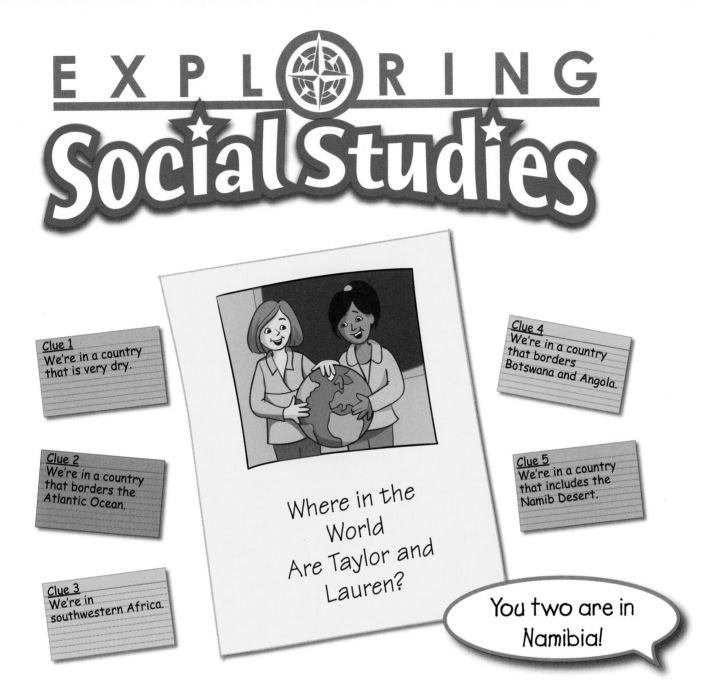

Clue 1
We're in a country that is very dry.

Clue 2
We're in a country that borders the Atlantic Ocean.

Clue 3
We're in southwestern Africa.

Clue 4
We're in a country that borders Botswana and Angola.

Clue 5
We're in a country that includes the Namib Desert.

Where in the World Are Taylor and Lauren?

You two are in Namibia!

Where in the World Are…
World geography

Improve geography and research skills with this weekly activity. At the end of the week, pick two students to research a country of their choice and write five clues about it (each clue on a separate index card). Take a photo of the pair holding a globe. On Monday, post the photo outside your classroom with the title shown. Then have the researchers post one clue each day. On Friday, classmates place in a container their guesses as to the country's identity. At the end of the day, let the researchers reveal the mystery country and recognize students who correctly identified it. Then choose two other students to be next week's world travelers.

Linda Marshall, Poquoson Elementary, Poquoson, VA

Sing a Song of Regions
U.S. geography

Help students tune in to United States regions and state locations using the catchy ditties on page 277. Give each student a copy of page 277 and a blank U.S. map. Model each song for students. Then provide time for them to practice in pairs or small groups. As students sing, challenge them to point to each state as they say its name.

Barbara Benton, University Laboratory School, Louisiana State University
Baton Rouge, LA

Video Game Voyage
Explorers

Use students' love of video games to fuel this exciting activity about explorers. Assign each student an explorer to research. After he has collected his information, have each child complete a copy of page 278, which guides him in designing three levels of a video game based on his explorer. Provide time for each student to give an oral presentation that describes his explorer's voyage and the strategies a player can use to navigate through the video game.

Andrea LaMantia, Hillcrest Elementary, New City, NY

Dude, Is That Democracy?
Government

For a fun introduction to a government unit, write two choices on the board, such as "extra recess" and "extra reading time." Have students vote for their favorite choice; then explain that they have just participated in democracy. After discussing the definition of *democracy*, divide students into four groups and give each group two different cards from page 279. Each card features an example of democracy. Explain that groups will be asked to mime each of their examples for the rest of the class. After giving groups several minutes to plan their presentations, have groups take turns miming their examples until all cards have been used.

Diane Coffman, Lawrence, KS

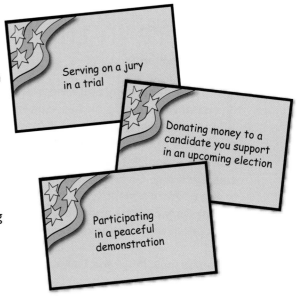

Sing a Song of Regions

The Northeast
(sung to the tune of "Ten Little Indians")

Maine, New Hampshire, Vermont, Massachusetts,
Rhode Island, Connecticut, New York,
Pennsylvania, New Jersey, Maryland, and Delaware—
These are the Northeast states!

The Southeast
(sung to the tune of "Clementine")

West Virginia and Virginia,
Carolinas (North and South).
Then there's Georgia, and there's Florida,
Alabama in the south.

Mississippi, Louisiana,
Arkansas, and Tennessee.
Add Kentucky, and we're finished
In the Southeast, you and me!

The Midwest
(sung to the tune of "I've Been Working on the Railroad")

North Dakota, South Dakota,
Nebraska, and Kansas too.
Add Missouri and add Iowa.
Now we're halfway through!

Minnesota and Wisconsin,
Illinois, and Indiana too.
Add Ohio and Michigan.
The Midwest—we know you!

The Southwest
(sung to the tune of "Are You Sleeping?")

Arizona, Arizona,
New Mexico, New Mexico,
Oklahoma, Oklahoma,
Texas too. Texas too.

The West
(sung to the tune of "On Top of Old Smoky")

Montana, Wyoming,
Colorado, Utah,
Idaho and Nevada,
And California.

Hawaii and Oregon
And Washington too.
Add Alaska—we're finished.

Note to the teacher: Use with "Sing a Song of Regions" on page 276.

Name _____

VIDEO GAME VOYAGE

Explorer: _____
Complete each step.

Level 1: Getting Ready

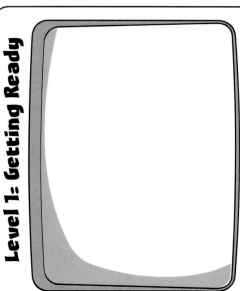

1 Name the place where the explorer's journey began. Tell about an obstacle the explorer met while getting ready for or starting the trip.

2 Tell how to get a bonus point or an extra power at the start of the voyage.

3 Draw a picture above showing how to earn the bonus point or extra power.

Level 2: The Voyage

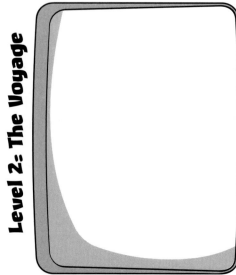

1 Describe the route your explorer took. Explain how it can be an obstacle in your game.

2 Tell how to get a bonus point or an extra power during the voyage.

3 Draw a picture above showing how to earn the bonus point or extra power.

©The Mailbox® • TEC44033 • Oct./Nov. 2007

Level 3: The Destination

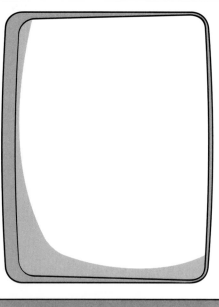

1 Name something valuable found at the destination. Tell how it can be a reward for overcoming an obstacle in your game.

2 Tell how to get a bonus point or an extra power using the valuable item.

3 Draw a picture above showing how to earn the bonus point or extra power.

Note to the teacher: Use with "Video Game Voyage" on page 276.

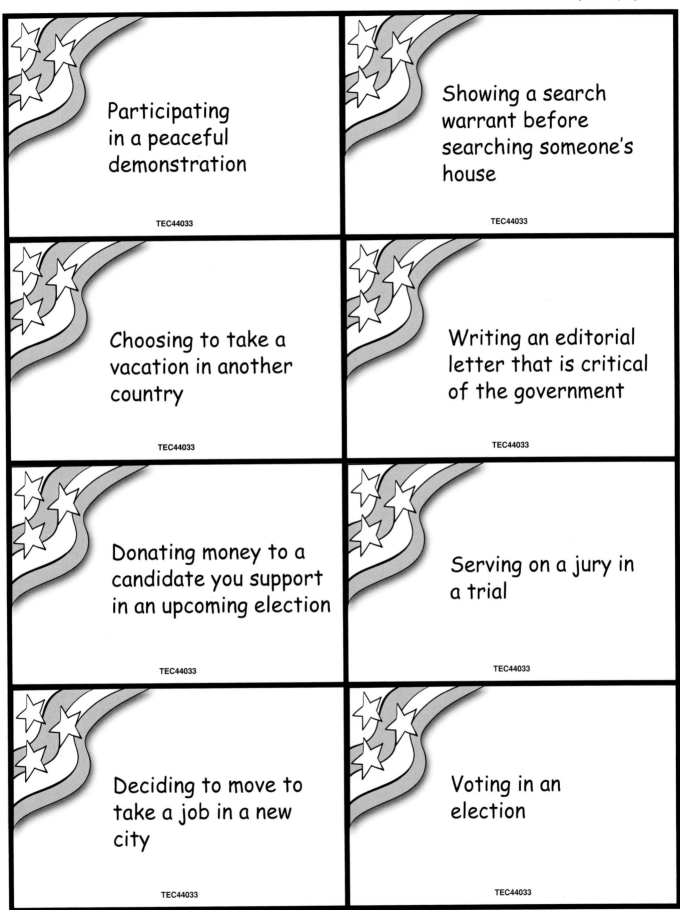

Participating in a peaceful demonstration

TEC44033

Showing a search warrant before searching someone's house

TEC44033

Choosing to take a vacation in another country

TEC44033

Writing an editorial letter that is critical of the government

TEC44033

Donating money to a candidate you support in an upcoming election

TEC44033

Serving on a jury in a trial

TEC44033

Deciding to move to take a job in a new city

TEC44033

Voting in an election

TEC44033

Materials for each student:
9" manila or tan circle (crust)
colorful paper: red (sauce), yellow
    (cheese), green (green pepper)
scissors
fine-tip marker
pushpin
brad

Wheel labels: JUDICIAL BRANCH — is made up of the Supreme Court and other Federal Courts / settles differences about the meaning of laws / can rule that a law or the president's actions are unconstitutional

EXECUTIVE BRANCH — is headed by the president of the United States / heads the armed forces, manages the government, makes treaties, and proposes and carries out new laws / can veto a bill passed by Congress and nominates Supreme Court justices

LEGISLATIVE BRANCH — is made up of the Congress: the House of Representatives and the Senate / makes laws and passes taxes / can override a president's veto and approves Supreme Court justices

I'll Take a "Pizza" Government!
U.S. government

Help students review the branches of government with a study tool that resembles a pizza! Copy page 282 onto sturdy paper. Cut out each pattern to make a tracer. Place the tracers at a center along with the materials listed above. Each student traces the patterns on colorful paper (as indicated on the tracers), cuts out the tracings, and then labels the tan circle with the headings shown. Next, for each branch of government, he labels one red, one yellow, and one green cutout each with a different fact about that branch. He stacks the green pieces and pokes a hole in them by pushing the pin through all three layers at the marked point. After repeating these steps with the yellow and red pieces, the student stacks the cutouts atop the tan circle in order from largest to smallest and inserts the brad. Then he labels the back of each piece with an *E, L,* or *J* for self-checking. To use his tool, the child aligns each branch's pieces under the matching heading and peeks at the backs to check.

Lavone Novotny, Marion, OH

Totally Totem
Native Americans

For a perfect project for studying Northwest Coast Native Americans, try this activity. Each student draws lines on a 9" x 12" sheet of brown paper to create a section for each family member. In the middle of each section, he draws an animal that represents that person. The student then decorates the rest of the section with words and/or symbols that celebrate that family member's unique qualities. To complete the project, the child rolls the paper into a tube and tapes the edges together to create a totem pole. Display the completed poles on a classroom table.

Starin Lewis, Phoenix, AZ

DAD
strong
brave
loyal
smart

MOM
gentle
beautiful
gracious
kind

JIMMY
loyal
playful
funny
happy

ME
athletic
studious
graceful
sensitive

Teatime
The American Revolution

Review the causes and effects of the Revolutionary War with this "tea-rific" project for individuals, pairs, or small groups. Have each child cut out a paper teapot shape and four tea bags. Then have her complete the following steps:

1. Label each tea bag with a cause and an effect related to the American Revolution or, specifically, to the Boston Tea Party. Color the tea bags. Then glue them on the corners of a 12-inch tagboard square.
2. Decorate the teapot and glue it on the square's center.
3. Tape a real tea bag to the teapot.

Mount the finished projects on a display titled "Trouble's A-brewing in Boston!"

Jeri Gramil, St. John Regional Catholic School, Frederick, MD

State Your Data!
U.S. regions, data analysis

To integrate a regional study of the United States with math, assign each of five groups a different region of the United States. Each group uses reference materials to locate the following information about each state in its region:

- area in square miles
- highest point
- lowest point
- population
- highest recorded temperature
- lowest recorded temperature

The group organizes its data in a table. Then it analyzes the data and writes three comparative statements about the region's states and one generalization about the region. Provide time for groups to share and compare their work.

Terry Healy, Manhattan, KS

> Wow! Wisconsin is about three-fourths the size of Minnesota!

Pizza Slices

Use with "I'll Take a 'Pizza' Government!" on page 280.

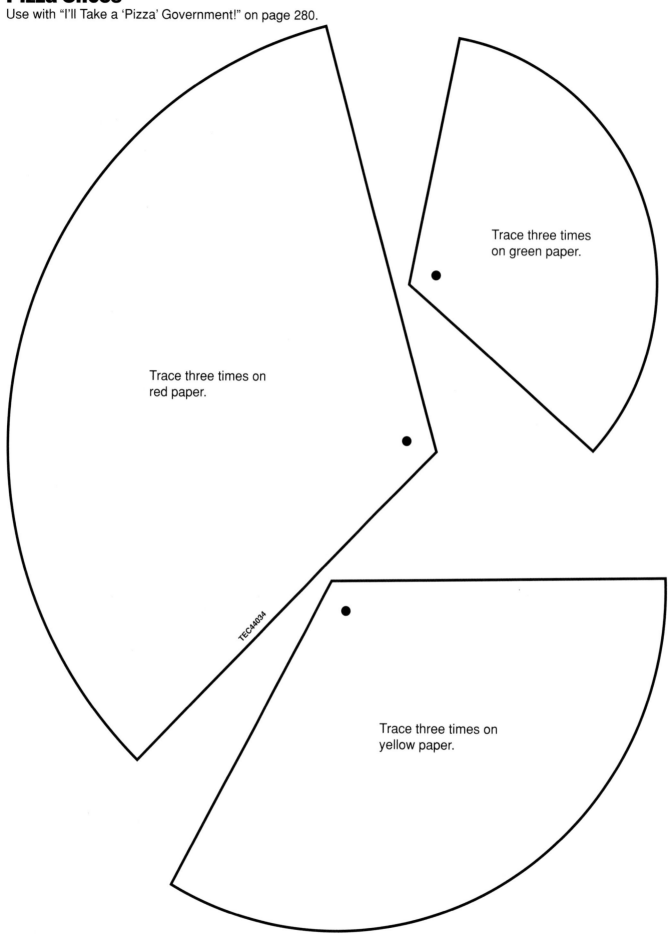

Trace three times on green paper.

Trace three times on red paper.

TEC44034

Trace three times on yellow paper.

Regions Relay
U.S. regions

All you need for this geography version of Around the World is a pencil and a copy of a U.S. map. Begin by asking the first two students to stand. Then name a region. The first student to correctly name a state in that region moves to stand beside the next classmate while you mark off that state on your map. The student who did not answer first sits down. Continue playing in this manner, alerting students that once a state has been named it cannot be used again. The last student standing wins.

Juli Engel, Midland, TX

Midwest region.

Illinois!

What's Going On?
Current events

World News

U.S. News

State News

Local News

To integrate comprehension and summarizing skills with current events, pin on a bulletin board the labels shown. Each Monday, share headlines and summaries of several interesting articles from weekend newspapers. Then send one student home with a newspaper from that day so he can read and summarize an article of his choice. After the student shares his summary the next day, post his article and summary below the appropriate label on the display. Choose a different student each night to complete the assignment, requiring that she select an article from a category that hasn't been featured yet. At the end of week, clear the board so you're ready to start anew on Monday!

Gretchen Gottschalk, Brookridge Elementary, Brooklyn, OH

Liberty Belles
Revolutionary War

Men weren't the only ones who fought for freedom during the American Revolution—ladies also did their part! To learn more about extraordinary female freedom fighters of that era, assign a woman from the list shown to each group of two or three students. Then have each group research its heroine and complete a copy of the form on page 284. Showcase the finished forms on a display titled "Liberty Belle Biographies."

Terri Myers, Ringgold, GA

Abigail Adams
Sarah Franklin Bache
Anne Bailey
Margaret Corbin
Mary Ludwig Hays McCauley
   (Molly Pitcher)
Sybil Ludington
Betsy Ross
Deborah Samson
Mercy Otis Warren
Martha Washington
Phillis Wheatley
Prudence Wright

Liberty Belles

Research your assigned freedom fighter.
Then write your information on the lines below.
Use the back of this page if you need more space.

Name of woman: _____

Birthdate: _____

Death date: _____

Birthplace: _____

Role in the Revolutionary War: _____

_____

_____

_____

_____

_____

Other interesting facts: _____

_____

_____

_____

EXPLORING Social Studies

Remembering Who Did What
History

Use this simple game to review the contributions of historical figures. Write the name of each person on a separate paper strip and his or her contribution on a strip of a different color. Then tape one strip to each child's back. (If you have an odd number of students, play along.) Next, have students circulate, asking relative questions of their classmates until every child finds his or her correct partner and each pair locks elbows. Then verify the matches, redistribute the strips, and play another round!

Leigh Anne Newsom, Cedar Road Elementary, Chesapeake, VA

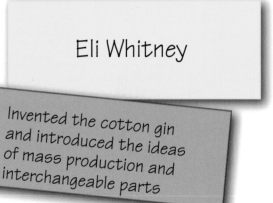

Eli Whitney

Invented the cotton gin and introduced the ideas of mass production and interchangeable parts

World Market
Economics

To make students aware of all the places that items they use come from, give each child a copy of page 286. Have her complete the form at home, recording information from clothing labels, electronics, and other household items representing as many different countries as possible. The next day, have students share their findings. If desired, post the completed forms around a large world map. Then have each student use yarn to connect each item on her form to each corresponding place on the map.

Terry Healy, Marlatt Elementary, Manhattan, KS

It's Our Right!
Citizenship

Begin this small-group activity by discussing general students' rights, such as the right to learn or the right to be safe. Then have each group write on a large index card an example of a situation in which a student's rights are either being respected or violated. Instruct the groups to plan a brief skit based on the card's scenario. After each group presents its skit, have the other groups identify the right that was enacted. Follow up the activity with a discussion of students' rights, the meaning of each right, and each student's responsibility to uphold those rights.

Stephanie Contreras, Autrey Mill Middle School, Alpharetta, GA

Two students are telling jokes and laughing during a math lesson. The other students around them have trouble hearing the teacher. (The right to learn is being violated.)

World Market

Name of item: _____

Where the item was made: _____

How the item is used: _____

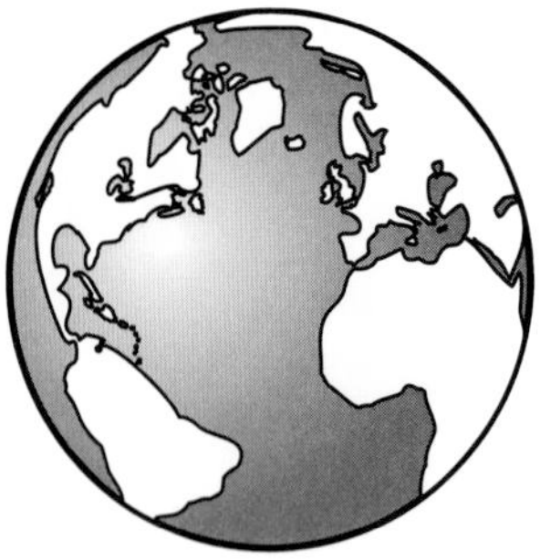

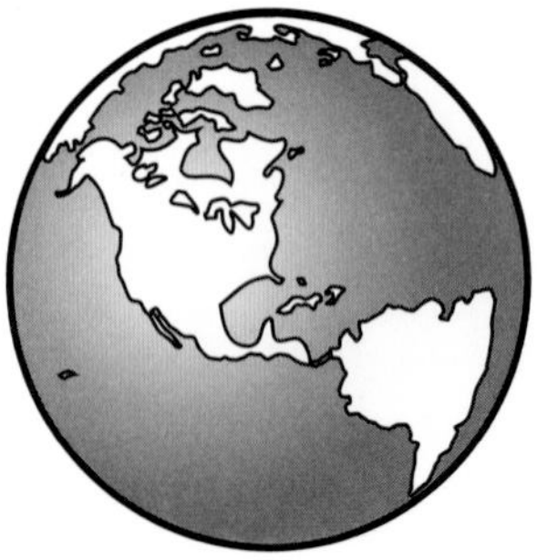

Name of item: _____

Where the item was made: _____

How the item is used: _____

Name of item: _____

Where the item was made: _____

How the item is used: _____

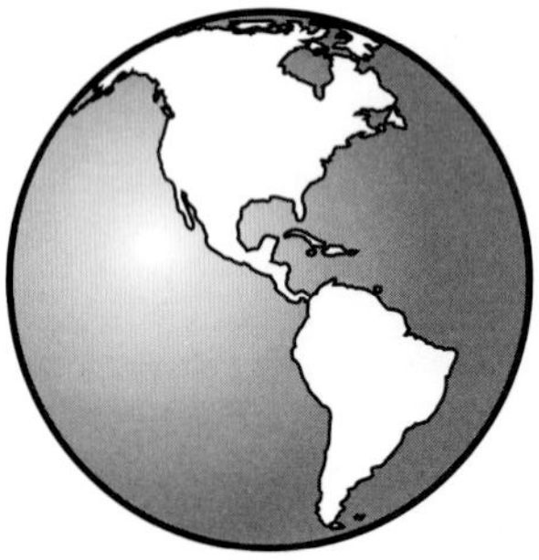

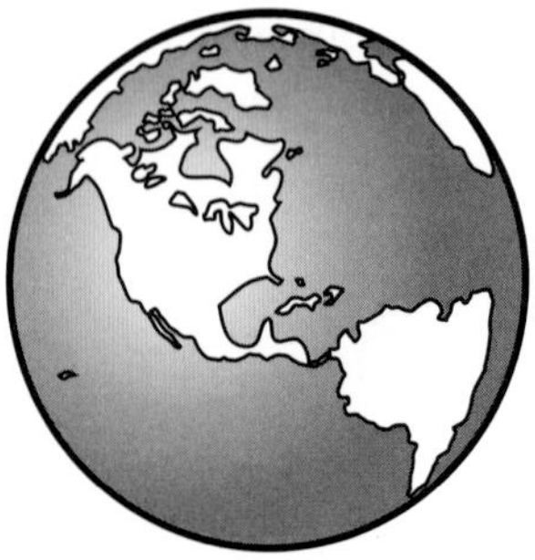

Name of item: _____

Where the item was made: _____

How the item is used: _____

Name of item: _____

Where the item was made: _____

How the item is used: _____

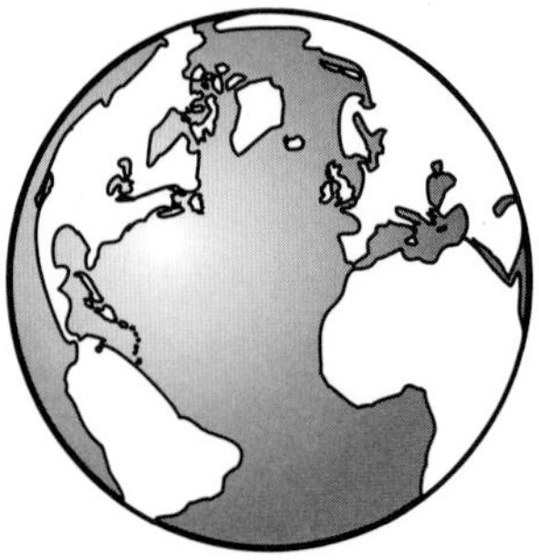

EXPLORING Social Studies

Picture This!
U.S. regions

U. S. Regions
The Northeast: New England states
The Northeast: Middle Atlantic states
The Southeast
The Southwest
The Midwest: Great Lakes states
The Midwest: Great Plains states
The West: Mountain states
The West: Pacific states

For a fun and easy-to-manage activity on U.S. regions, divide the class into eight teams (one for each region listed). Have each group research its region's land features, climate, population, economy, and history. After students have collected their findings, ask them to pretend that they have just used a magic camera to take a picture of each of their regions. Explain that this camera is capable of capturing several major aspects of a region in just one shot. Have each group illustrate its photo on poster board, making sure to include items that represent important information about its region. If desired, have the group glue decorated strips of paper around the edges of its photo to create a frame. Post the giant snapshots on a display titled "Picturing U.S. Regions."

Money Matters
Economics

Use the prompts below to get students thinking about how the economic principles of supply and demand affect their lives. Encourage students to use the terms *supply* and *demand* in their responses.

- There are many houses for sale in your neighborhood. Some have been for sale for months. Your family is planning to move, and your house has been for sale for three months. How might the situation in your neighborhood affect you and your family?

- How might rising oil prices affect the cost of food sold in your local grocery store? How might it affect your family?

- The U.S. Postal Service has announced an increase in the cost of mailing a package. Your mother buys most of her holiday presents from online catalogs. How might this affect her decisions about what to give you for the holidays next year?

> Brian
>
> The supply of houses in our neighborhood is high, but the demand is low. That means that the price of houses in our neighborhood is falling. My dad may have to lower the price for our house so that it sells more quickly. If he doesn't, the house might not sell for a long time. But if the house does sell for a lower price, it means we won't have as much money to spend on our new house. Maybe we'll even have to get a smaller house and I'll have to share a bedroom with my little brother. Yuck!

snow shoes
beaver trap
MICHIGAN OR BUST

Pack Your Bags!
State history, immigration

For this unique exploration, have pairs of students research the early explorers, settlers, or immigrants who came to your state. From their research, have each duo list items that a person from your state's past might have packed as he or she traveled to and in your state. Next, instruct the pair to create a suitcase by covering a shoebox and its lid with paper and adding a paper handle and luggage tag. Then have the partners "pack" their suitcase with objects from their homes, pictures, and cutouts that represent their selected items. Provide time for groups to examine each other's suitcases and discuss the contents.

Michelle Bauml, Houston, TX

State Biography Tea
Famous people

The important people in your state's history come alive when you hold a State Biography Tea. Have each student research and write a short report about a historic figure's contribution to your state's development. Have the student also make business cards for his person by writing the person's name on ten index cards. On the day of the tea, ask students to come to school dressed as their people and share their reports. Afterward, have them circulate around the room (in character) and exchange business cards, jotting down on the cards important information about their characters. When all cards have been exchanged, invite the class to enjoy punch and cookies. Then have students use the cards they collected to answer the questions shown.

Ginger Alleman, Decker Prairie Elementary, Magnolia, TX

Questions

1. Describe your person and his or her contribution to our state.
2. Name the most important person you met during the tea, and tell why you think he or she is important to our state's history.
3. Which of the people represented would you most like to meet in person? Why?

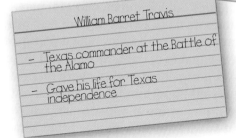

> William Barret Travis
>
> - Texas commander at the Battle of the Alamo
> - Gave his life for Texas independence

MANAGEMENT TIPS AND TIMESAVERS

Management Tips and Timesavers

License to Learn

Monitor student behavior with this unique method of classroom management. Create pockets by stapling to a bulletin board the bottoms and sides of car cutouts that students have made and personalized. In each car pocket, stack three paper strips front to back (one green, one yellow, and one red, in that order) to represent traffic lights. Each day, as long as a child's behavior is appropriate, his green strip stays on top. If he receives a warning, move his green strip behind the red one so that just his yellow strip is visible. If he receives another warning, move his yellow strip to the back so that only his red strip is visible. Then have him complete a copy of the traffic ticket on page 292 for your files. If a student receives a predetermined number of traffic tickets, summon his parent to school for a conference (send home a copy of the parent note on page 292 for the parent to sign and return). Reward students whose green strip is visible for an extended period of time. On days when no child's red strip is visible, reward the entire class!

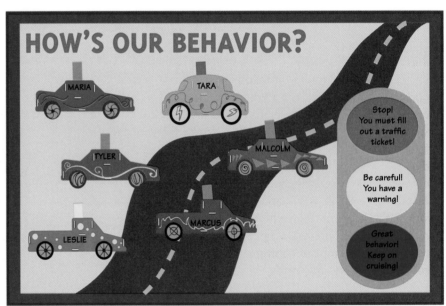

HOW'S OUR BEHAVIOR?

MARIA TARA TYLER MALCOLM LESLIE MARCUS

Stop! You must fill out a traffic ticket!

Be careful! You have a warning!

Great behavior! Keep on cruising!

Stacy Lewicki, Rolling Hills Primary School, Vernon, NJ

Desktop Job Sticks

Assigning classroom jobs is a breeze with this clever system! Simply write each classroom job on a separate craft stick. Next, attach the hook side of a small Velcro fastener to the back of each stick and a loop side near the outer edge of each child's desktop. Then affix a labeled stick to each child's desk. The next week, change jobs by having each student pass her stick to the child on her right.

Cynthia Sickles, Somerville School, Ridgewood, NJ

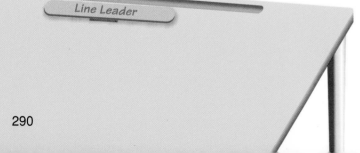

Line Leader

290

Clearly Organized

Keep student information organized with clear plastic sheet protectors and a three-ring binder. Label a page protector for each student. Then place in it pages listing the child's contact information, the child's class schedule, and any other important information. Behind those pages, store notes from home and any other correspondence related to that child. Arrange the protectors in the binder in alphabetical order. The next time you need a student's information, it'll be right at your fingertips!

April LeFevers, Horace Maynard Middle School, Maynardville, TN

Friday Folders

Inform parents about their child's progress and any upcoming events with this folder idea. Have each student bring in a two-pocket folder. Label the inside pockets as shown. Then staple a signature sheet to the front of the folder. Each Friday, return to students the papers you graded during the week. Have each child place her papers in the correct pocket along with any memos, book order forms, or permission slips that need to go home. Instruct each student to take her folder home over the weekend, have a parent sign and date the outer sheet and also sign papers as requested, remove the contents that can stay at home, and return the folder on Monday.

Lynn Tharrett, A. A. Kingston Middle School, Potsdam, NY

Personalized Borders

Are you looking for a creative way to jazz up your bulletin boards? Try this two-step idea. Using a product such as Wonder Under adhesive, fuse a piece of your favorite fabric to a piece of poster board. Then trim the poster board's outer edge to create an interesting and repeating pattern. In no time at all, you'll have the coolest borders at your school!

Amy Louden, Perrywood Elementary, Upper Marlboro, MD

Traffic Ticket and Parent Note

Use with "License to Learn" on page 290.

TRAFFIC TICKET

Name _____

Date _____

Offense: _____

_____

_____

_____

What I should have done instead: _____

_____

_____

_____

_____

student signature

©The Mailbox® • TEC44032 • Aug./Sept. 2007

Dear _____,

I would like to meet with you to discuss your child's recent behavior in class. Would _____ at _____ AM/PM be a convenient time for you? Thank you in advance for meeting with me to help your child.

Sincerely,

_____

☐ Yes, I will be able to attend.

☐ No, I will not be able to attend.
A better time would be on _____
at _____ AM/PM.

_____
parent signature

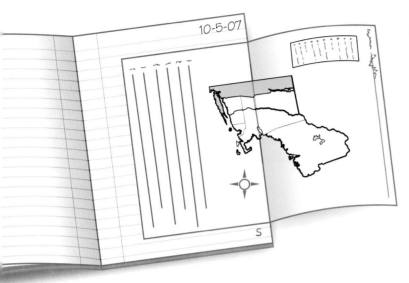

In One Place

Help students organize their subject area notes and handouts. Have each student designate the first three pages of a composition notebook for each subject as a table of contents. As each child writes notes in the book, have him date, label, and number the page of each lesson's notes before adding the listing to his table of contents. Also have students fold each handout in half, glue the bottom half to a numbered page, and list the handout in the table of contents. With this system, you can say goodbye to lost notes and handouts and say hello to organized students!

Bette Cobb, Prattville Intermediate, Prattville, AL

Quick Cleanup

To make cleanup after a paint project a snap, put the paint on a piece of aluminum foil. Students can use different areas of the foil to mix colors. Then, when they've finished painting, all they have to do is crumple up the foil with the paint inside and toss it in the trash. Neat and easy!

Debby Sato, Jefferson Elementary, Honolulu, HI

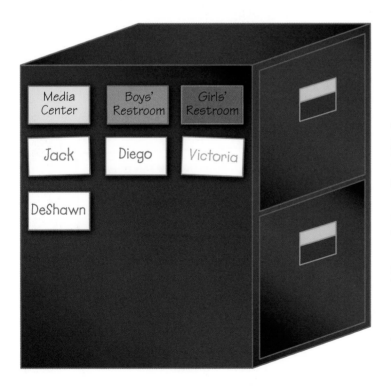

Multipurpose Nametags

With the help of some magnetic tape, your students' desk nametags can perform many functions! Have each child write her name on an index card and affix a strip of magnetic tape to the back to make a simple nametag. The child places the card on a metallic part of her desk to identify her seat. When permitted to go to the media center or restroom, she simply removes her nametag and places it on a corresponding section of a designated metallic surface. Then, on the way back into the room, she picks up her tag and returns it to her desk.

Jody Kadel, Clinton Elementary, Clinton, UT

Management Tips and Timesavers

Catch a Classmate

To promote positive behavior, tape baseball cards or magazine pictures of baseball players on the outside of a folder. Place copies of the baseball patterns from page 295 nearby. When a student observes a classmate demonstrating positive behavior, he nominates her for the class all-star team by filling out a baseball and placing it in the folder. At the end of the week, read aloud the nominations. Then complete a copy of the certificate on page 295 for each nominated child to take home.

Brooke Beverly, Julia Bancroft School, Auburn, MA

Stephanie is an all-star because she ate lunch with our new classmate, Min.

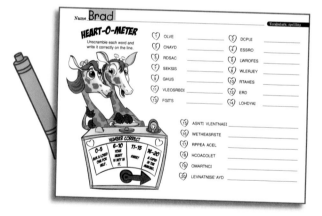

Name Brad

Vocabulary, spelling

HEART-O-METER
Unscramble each word and write it correctly on the line.

1. OLVE
2. CNAYD
3. RDSAC
4. SEKSIS
5. GHUS
6. VLEOSRBDI
7. FGITS

8. DCPUI
9. ESSRO
10. LWROFES
11. WLERJEY
12. RTAHES
13. ERD
14. LOHDYAI

15. ASNTI VLENTNAEI
16. WETHEASRSTE
17. RPPEA ACEL
18. HCOACOLET
19. OMARTNCI
20. LEVNATNISSE AYD

NUMBER CORRECT
0–5 ASK A LOVED ONE FOR HELP.
6–10 YOUR HEART IS NOT IN IT.
11–15 SWEET
16–20 A CUPID IN THE MAKING

Nameless No More

Say goodbye to no-name papers with this easy tip. Before each student turns in his paper, have him highlight his name with a colorful highlighter. This alerts a student who's forgotten to sign his paper. If students put their work in a box or folder instead, simply place a highlighter beside the receptacle.

Doreen Placko, St. Patrick School, Wadsworth, IL

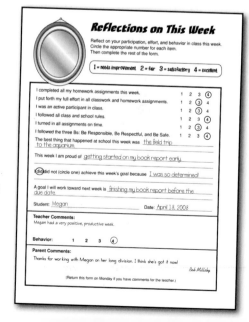

Reflections on This Week

Reflect on your participation, effort, and behavior in class this week. Circle the appropriate number for each item. Then complete the rest of the form.

1 = needs improvement   2 = fair   3 = satisfactory   4 = excellent

I completed all my homework assignments this week.	1 2 3 ④
I put forth my full effort in all classwork and homework assignments.	1 2 ③ 4
I was an active participant in class.	1 2 ③ 4
I followed all class and school rules.	1 2 3 ④
I turned in all assignments on time.	1 2 ③ 4
I followed the three Bs: Be Responsible, Be Respectful, and Be Safe.	1 2 3 ④

The best thing that happened at school this week was the field trip to the aquarium.

This week I am proud of getting started on my book report early.

I did/did not (circle one) achieve this week's goal because I was so determined!

A goal I will work toward next week is finishing my book report before the due date.

Student: Megan   Date: April 18, 2008

Teacher Comments:
Megan had a very positive, productive week.

Behavior: 1   2   3   ④

Parent Comments:
Thanks for working with Megan on her long division. I think she's got it now!
Bob Malloby

(Return this form on Monday if you have comments for the teacher.)

Weekly Reflections

Help students take ownership of their progress and set achievable goals one week at a time using the form on page 296. On Friday, have each child complete a copy of the form. Collect and quickly review the papers, adding your own evaluation and comments. Then send the forms home with students. Collect the returned forms with parent comments on Monday.

Katie Jensen, St. Timothy's School, Los Angeles, CA

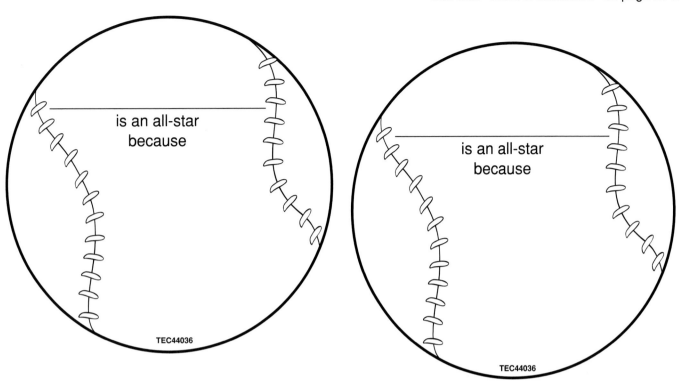

_____
is an all-star
because

TEC44036

_____
is an all-star
because

TEC44036

IS AN ALL-STAR!

_____ was nominated
student

for our class all-star team because

_____

_____

_____

C O N G R A T S !

Signed _____ Date _____

TEC44036

Reflections on This Week

Reflect on your participation, effort, and behavior in class this week.
Circle the appropriate number for each item.
Then complete the rest of the form.

1 = needs improvement   2 = fair   3 = satisfactory   4 = excellent

I completed all my homework assignments this week.	1 2 3 4
I put forth my full effort in all classwork and homework assignments.	1 2 3 4
I was an active participant in class.	1 2 3 4
I followed all class and school rules.	1 2 3 4
I turned in all assignments on time.	1 2 3 4
I followed the three Bs: Be Responsible, Be Respectful, and Be Safe.	1 2 3 4

The best thing that happened at school this week was _____
_____

This week I am proud of _____
_____

I did/did not (circle one) achieve this week's goal because _____
_____

A goal I will work toward next week is _____
_____

Student: _____   Date: _____

Teacher Comments:

Behavior: 1   2   3   4

Parent Comments:

(Return this form on Monday if you have comments for the teacher.)

©The Mailbox® • TEC44036 • April/May 2008

Management Tips and Timesavers

Storage Solution

Looking for a simple way to organize your bulletin board borders? Try clear plastic zippered bags, such as the ones comforters or sheet sets are sold in. Roll each border separately and secure it with a rubber band. Then place the rolled borders inside a bag. When it's time to change a display, you'll be able to see all your borders at a glance.

Bev Mullins, Benjamin Franklin Middle School, Rocky Mount, VA

On-Task Timer

Use this visual strategy to help minimize off-task behavior. Place a large sand timer in view of your students. (To make a timer, partially fill a small empty plastic bottle with colored sand and use a Tornado Tube connector to connect it to a second empty plastic bottle of the same size.) If students become inattentive, flip the timer and allow the sand to begin falling. After each student refocuses, lay the timer on its side to stop the sand's flow. Each time the class gets off track, stand the timer up, allowing more sand to fall. If the timer runs out of sand, reduce students' recess time to account for the lost instructional time.

Stacy Lewicki, Rolling Hills Primary, Vernon, NJ

Test-Taking Helpers

Give students privacy and reduce test-taking anxiety with these colorful dividers. Cover several half-size trifold presentation boards with colorful paper. Attach a colorful copy of the tips on page 298 to the center front and back of each board; then decorate the sides as desired. Place the boards between test-takers to help eliminate the temptation to look at another student's answers and to provide tips that can help a nervous child relax!

Deb Gribben, Twin Hickory Elementary, Glen Allen, VA

Test-Taking TIPS

1. Read and follow all the directions.

2. Read each question carefully.

3. Underline the key words in the directions and the questions.

4. Read all the answer choices before you choose an answer.

5. If you feel nervous, take a slow, deep breath.

6. Don't get stuck. Keep going! If you don't know the answer to a question, skip it and go to the next question.

7. Answer as many questions as you can without rushing. Then go back and try to answer the questions you skipped.

8. If you have extra time when you finish the test, check over your answers.

Note to the teacher: Use with "Test-Taking Helpers" on page 297.

OUR READERS WRITE

OUR READERS WRITE

Make It Shine!

To encourage my students to write neatly, I introduce the Penmanship Pixie at the beginning of each year. They know it's me, of course, but they love the silly persona! As I grade students' work, I look for excellent penmanship. On each sample I find, I attach a copy of a handwriting award from page 301 embellished with a bit of glitter and a small treat, such as a sucker. Then I return the fairy-dusted page along with the rest of the student's work and watch for the smile!

Jennifer Hoff, Edison Elementary, Stickney, IL

One, Two, Three, Comma!

Remembering where to put the commas in large numbers was giving my students trouble until we came up with this simple chant. When a student writes a large number, she counts three digits from the right as she says, "One, two, three, kick!" When she says the word *kick*, she writes a comma, "kicking" the comma into place. She repeats the chant until all of the commas are in place!

Kim Minafo, Dillard Drive Elementary, Raleigh, NC

One, two, three, kick!
One, two, three, kick!

3,527,016

Geographic Reminder

I use this colorful layering activity to help my students understand our location in the world. To begin, I cut a class supply of construction paper rectangles in five different sizes so that when stacked, each rectangle is smaller than the previous one. Next, I have each child label five rectangles from largest to smallest using the names of our continent, country, state, county, and city. Then the student glues the pieces together in order. The resulting project is a memorable model that represents the relationships between the designations of the place where we live.

Melanie Guido, St. Francis–St. Stephen's School, Geneva, NY

Our continent: North America
Our country: United States of America
Our state: New York
Our county: Ontario
Our city: Geneva

Steven

_____, this handwriting really stands out!

WELL DONE!

The Penmanship Pixie

©The Mailbox® • TEC44032 • Aug./Sept. 2007

_____, this handwriting really stands out!

WELL DONE!

The Penmanship Pixie

©The Mailbox® • TEC44032 • Aug./Sept. 2007

OUR READERS WRITE

Shamrock Shuffle

In March, my students review important topics by playing Shamrock Shuffle. Each student cuts a paper shamrock in half puzzle-style and labels one half with a question and the other half with its answer. After collecting the questions in a bag, I collect and redistribute the answers. To play, the first student draws and reads aloud a question. The class-mate who thinks he holds the matching answer calls it out. To check, the two students try to fit their puzzle pieces together. If the pieces match, the answering student draws the next question. We continue until all shamrocks have been reassembled.

What type of rocks form from magma?

igneous rocks

Irene M. Taylor, Piscataway, NJ

Math Calendar Test

To keep math skills sharp all year long, I give students a monthly "calendar test." Before each new month, I label a calendar grid with math review problems (one per day) and make a copy for each child. I send the calendar home on the first school day of the month. Students have all month to complete the calendar test, which I offer to precheck up to two days before its due date. On the due date, we go over the answers together and correct any errors.

Rebecca Blanchard, Harris Road Middle School, Concord, NC

BLAST OFF!

Beginning with a bold topic sentence
Lots of supporting details
At least five adjectives
Simile or metaphor
Transition or time-order words

Organized ideas
Four or five paragraphs
Final, concluding statement

Editing Helper

An easy-to-remember acronym helps my students edit rough drafts for errors other than spelling and punctuation. I post in my classroom a sign labeled with the acronym shown. (If desired, give each child a copy of the bookmark on page 304.) By the time testing rolls around in the spring, my students know the acronym by heart!

Deb Gribben, Twin Hickory Elementary, Glen Allen, VA

302

Name			**March**			Calendar Test
Sunday	Monday	Tuesday	Wednesday	Thursday	Friday	Saturday
						1 3,000 − 1,296
2 1,487 x 5	3 700 ÷ 12	4 $1.45 x 32	5 80,000 − 57,689	6 6)7.511	7 $\frac{4}{5} \div \frac{2}{3}$	8 615 x 62
9 Simplify: $\frac{12}{10}$	10 Which is larger? $\frac{1}{2}$ or $\frac{3}{8}$	11 4)2.32	12 $2\frac{1}{3} \times \frac{3}{8}$	13 $0.99 x 54	14 $\frac{6}{9} + \frac{3}{4}$	15 Simplify: $\frac{24}{21}$
16 $1\frac{1}{2} \times 1\frac{1}{2}$	17 $\frac{1}{8} + \frac{3}{5}$	18 Which is larger? $\frac{3}{5}$ or $\frac{3}{4}$	19 Simplify: $\frac{34}{5}$	20 1.36 x 5.4	21 $4\frac{1}{2} \times 6$	22 $\frac{3}{4} - \frac{5}{16}$
23 Draw acute < KBC. Draw HL.	24 $\frac{4}{8} + \frac{4}{16}$ Draw a rhombus	25 $7\frac{1}{9} − 2\frac{2}{3}$	26 Write as a decimal: 16%	27 Simplify: $\frac{55}{6}$	28 0.25 x 32	29 Write as a decimal: 68%
30	31					

Personal Whiteboards

Instead of purchasing individual whiteboards, I give each student a sheet of sturdy white cardstock placed in a plastic page protector. After I call out a question, each child writes on his "board" with a dry-erase marker and then holds it up so I can check his answer. If I want to share a student's work with the class, I simply remove the cardstock and place the page protector right on the overhead projector!

Kristine Ford, Holmesburg Baptist Christian School Philadelphia, PA

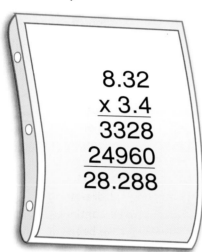

$$8.32$$
$$\times\ 3.4$$
$$\underline{3328}$$
$$\underline{24960}$$
$$28.288$$

Got the Picture?

For a unique parts of speech activity, I have each child cut out eight adjectives from old magazines or newspapers. The student uses the cutout adjectives in a paragraph that describes an imaginary person (see the example). Then she swaps papers with a classmate, reads her partner's paragraph, and illustrates the character. After partners share their pictures, I post the artwork and paragraphs on a display titled "Got the Picture?"

Shawna Miller
Wellington Elementary
Flower Mound, TX

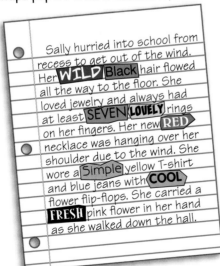

Sally hurried into school from recess to get out of the wind. Her WILD Black hair flowed all the way to the floor. She loved jewelry and always had at least SEVEN LOVELY rings on her fingers. Her new RED necklace was hanging over her shoulder due to the wind. She wore a Simple yellow T-shirt and blue jeans with COOL flower flip-flops. She carried a FRESH pink flower in her hand as she walked down the hall.

Statistical Sing-Along

If my students become confused about mean, median, mode, and range, I teach them the simple song shown below. In no time, they're singing a different tune!

Marcia Richey, John C. Fremont Elementary, Carson City, NV
and Jennifer Ward-DeJoseph, Empire Elementary, Carson City, NV

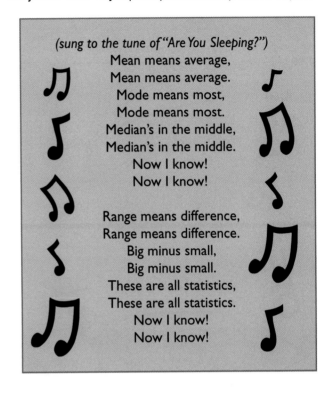

(sung to the tune of "Are You Sleeping?")
Mean means average,
Mean means average.
Mode means most,
Mode means most.
Median's in the middle,
Median's in the middle.
Now I know!
Now I know!

Range means difference,
Range means difference.
Big minus small,
Big minus small.
These are all statistics,
These are all statistics.
Now I know!
Now I know!

S.N.A.C.K. Time

Once a week, I use our class set of weekly periodicals in an activity called "S.N.A.C.K.," or "Stop Now and Consume Knowledge." I give each student a magazine and divide the class into groups of four. Each group reads the entire magazine and plans a brief presentation on a favorite article. After the presentations, I serve students a simple snack. My kids love the chance to interact with each other, and I love the reading practice they get.

Norene Carr, Fox River Grove Middle School, Fox River Grove, IL

Climb and Slide

This little ditty helps my students remember the difference between latitude and longitude. I even have students act it out, pretending to climb the rungs of a ladder while singing about latitude and pretending to slide down a rope when singing about longitude.

Kim Minafo, Dillard Drive Elementary, Raleigh, NC

Latitude and Longitude Song
(sung to the tune of "The Mulberry Bush")

We're climbing the lines of latitude,
Latitude, latitude.
We're climbing the lines of latitude
And sliding down longitude.

303

Editing Helper Bookmarks

Use with "Editing Helper" on page 302.

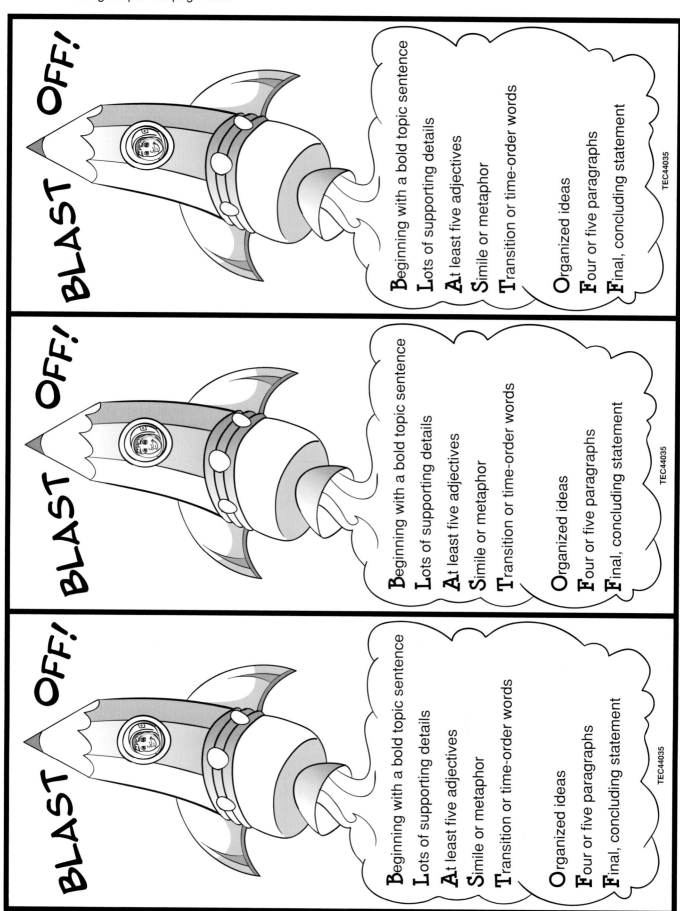

BLAST OFF!

- **B**eginning with a bold topic sentence
- **L**ots of supporting details
- **A**t least five adjectives
- **S**imile or metaphor
- **T**ransition or time-order words

- **O**rganized ideas
- **F**our or five paragraphs
- **F**inal, concluding statement

TEC44035

BLAST OFF!

- **B**eginning with a bold topic sentence
- **L**ots of supporting details
- **A**t least five adjectives
- **S**imile or metaphor
- **T**ransition or time-order words

- **O**rganized ideas
- **F**our or five paragraphs
- **F**inal, concluding statement

TEC44035

BLAST OFF!

- **B**eginning with a bold topic sentence
- **L**ots of supporting details
- **A**t least five adjectives
- **S**imile or metaphor
- **T**ransition or time-order words

- **O**rganized ideas
- **F**our or five paragraphs
- **F**inal, concluding statement

TEC44035

That's a radius!

"Geo-licious"!

For a tasty geometry review, I give each student a paper plate on which I've placed some shoestring licorice, pretzel sticks, and mini marshmallows. Students use the items to make different geometric figures such as the following:

- Licorice: circle, different types of lines (perpendicular, intersecting, and parallel)
- Pretzel sticks: ray, line, line segment; chord, diameter, and radius of a licorice circle; different types of triangles (with marshmallows as vertices)
- Mini marshmallows: vertices for pretzel stick rays and different types of angles

After the review, we snack on our munchable manipulatives!

Wendy Twaddell, Brecknock Elementary, Denver, PA

800

Numbers inside the suitcases: 1, 3, 5, 10, 15, 20, 25, 30, 35, 40, 45, 50, 60, 70, 90, 100, 200, 300, 400, 500, 600, 700, 800, 900, and 1,000

Choose a Suitcase!

To review for any test, we play a game inspired by the game show "Deal or No Deal." Inside each of 25 folded sheets of construction paper (suitcases), I write one of the numbers above. Then I have one person from each of four teams choose a suitcase and set it aside without opening it.

To play, I ask Team 1 a question. If the question is answered correctly, Team 1 chooses a suitcase and reveals the number inside. If incorrect, Team 1 does not choose a suitcase. Then I repeat these steps with the other teams. If Team 1 answers correctly on its next turn, it decides whether to keep the case it has or discard it and pick another one. If Team 1 chooses a new case, it must reveal the case's number. The game continues until time is up or all cases have been chosen. Then each team decides whether to keep its last case or open the mystery case it picked before the game. The team with the highest number wins.

Renae Henderson, Holy Cross Elementary, Dewitt, NY

Nico, we know you will do GREAT on your test. Just do your best and stick with it! We love you!

Mom and Dad

Don't Stress the Test!

I ease testing stress by sending a letter to each student's family about a month before state testing begins. In it, I ask each parent to secretly write an encouraging note to his or her child and to make a sign to hang on his desk. I also send home a manila envelope with instructions to seal the note and sign inside before returning it to school with their child. On the Monday of testing week, I distribute the special stress-busters. I know they work because of all the smiles that appear!

Amy Bruening, Sacred Heart School, Yankton, SD

On Target

I use concentric circles to demonstrate how the parts of the human body are interconnected. I draw on the board a four-ring target and label its center circle "cells." As I explain how cells relate to tissues, organs, and body systems, I label the next three rings. In social studies, I use a five-ring target to show how our city, parish (or county), state, country, and continent are related.

Theresa Cress, Bellingrath Hills Elementary, Greenwell Springs, LA

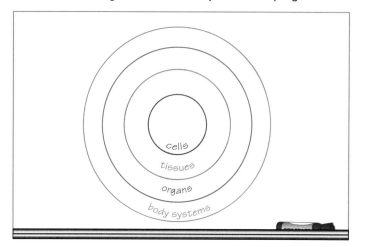

Let's Twist

I play this version of a familiar game with my students to practice basic parts of speech. Using permanent markers, I draw colorful circles on an inexpensive plastic tablecloth to make it look like a Twister game mat. I label each circle with a part of speech. Then I make a spinner similar to the one shown. To play, I have a small group of students remove their shoes. I ask a student volunteer to spin the spinner as I call out a word that matches one of the parts of speech. Each player places the corresponding body part on an appropriate circle. Play continues in this manner as time allows. For a more challenging version, I use two mats and label the circles on the second mat with the following: *pronoun, interjection,* and *conjunction.*

Autumn Arnold, The Chatsworth School, Reisterstown, MD

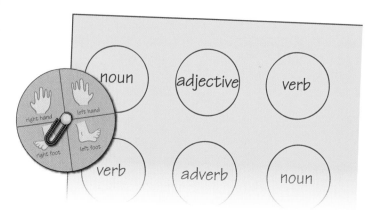

To Hyphenate or Not to Hyphenate

To obtain words for this vocabulary activity, I have small groups of students use a dictionary to list on a copy of a recording sheet (see page 307) as many hyphenated words as they can. After an appropriate amount of time, I collect the lists. Next, I draw on the board a T chart and label its columns "Hyphenated" and "Nonhyphenated." Then I call out a word (either a word from one of the lists or a nonhyphenated word of my choice). Each group decides whether the announced word should be hyphenated or not. After the groups share their decisions with the class, I have a student from a group that provided a correct answer record the word in the appropriate column of the chart.

Patricia Twohey, Smithfield, RI

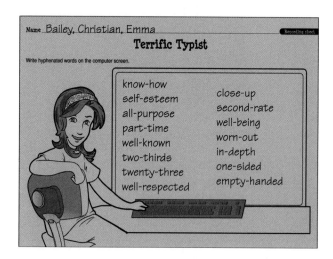

Bags of Knowledge

During the last week of school, I like to have my students reflect on what they've learned during the year. To do this, I have each child personalize a lunch-size paper bag and then fill it with colorful paper strips, each labeled with a different example of something new she learned during the year. Students write a variety of things on their slips,  from vocabulary words to math formulas. I encourage each child to take her bag home as a reminder of all the wisdom she has acquired.

Kim Minafo, Apex, NC

Name

Terrific Typist

Write hyphenated words on the computer screen.

Note to the teacher: Use with "To Hyphenate or Not to Hyphenate" on page 306.

Answer Keys

Page 9
Answers for synonyms will vary.

<u>STUDENT</u>
<u>BACKPACK</u>
<u>FRIEND</u>
<u>TEACHER</u>
<u>SUPPLIES</u>

Page 10
1. might've
2. who's
3. I'm
4. you're
5. they'd
6. couldn't
7. let's
8. haven't
9. there's
10. he'll
11–15. Answers will vary.

Page 11
1. 5 hours, 35 minutes
2. 6 hours, 50 minutes
3. 14 hours, 22 minutes
4. 22 minutes
5. 1 hour, 25 minutes
6. 4 hours, 50 minutes
7. 15 hours, 20 minutes
8. 32 minutes
9. Mimi and Grandpop Norwood
10. Granny and Gramps Smith

Page 12
A = (11, 12)
B = (4, 13)
C = (7, 5)
D = (8, 10)
E = (1, 11)
E = (9, 15)
F = (9, 3)
L = (2, 16)
L = (14, 5)
N = (3, 7)
O = (1, 1)
R = (6, 9)
S = (11, 7)
T = (2, 5)
W = (11, 2)

<u>WELL DONE</u>!

Page 15
1. We **are** going to have a <u>huge</u> party for **Halloween** and invite all <u>our</u> **friends**.
2. <u>Matt</u> couldn't find <u>a</u> costume to **wear**, but he came to the party anyway<u>.</u>
3. **All** my <u>friends</u> **were** having a wonderful time at <u>my</u> party.
4. We played <u>a</u> game, but first we had to **separate** the <u>girls</u> from the **boys**.
5. <u>The</u> team that **won received candy bars, puzzle books, and movie tickets**.
6. Haley said, "**The** party is great! **It's** the best <u>one</u> I have ever been **to**."
7. **There** were **a lot** of <u>laughs</u> and great food for everyone.

"<u>BOO-BERRY</u>" PIE and "<u>I SCREAM</u>"

Page 16
1. 24 girls
2. 28 boys
3. butter
4. 4 more boys
5. caramel
6. cheese

Graph may vary.

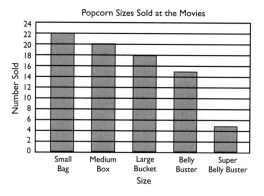

Popcorn Sizes Sold at the Movies

Page 17
1. maize
2. squash
3. pilgrim
4. turkey
5. pumpkin
6. harvest
7. family
8. carve
9. cranberry
10. potato

1. Answers will vary.
2. (fēst)

D B A C
thanks·giv·ing (thăngks-gĭv´ ĭng) *n* **1.** an act of giving thanks; an expression of gratitude **2. Thanksgiving** a holiday for giving thanks, celebrated on the fourth Thursday of November in the United States and on the second Monday of October in Canada

Page 18
A. (7 × 4) + 1 = 29
B. (24 ÷ 6) − 2 = 2
C. (4 × 5) + 6 = 26
D. (9 + 8) − 3 = 14 or (8 + 9) − 3 = 14
E. (36 ÷ 3) + 4 = 16
F. (12 ÷ 2) + 5 = 11
G. (8 + 7) × 4 = 60 or (7 + 8) × 4 = 60
H. (14 ÷ 7) + 1 = 3
I. (25 ÷ 5) + 5 = 10

Page 21
1. yellow
2. blue
3. blue
4. yellow
5. yellow
6. yellow
7. blue
8. blue
9. yellow
10. blue

<u>CHOCOLATE COINS</u>

Page 22
A. green; 1, 5, 25
B. green; 1, 2, 3, 4, 6, 12
C. red; 1, 97
D. red; 1, 101
E. red; 1, 2
F. red; 1, 11
G. green; 1, 2, 3, 6, 9, 18
H. red; 1, 59
I. green; 1, 2, 3, 6
J. green; 1, 2, 7, 14
K. green; 1, 2, 5, 7, 10, 14, 35, 70
L. red; 1, 3

Bonus Box: 2

Page 23

1. I will arrive at school (promptly) at 8:30 AM.
2. I will wait (patiently) for the school bus.
3. I will dress for school (quickly) each morning.
4. I will play (nicely) with my classmates at recess.
5. I will write all my homework assignments (correctly).
6. I will (neatly) organize the supplies in my desk.
7. I will listen (attentively) to the teacher.
8. I will (carefully) proofread all my written work.
9. I will (always) do my homework before watching TV.
10. I will (regularly) go to bed on time.
11. I will (never) leave my backpack at school.
12. I will study (hard) for all my tests.

Sentences will vary.

Page 24

Blake—range, 11; median, 12; mode, 12; mean, 14
Mandy—range, 12; median, 33; mode, 40; mean, 34
David—range, 31; median, 40; mode, 25; mean, 40
Anna—range, 28; median, 46; mode, 51; mean, 41
Trevor—range, 33; median, 23; mode, 23; mean, 27

Page 27

1.	LOVE	11.	LOVEBIRDS
2.	CUPID	12.	RED
3.	CANDY	13.	GIFTS
4.	ROSES	14.	HOLIDAY
5.	CARDS	15.	SAINT VALENTINE
6.	FLOWERS	16.	SWEETHEARTS
7.	KISSES	17.	PAPER LACE
8.	JEWELRY	18.	CHOCOLATE
9.	HUGS	19.	ROMANTIC
10.	HEARTS	20.	VALENTINE'S DAY

Page 28

A.	12.39	I.	12
M.	37	T.	50½
I.	21	F.	6
W.	8	T.	25
L.	9	H.	5.0
A.	4	L.	6.09

WILLIAM H. TAFT

Page 29

1.	successful	6.	heroic	11.	quietly
2.	backward	7.	musical	12.	friendship
3.	payment	8.	foolish	13.	fasten
4.	governor	9.	speechless	14.	goodness
5.	courageous	10.	childlike	15.	duckling

Page 30

A.	5/8	F.	5/6	K.	1/3
B.	3/4	G.	1/2	L.	17/30
C.	13/24	H.	3/10	M.	17/24
D.	5/12	I.	1/14	N.	11/14
E.	7/12	J.	8/15	O.	11/12

Page 33

1. Use reusable mugs instead of disposable cups.
2. Ride your bicycle or use public transportation.
3. Cooperate with your neighbor to combine errands and save gas.
4. Defrost frozen foods to reduce cooking time.
5. Perform an energy audit to determine how much energy your family uses.
6. While on long trips, unplug home computers to prevent energy waste.
7. Avoid buying products that cannot be recycled or that have unnecessary packaging.
8. Think of ways to improve the land, air, and water in the surrounding area.

Page 34

Bonus Box: trapezoid, rectangle, parallelogram, square, rhombus

Page 35

Answers may vary.

In 1862, France was trying to take over Mexico and set up a new government there.

Cinco de Mayo celebrates a Mexican victory over the French on May 5, 1862, at the Battle of Puebla.

The Mexican army won even though the French army was larger and better armed.

France withdrew its troops a few years later because of resistance by many Mexicans and pressure from the United States.

Some Mexican towns and U.S. cities celebrate Cinco de Mayo with parades.

In the United States, people often celebrate Cinco de Mayo with folk dancing and Mexican music.

Page 37

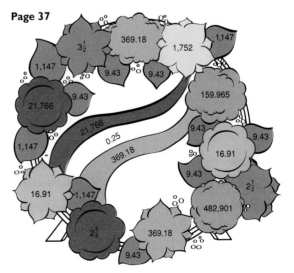

1. 21,766	2. 16.91	3. 1,752	4. 3½	5. 482,901	6. 1,147
7. 369.18	8. 2½	9. 9.43	10. 0.25	11. 2⅝	12. 159.965

Page 40
1. 2 hours 2 minutes, 53 minutes
2. 1 hour 39 minutes, 36 minutes
3. 3 hours 9 minutes, 39 minutes
4. 75 minutes, yes; Ryan will have time because it only takes 1 hour 15 minutes to see both sites.

Page 41
Estimated angle measurements will vary.
Actual measurements:
A. 80°   H. 38°
B. 143°   I. 70°
C. 95°   J. 155°
D. 135°   K. 90°
E. 85°   L. 160°
F. 42°   M. 65°
G. 100°

Acute angles: A, E, F, H, I, M
Obtuse angles: B, C, D, G, J, L
Right angle: K

Page 42
Facts: 1, 3, 4, 6, 9
Opinions: 2, 5, 7, 8, 10

Underlined text may vary.
¹· Hot dogs have been eaten in American baseball parks <u>since 1893</u>. ²· However, Americans <u>adored</u> hot dogs even before then. ³· The <u>first</u> Coney Island hot dog stand opened <u>in 1871</u>. ⁴· The stand <u>sold</u> nearly <u>4,000</u> hot dogs in its first year. ⁵· Customers went <u>crazy</u> for the <u>delicious</u> hot dogs. ⁶· <u>Today</u>, hot dogs are <u>sold</u> across the country. ⁷· There are many <u>delicious</u> ways to eat a hot dog. ⁸· The <u>best</u> New York hot dogs are covered in steamed onions and mustard. ⁹· A Kansas City–style hot dog has <u>sauerkraut</u> and melted <u>Swiss cheese</u>. ¹⁰· No matter what tops a hot dog, it's the <u>coolest</u> food in the nation.

Page 43
Answers may vary.

Family: He has two sons, a daughter, and a wife.
Community: He coaches a sports team.
Home: He lives in the city.
Hobby: He enjoys getting out into nature away from the city.
Career: He is a teacher.

Page 65
1. "Books are being stolen from the library every Saturday," stated the librarian.
2. Detective Smith wrote the information on his pad and started to question more people.
3. "After asking all the right questions, I still don't know who the bandit is," declared the detective.
4. Suddenly, he spotted a book that looked out of place.
5. Right next to the book was the clue he'd been looking for.
6. It was a poem titled "I'm the Book Bandit."
7. The detective used the clues, and now he knows who the bandit is.

The book bandit is Suspect 3.

Page 68
1. D   9. E
2. F   10. D
3. INT   11. F
4. INT   12. INT
5. F   13. IMP
6. IMP   14. D
7. E   15. E
8. IMP

Page 70

Simple
2 4 [24 pounds] 8 10

Compound
1 6 [26 pounds] 7 12

Complex
3 5 [28 pounds] 9 11

Page 76
1. parents'
2. tractor's, Bernard's
3. Miss Lizzy's, barn's
4. Mrs. Jones's
5. family's, neighbor's, pie's
6. children's, grandpa's
7. Miss Lizzy's
8. farmhands', tonight's

Page 77
1. A   5. R   9. O
2. H   6. O   10. V
3. O   7. R   11. I
4. R   8. M   12. E

Page 97
1. B   5. C
2. C   6. A
3. B   7. C
4. A   8. B

Page 118
Answers may vary.
1. noun, verb
   Old English
2. 3
   helmeted
3. 3
   kəm-'pyü-tər
4. väl-'ka̅-no̅
   volcanoes, volcanos
5. lava
   2
   molten rock that comes from a volcano
6. noun
7. light
   both
   6
8. electricity
   i-lek-'tri-sə-te̅
   the first

Page 122
Some answers may vary.

Andy and his best friend, Joe, were walking to school when they spotted the Guminator. Neither Andy nor Joe thought they were in danger, but as they turned a corner, Andy yelled, "Watch out, Joe! The Guminator is aiming his atomic gumball chewer at us, and I don't think we can outrun it!"

"Maybe we should duck or run or something…oh, I don't know what to do!" blubbered Joe.

"Those who hesitate are toast!" bellowed the Guminator as he blasted the boys with wads of sticky gum. Soon their hair and clothes were covered with colorful splotches. They were worried, for they knew better than to go to class with gum all over them. Yet if they didn't, they'd be late for school!

All of a sudden, a dazzling pink figure appeared. "It's Super Bubbleman! He's come to our rescue!" exclaimed Joe.

The Guminator froze in his tracks, for he saw that Super Bubbleman had not one but two things that could spoil his fun: ice cubes and a jar of peanut butter. The Guminator knew he was really in trouble if Super Bubbleman had some gum removers with him, so he left in a hurry.

"Oh, thank you, Super Bubbleman," chorused Andy and Joe. "You'll be our hero forever!"

Page 126

810 − 70 = 740	1,390 − 220 = 1,170	650 − 50 = 600	8,350 − 6,940 = 1,410
4,360 − 1,340 = 3,020	590 − 220 = 370	1,700 − 140 = 1,560	280 − 20 = 260
860 − 120 = 740	4,440 − 780 = 3,660	910 − 380 = 530	1,230 − 570 = 660
2,600 − 1,110 = 1,490	9,120 − 2,010 = 7,110	390 − 220 = 170	570 − 100 = 470

100 + 300 = 400	3,200 + 2,700 = 5,900	6,200 + 2,400 = 8,600	500 + 200 = 700
1,200 + 1,200 = 2,400	700 + 200 = 900	900 + 500 = 1,400	32,100 + 4,900 = 37,000
4,100 + 900 = 5,000	8,800 + 5,400 = 14,200	800 + 500 = 1,300	12,200 + 7,200 = 19,400
800 + 300 = 1,100	2,700 + 900 = 3,600	900 + 600 = 1,500	3,400 + 1,000 = 4,400

Pets Galore

Music 'n' More

Jewelry Boutique

Shoe Colony
Shoe Colony

Sports Scene

Pets Galore

Music 'n' More

Page 127

Answers may vary. Accept reasonable responses.

1. about 600 books
2. about 3 DVDs
3. about 40 pounds
4. about 30 bags
5. about 300 issues
6. about 50 boxes
7. about 4,200 gumballs
8. about $100.00
9. about 420 cartons
10. about 40 hours

Page 132

A. 180 sq. yd.
B. 900 sq. yd.
C. 600 sq. yd.
D. 1,980 sq. yd.
E. 6,250 sq. yd.
F. 5,040 sq. yd.
G. 3,024 sq. yd.
H. 8,000 sq. yd.
I. 5,580 sq. yd.
J. 1,200 sq. yd.

Page 137

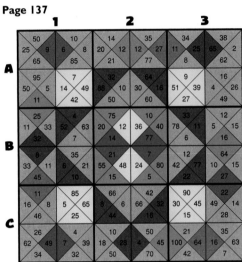

Page 138

	Number	Factors	Number of Factors
A.	15	1, 3, 5, 15	4
B.	36	1, 2, 3, 4, 6, 9, 12, 18, 36	9
C.	7	1, 7	2
D.	25	1, 5, 25	3
E.	16	1, 2, 4, 8, 16	5
F.	64	1, 2, 4, 8, 16, 32, 64	7
G.	30	1, 2, 3, 5, 6, 10, 15, 30	8
H.	1	1	1
I.	20	1, 2, 4, 5, 10, 20	6

Page 141

Metric Conversion Chart
1 liter (L) = 1,000 milliliters (mL)

Customary Conversion Chart
1 cup (c.) = 8 fluid ounces (fl. oz.)
1 pint (pt.) = 2 cups
1 quart (qt.) = 2 pints
1 gallon (gal.) = 4 quarts

A. 6
B. 16
C. 64
D. 20
E. 8
F. 6
G. 80
H. 10,000
I. 3
J. 25

Page 142

1. 1,300
2. 32
3. 150
4. 19,200
5. 4,000
6. 1
7. 10
8. 1,000,000
9. 9
10. 544,000,000
11. 227,000
12. 800

Page 143

1. T
2. Y
3. R
4. U
5. H
6. E
7. A
8. W
9. S
10. N
11. P
12. G

THEY ARE ALWAYS ROUNDING THINGS UP!

Page 148

Answers may vary.
One possible solution is shown.

Page 149

A. $\frac{1}{2}$
B. $\frac{1}{5}$
C. $\frac{3}{5}$
D. $\frac{17}{50}$
E. $\frac{2}{25}$
F. $\frac{11}{25}$
G. $\frac{29}{50}$
H. $\frac{9}{10}$
I. $\frac{3}{4}$
J. $\frac{31}{100}$
K. $\frac{91}{1,000}$
L. $\frac{7}{100}$
M. $\frac{89}{100}$
N. $\frac{1}{20}$
O. $\frac{79}{100}$
P. $\frac{11}{1,000}$
Q. $\frac{9}{100}$
R. $\frac{3}{50}$
S. $\frac{4}{5}$
T. $\frac{3}{100}$

Page 150

1. 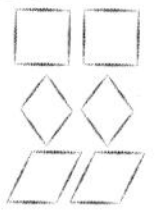 ; translation, rotation, or reflection
, translation or reflection
, translation
2.  , translation or reflection
3.  ; translation, rotation, or reflection
4.  ; translation, rotation, or reflection
5.  , translation or reflection

Page 153

1. I, reflection
2. M, rotation
3. P, rotation
4. L, rotation
5. B, translation
6. I, rotation
7. M, reflection
8. R, rotation
9. E, rotation then reflection
10. C, translation

It was a PRIME place to CLIMB!

Page 154

Order of letters on each box may vary.
Cliff Hangers: Y, R, A, S; RAYS
Crazy About Climbing: E, O, C, N; CONE
Climb Time: E, C, B, U; CUBE
Over the Wall: N, E, L, I; LINE
Storage: A, E, A, R; AREA

Page 159

1. $90
2. $654
3. $300
4. $24
5. $168
6. $48

Transportation: $90
Lodging: $654
Meals: $300
Dragon-slaying license: $24
Suit of armor: $168
Land claim: $48

Page 160

1. 7 horses
2. 13 stalls
3. 16 horses
4. 207 bales
5. 4 carriages
6. 1 more carrot

Page 161

1. T, 7 R3
2. E, 3 R10
3. H, 7 R6
4. S, 5 R4
5. G, 6 R5
6. N, 4 R7
7. I, 8 R1
8. N, 7 R8
9. K, 2 R9
10. Y, 2 R11
11. W, 2 R2
12. L, 8 R12

They watch the "KNIGHTLY" NEWS!

Page 164

A. triangular pyramid; four faces, six edges, four vertices
B. triangular prism; five faces, nine edges, six vertices, rectangle
C. square pyramid; five faces, eight edges, five vertices, square

Page 167

1. F
2. B
3. H
4. D
5. G
6. C
7. E
8. A
9. quadrilateral
10. decagon
11. hexagon
12. octagon
13. triangle
14. pentagon
15. heptagon

Page 168

1. A (orange)
2. D (green)
3. O (blue)
4. E (red)
5. C (multicolored)
6. H (purple)
7. R (yellow)
8. N (pink)

A DODECAHEDRON

Page 173

1. $\frac{39}{40}$
2. $\frac{6}{11}$
3. $5\frac{1}{2}$
4. $5\frac{1}{9}$
5. $1\frac{7}{15}$
6. $11\frac{7}{10}$
7. $\frac{1}{12}$
8. 1
9. $\frac{7}{18}$
10. $7\frac{1}{2}$

Page 174

	Estimate	Actual Answer
1.	120	114.52
2.	800	718.74
3.	110	107.02
4.	600	569.408
5.	30	30.98
6.	200	199.05
7.	175	175.00
8.	5	4.54

Justin made the hole in one.

Page 177

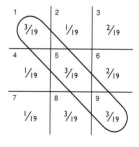

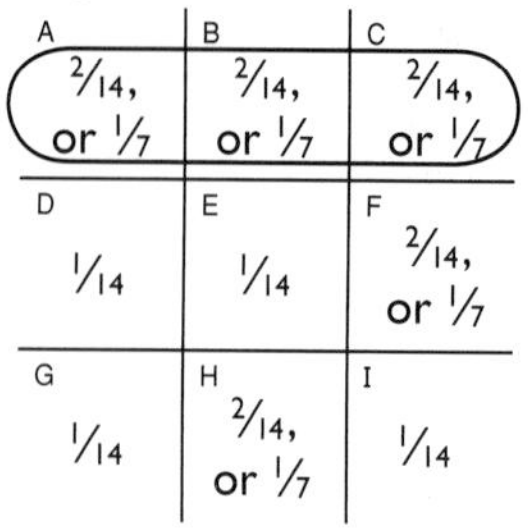

A $\frac{2}{14}$, or $\frac{1}{7}$	B $\frac{2}{14}$, or $\frac{1}{7}$	C $\frac{2}{14}$, or $\frac{1}{7}$
D $\frac{1}{14}$	E $\frac{1}{14}$	F $\frac{2}{14}$, or $\frac{1}{7}$
G $\frac{1}{14}$	H $\frac{2}{14}$, or $\frac{1}{7}$	I $\frac{1}{14}$

1 $\frac{3}{19}$	2 $\frac{1}{19}$	3 $\frac{2}{19}$
4 $\frac{1}{19}$	5 $\frac{3}{19}$	6 $\frac{2}{19}$
7 $\frac{1}{19}$	8 $\frac{3}{19}$	9 $\frac{3}{19}$

Page 178

1. $\frac{1}{7}$
2. $\frac{5}{10}$, or $\frac{1}{2}$
3. $\frac{8}{12}$, or $\frac{2}{3}$
4. $\frac{2}{54}$, or $\frac{1}{27}$; $\frac{13}{54}$; $\frac{26}{54}$, or $\frac{13}{27}$
5. $\frac{4}{10}$, or $\frac{2}{5}$
6. $\frac{12}{20}$, or $\frac{3}{5}$; $\frac{8}{20}$, or $\frac{2}{5}$
7. $\frac{6}{8}$, or $\frac{3}{4}$
8. $\frac{10}{12}$, or $\frac{5}{6}$

1.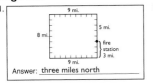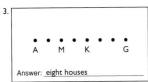
Answer: three miles north

2.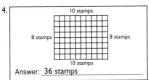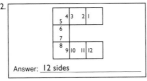
Answer: 12 sides

3. • • • • • • • •
   A   M   K   G
Answer: eight houses

4.
Answer: 36 stamps

5. R R R RY RB RB RB RBY B B B BY
Answer: Four cookies have red and blue sprinkles; one cookie has yellow sprinkles.

Page 183

1. nine combinations
   pizza parlor, three friends
   pizza parlor, five friends
   pizza parlor, seven friends
   skating rink, three friends
   skating rink, five friends
   skating rink, seven friends
   pottery-making shop, three friends
   pottery-making shop, five friends
   pottery-making shop, seven friends

2. 11 combinations

Quarters	Dimes	Nickels
2	0	1
1	3	0
1	2	2
1	1	4
1	0	6
0	5	1
0	4	3
0	3	5
0	2	7
0	1	9
0	0	11

3. nine combinations

Sport	Music Lesson
soccer	piano
soccer	violin
soccer	drums
volleyball	piano
volleyball	violin
volleyball	drums
gymnastics	piano
gymnastics	violin
gymnastics	drums

4. six ways

Left	Middle	Right
Eddie	Brandon	Jake
Eddie	Jake	Brandon
Brandon	Eddie	Jake
Brandon	Jake	Eddie
Jake	Eddie	Brandon
Jake	Brandon	Eddie

Page 187

A. 14, 16, 18
B. 12, 20, 28
C. 5, 11, 20
D. 2, 11, 26
E. 18, 23, 29
F. 8, 11, 12
G. 10, 16, 26
H. 9, 20, 30
I. 6, 7, 10
J. 5, 2, 0

Page 188

Wording for rules may vary.
1. 40, 30, 35; Alternate subtracting 10 and adding 5.
2. 19, 25, 32; Add 2, add 3, add 4, and so on.
3. 23, 17, 11; Subtract 6.
4. 9, 3, 1; Divide by 3.
5. 50, 100, 90; Alternate multiplying by 2 and subtracting 10.
6. 41, 49, 57; Add 8.
7. 97, 193, 385; Multiply by 2 and then subtract 1.
8. 20, 10, 5; Divide by 2.
9. 48, 96, 192; Multiply by 2.
10. 51, 76, 106; Add 5, add 10, add 15, and so on.

Page 201

Order of answers in each category may vary.

Antonyms
happy : depressed as seal : open
comfort : annoy as soothe : vex
loud : faint as quiet : noisy
guilty : innocent as broad : narrow

Synonyms
thin : narrow as yell : shout
steal : plunder as launch : start
trouble : bother as scalding : hot
early : premature as rough : coarse

Students' analogies will vary.

Object—Action
broom : sweep as kitten : purr
phone : ring as bird : chirp
tornado : destroy as oven : bake
earthworm : dig as horse : gallop

Part—Whole
keyboard : computer as player : team
student : class as musician : band
country : continent as fin : fish
letter : alphabet as tree : forest

Page 221

Appetizers
Buffalo Wings—$3.90
Spicy French Fries—$1.75
Mozzarella Sticks—$2.25

Soups and Salads
Chicken Soup—$1.85
French Onion Soup—$2.15
House Salad—$2.65
Caesar Salad—$3.35

Beverages
Milk—$0.95
Soda—$1.69
Tea—$1.79

Entrées
Hamburger—$5.45
Cheeseburger—$5.60
Chicken Fingers—$5.95
Pizza—$9.95

Sides
French Fries—$1.45
Onion Rings—$1.95

Desserts
Chocolate Cream Pie—$2.45
Apple Pie—$2.35
Ice Cream—$2.50
Milk Shake—$3.09

Answers for the total cost of a meal will vary.

Page 226

1. cylinder
2. triangular prism
3. rectangular prism
4. square pyramid
5. cube
6. triangular pyramid
7. sphere
8. pentagonal prism

Page 231

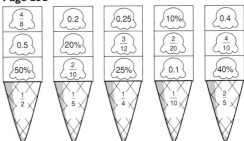

Page 232

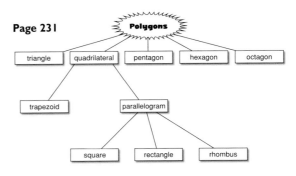

Page 237

Topic sentences (in bold) and order will vary.

Many people like to eat turkey.
Turkey is high in protein and low in fat.
White meat has less fat and fewer calories than dark meat.
Forty-five million turkeys are eaten each Thanksgiving.
Twenty-two million turkeys are eaten each Christmas, and 19 million are eaten each Easter.

Turkeys have some special body features.
All male turkeys and some female turkeys have beards. These beards are black hairlike feathers on their breasts.
A turkey can see movement from almost 100 yards away.
When turkeys are excited, their heads change colors.
Though they don't have ears like humans, turkeys have good hearing.

Some turkeys are raised by farmers.
Domesticated turkeys, which are raised on farms, cannot fly.
The leading turkey-producing states in 2003 were Arkansas, Minnesota, Missouri, North Carolina, and Virginia.
In 2003, turkey growers in the United States raised 270 million turkeys.
The heaviest domesticated turkey ever raised weighed 86 pounds.

Wild turkeys are different from domesticated turkeys.
Wild turkeys can fly as fast as 55 miles per hour for short distances.
A wild turkey can run as fast as 20 miles per hour.
Wild turkeys stay in trees at night.
Today wild turkeys can be found in every state except Alaska.

ISBN-13: 978-156234854-0
ISBN-10: 156234854-X

9 781562 348540